THE MYSTERY OF SALVATION

The Story of God's Gift

A Report by
the Doctrine Commission
of the General Synod
of the Church of England

MOREHOUSE PUBLISHING
Harrisburg, PA

Published 1995 for the General Synod of the Church of England by Church House Publishing

First American edition published by Morehouse Publishing, *Editorial Office*, 871 Ethan Allen Hwy, Ridgefield, CT 06877; *Corporate Office*, P.O. Box 1321, Harrisburg, PA 17105

A catalog record for this book is available from the Library of Congress.

ISBN 0-8192-1671-2

Cover design by Leigh Hurlock

Cover photograph used with the permission of Coventry Cathedral Council

Printed and bound in England by The Cromwell Press Ltd, Melksham, Wiltshire

Contents

The Doctrine Commission
1989 – 1995

CHAIRMAN
The Right Revd Alec Graham
Bishop of Newcastle

MEMBERS
The Revd Dr Paul Avis
Vicar of Stoke Canon, Poltimore with Huxham, and Rewe with Netherexe, and Prebendary of Exeter

Dr Richard Bauckham
Professor of New Testament Studies in the University of St Andrews, previously Reader in the History of Christian Thought in the University of Manchester

Dr Christina Baxter (from 1991)
Dean of St John's College, Nottingham, and Vice-Chairman of the House of Laity of the General Synod

The Revd Dr David Brown
Van Mildert Professor of Divinity in the University of Durham, and Canon of Durham; previously Fellow of Oriel College, Oxford

The Right Revd Colin Buchanan (until 1991)
Vicar of St Mark, Gillingham, and Honorary Assistant Bishop in the Diocese of Rochester

Dr Sarah Coakley (until 1992)
Fellow of Oriel College, Oxford; subsequently Professor of Christian Theology, The Divinity School, Harvard University

Dr Ruth Etchells (until 1991)
formerly Principal of St John's College, with Cranmer Hall, Durham, and Senior Lecturer in the University of Durham

Lady (Sophie) Laws (from 1991)
formerly Lecturer in New Testament Studies at King's College, London

The Revd Dr John Muddiman (from 1990)
Fellow of Mansfield College, Oxford

The Revd Dr John Polkinghorne FRS
President of Queens' College, Cambridge, and Canon Theologian of Liverpool

The Right Revd Dr Geoffrey Rowell (from 1991)
Bishop of Basingstoke, Prebendary of Chichester and Emeritus Fellow of Keble College, Oxford

The Right Revd Dr Peter Selby (from 1991)
William Leech Professorial Fellow in Applied Christian Theology in the University of Durham; previously Bishop of Kingston-upon-Thames

The Revd Dr Derek Stanesby (until 1991)
Canon of Windsor

The Right Revd Stephen Sykes (from 1990)
Bishop of Ely

The Right Revd John B. Taylor
Bishop of St Albans

The Right Revd Dr Rowan Williams (until 1991)
Bishop of Monmouth; previously Lady Margaret Professor of Divinity in the University of Oxford

The Very Revd Dr Tom Wright
Dean of Lichfield, and Canon Theologian of Coventry; previously Fellow of Worcester College, Oxford

CONSULTANT
The Revd Andrew Wingate
Principal of the College of the Ascension, Selly Oak, and Assistant Secretary of the USPG

SECRETARY
The Revd Dr John Clark
Vicar of Chevington; previously Vicar of Longframlington with Brinkburn

Preface

This Report, like its two predecessors, is published under the authority of the House of Bishops and is commended by the House to the Church for study.

On behalf of the House of Bishops

+ **George Cantuar**

Chairman

Foreword

This report by the Doctrine Commission of the General Synod of the Church of England on the subject of salvation is the third in a series. *We Believe in God* was published in 1987, and in 1991 it was followed by *We Believe in the Holy Spirit.* These three reports have several common features. They all treat major themes which lie at the heart of the Christian religion. They seek to do so in a way which, it is to be hoped, will make the Christian faith more readily comprehensible and more easily accessible to a non-specialist and enquiring public, which may include regular worshippers as well as enquirers and seekers who stand on the margin of the Church's life. This report, like the others, has been prepared by a group of theological teachers and thinkers who have been appointed to the Commission by the Archbishops of Canterbury and York, and who represent a wide spread of professional expertise and of theological standpoint. We have tried to write in a non-technical way, though it has not always proved possible to avoid the use of technical terms. Our aim has been to express the Church's faith as received by us from Scripture and from the Church's subsequent understanding of its inheritance, in such a way that we are true to the tradition received and give fresh expression to it; we take account of the present context and of modern difficulties, and we indicate ways in which understanding of our subject may appropriately be expressed and set forward in our day. Thus we modestly hope that our work may be of service to parish study groups, to theological students, to other provinces of the Anglican Communion, and, indeed, to the wider Church.

Each of these reports has taken several years to compose, and all have been the fruit of corporate writing. This exercise has proved to be both time-consuming and worthwhile. At the first stage, papers on various topics associated with our central theme were prepared by members of the Commission and by others on whose services we were able to draw. After a while a pattern for the book emerged, and various members of the Commission undertook to write the first draft of entire chapters or of parts of chapters. These drafts were discussed, rewritten, amended, refined, until at last a form of words was achieved with which everyone who was a member of the Commission at the time of final drafting could concur. Thus this report, like its predecessors, comes with the unanimous support of the entire Commission, composed, as it is, of members who represent a diversity of viewpoint and background. We can all live with, endorse and happily commend the agreed text. We have been careful to phrase our report in such a way that we do not exclude some other expressions of Christian truth which have an honoured place in the Anglican tradition. Christian truth as a whole, and Christian teaching on this particular topic of salvation, are so rich and complex that one statement does not necessarily exclude all others. Our unanimity over such a wide field of issues associated with the topic, which surely is the nerve-centre of Christian faith, needs to be underlined, as also does our readiness to leave room for some other views and to leave some questions open; equally, on occasion we do not hesitate to express opinions critical of various points of view which we consider inadequate.

In this report, as in the two previous reports, we have been trying to weave together in a coherent and systematic way the biblical faith as understood and transmitted by the Church, while bearing in mind the intellectual climate and the practical concerns of our time. We have not set out to write a history of the doctrine of salvation, though we draw frequently on some of the numerous ways in which salvation has been understood through the Christian centuries, and in chapter 5 we provide some modern versions of traditional themes. Equally, we have not attempted a full examination of the complex biblical threads which combine to form this theme of salvation. We have, however, drawn extensively on the Scriptures throughout our report, particularly near the centre of our work in chapter 4, in which we concentrate on the witness of the New Testament. That chapter is immediately preceded by a chapter in which is examined the nature of the historical content and context of Christian faith, and in the first two chapters of the report an attempt is made to set the Christian doctrine of salvation within the context of today's world and of the Christian faith as a whole. Readers of the two earlier reports will notice a certain measure of continuity between the earlier reports and some parts of these two chapters. Common to all three reports has been the concern to root the subject under discussion within the world and the Church in our time. Common too has been the trinitarian nature of Christian faith which in all three reports has been treated with full seriousness. Linked with the basic trinitarian structure of Christian belief is our repeated reference, in all three reports, to Romans 8, to the Lord's cry of 'Abba, Father', and to the eventual remaking and transformation of the entire created order.

In our survey of the context in which this report is being prepared we have identified several features which require particular attention. To one of these features, the rise of feminist consciousness, we return on several occasions in the course of our report, as we touch on some of the ways in which it affects our subject and in which it affects the understanding and expression of Christian faith as a whole. For two other features of our context we reserve treatment near the end of our work in chapters 7 and 8, in which we address respectively the ways in which Christian understanding of salvation bears upon other faiths, and the future of the universe, in particular of individuals after death. When we were commissioned by the Archbishops to undertake this work, we were asked to give close attention to these two issues. Not surprisingly they have been the subjects at which we have had to work the hardest. In our consideration of other faiths we have been immensely helped by experts in this field, principally by the Revd Andrew Wingate, Principal of the College of the Ascension, Selly Oak, who was recruited to this Commission as a consultant for the preparation of this report. We have sought to identify the positive points which are being made by each of the three most frequently trodden approaches to this particular topic, and to advance understanding of it by combining these positive insights in such a way that we set discussion of the subject a step further forward. With regard to the future of the universe and to the life of human beings after death, we have sought to balance the bearing of the doctrine of salvation on this present age with its bearing on what the Nicene Creed calls 'the life of the world to come'. Here we encountered particular difficulty because the dualist assumptions about human beings (body and soul), which underlie much traditional Christian thinking on these subjects, are not commonly held nowadays; in any case, life after death is hedged about by mystery more than most other subjects, and it would be unwise to write with precision of detail about our future expectations. We have, therefore, treated it in a way which we consider takes account of the Church's understanding of the Scriptures, of the intellectual climate of our time, and of the mysteriousness which necessarily attends this element of Christian faith in particular.

In the central chapters we set out some of the principal features of the understanding of salvation in the New Testament, and we also provide some modern restatements of classical Christian ways of understanding salvation. These chapters are followed by one in which we include a treatment of some of the more important ideas which have been associated with our subject, among them forgiveness, suffering, sacrifice and sacrament. We are conscious of the impossibility of doing justice to such grand themes in so limited a compass, but they are all so closely linked with our general theme that our report would be the poorer without some reference to them and to the bearing of our subject upon them. Christian liturgies all reflect the Church's understanding of these truths, and as we are the Doctrine Commission of the Church of England we have provided an appended note on understandings of salvation to be found in the Book of Common Prayer and in the Alternative Service Book.

In our last two reports we quoted the Bible from the Revised Standard Version. In this report, however, we generally use the New Revised Standard Version. On this occasion, as on previous occasions, we have been fortunate enough to be able to draw on the advice and help of scholars who are not members of the Commission nor formally appointed as consultants to it. We wish particularly to express our appreciation to Dr Gavin D'Costa, now of Bristol

University, and Dr Grace Davie, of Exeter University, both of whom prepared papers for us and attended a residential session of the Commission. Dr D'Costa enriched our understanding of the relationship between Christianity and other faiths, and Dr Davie helped us to understand better the sociological factors which bear upon our subject. We also owe a debt of gratitude to those who have been of assistance to us in various ways, among them: Dr S. Alsford, Dr D. J. Davies, Dr L. J. Francis, Dr K. S. Harmon, Dr D. Hewlett, Dr C. Lamb, Dr B. Martin, Dr J. A. Williams, Dr M. Winter.

In the first book of his treatise *Of the Laws of Ecclesiastical Polity* Richard Hooker sums up a long discussion in these words: 'There resteth therefore either no way unto salvation, or if any, then surely a way which is supernatural, a way which could never have entered into the heart of man as much as once to conceive or imagine, if God himself had not revealed it extraordinarily. For which cause we term it the Mystery or Secret way of salvation.' In the following paragraph he continues in a similar vein: 'Behold how the wisdom of God hath revealed a way mystical and supernatural . . . This supernatural way had God in himself prepared before all worlds' (I.xi.5,6). It is our hope that our discussion of this mystery of faith will help our readers 'to comprehend, with all the saints, what is the breadth and length and height and depth, and to know the love of Christ that surpasses knowledge' (Eph. 3.18f); our work is offered to the Church at large and to a wider readership with that intention.

1

Posing the problem

To the drowning passengers of a sinking ship salvation does not need to be explained, only offered – and quickly. Discussion in such circumstances is as unnecessary as it is dangerous. Those trapped on the top storey of a blazing building require a different remedy for the danger that faces them, but they too are clear what salvation means in their situation. Their need is for a fireman's ladder, not a learned discussion.

Such illustrations may seem altogether too ordinary and material to furnish insight about the nature of salvation. For is not salvation a word from the technical language of theology, bearing centuries of confession on the part of Christians that Jesus Christ came down from heaven for us 'and for our salvation'? Are we not speaking here of the situation facing the whole of humanity rather than the specific needs of those facing the waves of the ocean or the flames of a burning house?

Yet the examples of danger from drowning or fire do illuminate the ease with which it is possible to speak of being saved when the nature of the peril is clear, and, by contrast, suggest a much greater difficulty when the danger being faced is either not clear or is the subject of controversy. What if the smoke alarm has a fault, or the smell is just that of bread overcooked? What if the water seeping across the cabin floor is not a fatal leak but simply the spilling of a drink or the appearance of condensation? Then the rescue called for, in either case most probably a mass evacuation, is unnecessary.

So if we are to speak of salvation in a Christian sense we have also to seek more clarity about the peril in which the world is believed to stand. To know the danger is to be more than half way to understanding what is required to deal with it. If God is said to be acting towards the world in order to save it, from what is it being saved? There are, of course, other questions too: how did this danger in which the world stands come about? And for what continuing purpose is humanity being saved in any case? But these further questions arise when we have understood what the human situation is, what is the danger in which we stood until God chose to act as saviour through the life and self-offering of Jesus Christ.

Most religious traditions, and certainly the Christian tradition, have a name for this peril, a diagnosis. In Christian terms, the peril from which humanity has to be, and has been, saved is the power of sin and its consequence, death. Yet this naming of the human peril arose in the context of a culture in which religious language was widely used and understood; controversy there certainly was, but there could be conversation that assumed that humankind had to reckon with a common destiny, and that such a destiny was determined by the power of a divine world towards which human beings had to turn if their lives were to have meaning and shape.

That world was one in which human beings were understood to have to reckon with a realm other than this, with a power beyond human powers, and with a reality beyond human imagining, let alone control; it was also a world where the human situation could be understood as a shared one. If all human beings have to reckon with a transcendent reality, then all human beings share the same fundamental peril and the same ultimate opportunity. In such a world it came naturally to speak of a universal saviour, for in such a world there was a universal peril with which humanity had to contend, a common disaster which men and women faced and from which they needed to be saved. Not only that: God's concern for the whole person is more naturally expressed in a culture which has not polarised our 'inner' and 'outer' worlds as modern culture does.

Is that the thought-world which we still inhabit and in terms of which it is still possible to speak of one who died for our salvation, the salvation not of believers only but of all who have been and are yet to be born? And if, as has been widely stated by those who have observed western culture, such a world has passed from us irrevocably (so far as we can tell), how can we continue to speak of salvation? Does our witness require that we first of all restore for ourselves and our fellow human beings a shared diagnosis of the peril in which we stand, and of the transcendent reality which human beings must face?

A concern, therefore, to address the question of salvation draws us inevitably into the discussion of how far our society is secularised, and of the extent to which that is a development which cannot be resisted, and so has to be accepted as the context within which the message of salvation has to be proclaimed. Secularisation is a hotly debated concept among sociologists, both as to what it is and whether it is a dominant feature of our culture. Similarly theologians have by no means been of one mind in their discussion of whether such a secularised world is to be accepted and valued, or opposed as inimical to the practice and proclamation of the Christian gospel.

Even in a secularised society, however, it is not to be assumed that 'salvation' has no meaning. Quite the contrary: much of modern literature, not to mention many of the television 'soaps', are about salvation (though they seldom use that word), trying out various versions of it and often rejecting them as inadequate.

The recently revived 1955 classic document of western secular society (written by an Irishman in French and translated into English), Beckett's *Waiting for Godot*, offers perhaps the most precise and profound exploration in twentieth-century secular literature, even using salvation language. It is a drama about waiting for salvation: but from what, to what, by what means – none of these are clear. The mysteriously salvific figure, Godot, is never defined. As the play ends, one of its two main characters says to the other:

> We'll hang ourselves tomorrow. Unless Godot comes.
> And if he comes?
> We'll be saved.

(Samuel Beckett, *Waiting for Godot* (Faber edn. 1961), Act 2, p. 94)

The play reflects the sense of many that 'salvation' means release from the sufferings and painlessness and accidie of human existence, though into what better kind of life is not clear. A more precisely religious dimension to this is not lacking in writers throughout the century, up to our own time, such as Peter Ackroyd, Muriel Spark and Margaret Drabble. Even in *Waiting for Godot* there are frequent references to Christ:

> One of the thieves was saved.
> It's a reasonable percentage. (Act 1, p. 11)

And the crazed philosopher, Lucky, speaks for the religious confusion and anguish of this century:

> Given the existence . . . of a personal God . . . with white beard . . . outside the time without extension who from the heights of divine apathia . . . loves us dearly with some exceptions for reasons unknown but time will tell and suffers . . . with those who . . . are plunged in torment . . . and what is more that as a result of the labours left unfinished . . . it is established beyond all doubt . . . what many deny that man is seen to waste and pine to shrink and dwindle . . . I resume for reasons unknown . . . the facts are there . . . the labour's abandoned, left unfinished. (Act 1, pp. 42–4)

This focuses a secularised society's problem with the very concept of salvation: 'The facts are there' – that humanity continues to suffer. Salvation, therefore, must lie somewhere in the unknown territory between that human suffering and the paradoxes of belief: 'divine apathia', God's 'dear love' of us and allowed torment of us. The conclusion bleakly reached by the large mass of those who think about it at all is that 'the labour's abandoned, left unfinished'. But by whom? By God? By humanity?

The sufferings of the present time, therefore, remain a common denominator between Christianity and the secularised world. But their theological meaning (if any) is wholly in dispute. What of the world to come? Would most of the secularised West, like Macbeth, 'jump the life to come' were all well in this one?

Here the language of poets and novelists and mass media is even more ambiguous. Inspector Morse, in one of the last episodes screened, said of a drug dealer who had destroyed several teenagers and then been killed in a car chase, 'I don't believe in hell, but when I meet people like him, I wish I did.' Beckett's tramps were not sure if they believed in hell – for them it was almost synonymous with death. Indeed, salvation from death preoccupies much of the western world, but the state beyond death remains a troubled question mark.

William Golding, Nobel prize novelist of the evil and the holy, spoke in *The Paper Men* for those for whom the latent sense of divine judgement remains a reality. His fugitive novelist fleeing from that symbolic Recording Angel, the literary biographer, comes face to face in his flight with a statue of Christ in a church, which he sees as the epitome of divine judgement, 'the universal intolerance'. He is delivered from the anguish of this sense of imminent divine wrath by an extraordinary revelation of God's mercy, expressed in golden light, and harmony of music and form and movement; death becomes

> Narrow steps to a door with a drumhead . . . I think that there was a dark calm sea beyond it, since I have nothing to speak with but metaphor. Also there were creatures in the sea that sang. For the singing and the song I have no words at all.

(William Golding, *The Paper Men* (Faber 1984), p. 161)

But this God-bestowed peace in the face of divine judgement is rare in twentieth-century writing, though perhaps it is not without significance that it is described by a novelist recognised as one of the greatest of this century. But for most of the western secularised world, what emerges most clearly is the sense of loss attendant on the conviction that there is no 'God up there' weighing and assessing and evaluating us, caring about us enough for it to matter how we go on.

> When you're young you prove how brave you are, or smart; then, what a good lover; then, a good father; finally, how wise or powerful or what the hell ever . . . But underlying it all, I see now, there was a presumption. That I was moving

on an upward path towards some elevation, where . . . God
knows what . . . I would be justified or even condemned – a
verdict, anyway. I think now my disaster really began when
I looked up one day – and the bench was empty: not a judge
in sight. And all that remained was the endless argument
with oneself – this pointless litigation of existence before an
empty bench.

(Arthur Miller, *After the Fall* (Penguin Plays 1968), Act 1)

Many serious writers have charted how the loss of a sense of ultimate
accountability has meant losing the shape and meaning to life.

Against such loss have been the stratagems of existentialism, hedo-
nism and the other 'isms' of our age. The language of despair and
hope are so intertwined and reversed as to become inextricable.
What is clear, as the century moves to its close, is that for many
people in our culture there are not only no more divine certainties,
but no 'divine'. And equally clear is the perplexed sense that the
language of computers is an inadequate exchange for the language of
the seer.

> . . . What anthems have our computers
> to insert into the vacuum caused
> by the break in transmission
> of the song upon Patmos?

(R. S. Thomas in 'Reply', *Experimenting with an Amen*
(Macmillan 1993))

So in attempting a contemporary understanding of the nature of
salvation, we must reckon with the fact that our prevailing culture
has little room for the sacred, or with a transcendent world on
which this one depends. However, while some cultural trends seem
hostile to faith, we have to take seriously the significant phenomenon of 'folk' or 'common' religion. This can comprise seasonal
church attendance, use of the 'rites of passage' provided by the
Church (baptisms, marriages, funerals), inherited beliefs which are
largely Christian (about God as creator, about Jesus as Son of God,
about the efficacy of prayer or meditation) and adherence to basi-

cally Christian moral values. Such 'folk' religion bears witness to the continuing quest for God. There is a religious component in many public observances; and there are on occasion less orthodox (from a Christian standpoint) manifestations of a transcendent world-view including new spiritualities, and even the more disturbing phenomena of witchcraft and Satanism. But for many people in modern western societies life is carried on without reference to a divine dimension, and all religious institutions reflect attempts to respond to that change in social attitudes.

If society as a whole does not assent to a transcendent dimension to life, such assent becomes a matter not of public doctrine but of individual choice. Alternatively, society fragments into smaller groupings each with its own frame of reference and religious outlook, and the individual chooses to which, if any, to belong. All religion therefore, even religion which claims universal truth or the capacity to offer universal salvation, comes to be seen in the society at large as a matter of personal choice, and therefore it becomes harder to treat universal truth claims as such. Such is the effect of the privatisation of values, a process by which the publicly accepted order of society is replaced by an order chosen by the individual and not subject to contradiction by the community at large.

Such a social situation, one in which there is no agreed human peril from which to be saved, easily also generates a wide range of more or less exotic pursuits by which individuals and groups seek to give shape to their lives, in a world in which no common peril is acknowledged and no generally accepted transcendent dimension is accepted. These are the privately chosen roads to salvation, the cults and movements of those who are forced to invent for themselves means of salvation to fill the vacuum left by the departure of a religious frame of reference.

Those movements are not to be criticised just because they are privately chosen: they may contain much that is good, and many of the insights which traditional religious belief has either promoted or neglected. For example, many of the movements and disciplines that promote a holistic view of the human situation and therefore promote ideals of human wholeness are affirmed by many Christians. On the other hand, some adherents of traditional religions, Christianity in particular, may see grounds for resisting some of the movements and cults of modern times: but they have to take seriously the extent to which they too, no less than those who have ceased to practise traditional religion, are part of a world where their own language and ritual, whatever the claims to truth they may make, are seen as personal choices of a way of salvation in a world where no generally necessary road to salvation is readily accepted.

A further effect of modern culture on religious belief and attitudes is the increased tendency to make ways of salvation available only within sects of the saved. As the way of salvation is not generally accepted in society, the need to belong to the community of the saved can only be fulfilled by the creation of units of intense belonging. Salvation is then seen as a crucial feature of identity, and to belong is to be joined to the community of the saved. Many Christian groups show such signs of exclusivity in belief and practice, and indeed such groups show many of the signs of institutional success. There is, however, an inevitable contradiction between the message of universal salvation in Jesus Christ and the proclaiming of that message by a group which holds that salvation tightly to itself. What cannot be avoided is the harsh question of how that message can be conveyed and lived out in a world in which transcendence no longer functions as part of the common currency, where there is no sense, therefore, of shared human peril and therefore no common quest for salvation.

We have also to accept the significance of the fact that this report makes its appearance at a particular time in our society's political history. 'Privatisation', of which we spoke earlier, is also a word in the language of politics and economics, spheres in which notions of individual responsibility have come to take on powerful signficance in a country which in recent years has moved sharply away from a much stronger view of the role of the State in welfare provision and in the direction of the economy. What has the gospel of salvation to say to those who have gained materially from these far-reaching political changes? And what to those who have lost by them? Release from debt is a strong biblical image of salvation, and an image grounded in experience; how is such language to be used and heard in a society where public debt has come to be regarded as economically dangerous, while private debt, seen as a crucial part of the engine of the economy and strongly promoted by the advertising of financial institutions, has increased by leaps and bounds? If a primary aspect of the gospel of salvation is that it is good news for the poor, when the Church speaks about salvation it has to bear in mind who the poor are in our time, how they come to be the poor, and what their experience of poverty is: their identity and their experience may indeed be a reflection of a common feature of all times and societies, but it also has a quality and a character particular to this time, and their salvation and ours has to be within history, our history.

So in considering the context in which the Christian understanding of salvation has to be understood and communicated, we take as examples three of the most pressing challenges of our particular time:

1. the impact of scientific cosmology on our human self-understanding;

2. the challenge of the social context, of which the issues raised by feminism have come to the fore and call for particular attention; and

3. the greatly increased awareness, in the world generally and in western societies in particular, of the variety of religious belief and the existence and antiquity of faith traditions as central to the development of other civilizations as Christianity has been to our own.

These three vital aspects of our context will now briefly be described in turn.

The context of contemporary science

In the twentieth century, science has learnt that the cosmos itself has a history. It has not always looked the same. A fraction of a second after the Big Bang, the whole universe was simply an expanding ball of energy. Such initial simplicity has given rise, after fifteen billion years of cosmic history, to a rich, evolved, complexity, of which we ourselves are far and away the most striking examples known to us. Four billion years ago, the Earth was lifeless, though its chemically rich shallow waters held the promise of the eventual development of replicating molecules and living beings. Humankind is a very late event in this story, our own variety of hominid, *Homo sapiens*, having only appeared within the last fifty thousand years. Many details of the evolutionary history of the universe are still unknown to us, but its general sweep appears well established and there are no pointers to a radical discontinuity of development setting humanity apart from the physical world which gave it birth. The universe is not just there to be the backdrop for the human drama; we are actors who have emerged from the scenery.

Within this apparently continuous story of human origin, the coming-to-be of consciousness is the most profoundly novel development in the course of cosmic history. A world which was once just a hot quark soup has become the home of beings endowed with self-awareness and the ability to understand that physical world of which they are a part. The unriven unity of evolutionary history encourages a view of men and women as being psychosomatic unities, integrated beings, and the most impressive example of the fruitful potency of matter-in-organisation, rather than their being soul–body hybrids, in whom a divinely provided spiritual component is housed within an evolutionarily constructed physical shell. Our ignorance of the true nature of humanity is so great that it is impossible to be dogmatic, but a dualism of soul and body, such as is associated with the philosopher René Descartes, has become an increasingly difficult position to hold in the twentieth century. It always suffered from an inability to give a convincing account of how the two contrasting substances, extended matter and thinking mind, could interact with each other. We now know, from studies of brain function, brain damage, and the effect of drugs, how intimately these two aspects of our nature influence each other. A plausible theory of the material and the mental must be capable of accommodating this interaction, and of acknowledging our emergence historically from the world of animals and, initially, inanimate matter.

The Christian may not find great difficulty in being pressed to move in the direction of a psychosomatic understanding of human nature. The concept of humankind as animated bodies rather than incarnated souls is generally characteristic of Hebrew thought. It is true that a dualist as well as a unitary view of human nature can be supported from Scripture, though the latter predominates. While Platonic notions have often influenced Christian theology, they should not be taken to be determinative of it.

Even if this picture of human psychosomatic unity is correct, there is no adequately worked out articulation of it available to us at present. A contemporary philosopher, Thomas Nagel, has spoken of our being able to indulge only in 'pre-Socratic flailings around'. The implied comparison is instructive: six centuries BC, the Greeks began to speculate that the variety of objects in the world might be but the manifestations of a single underlying stuff. Guesses at air or water as the basic substance were hopelessly awry, but the germinal idea has come to flower in our own time as physicists seek a unified theory of matter. Similarly, we may be centuries away from a psychosomatic theory of human nature, but it may still be the most hopeful direction in which to wave our arms. For our present purpose it would be imprudent to pin our thoughts on any particular contemporary speculation, but nevertheless it will be valuable to consider how a doctrine of salvation can be framed in psychosomatic terms. It would not be possible to speak of salvation in terms of the destiny of souls after death, if the soul is thought of as the detachable spiritual part of ourselves. If the essential human being is an embodied whole, our ultimate destiny must be the resurrection and transformation of our entire being.

To speak thus is not to abandon talk of the soul, but to seek its rede-finition. When we speak of salvation in terms of the destiny of souls we must be using the word to represent the essential nature which constitutes us in our individual particularities. That essence of humanity is certainly not merely the matter of the body, for that is continuously changing through wear and tear, eating and drinking. What provides continuity and unity through that flux of change is not material but (in a vague but suggestive phrase) the vastly complex information-bearing pattern in which that material is organ-ised. That 'pattern' can surely be considered as the carrier of memories and of personality. We are close to the Aristotelian notion of the soul as the 'form' of the body, found also in Aquinas. Language is here being stretched to a limit, but to think of the soul in this fashion is by no means to embrace a reductionist concept of human nature. 'Pattern' is a word with deliberately holistic over-tones, for its essence is the web of relationships in which the parts are organised. Eventually, an understanding of 'pattern' will have to be adequate to accommodate what has traditionally been spoken of in terms of the mind and heart and will.

'Information' is not to be construed in a narrow computer-model sense; there are good reasons for rejecting the strong programme of artificial intelligence, equating thought with computation, and for believing that thought transcends the mere execution of algorithms, however complex. Human beings are very much more than 'computers made of meat'. At present our understanding of that 'much more' is insufficient to provide us with a vocabulary precise enough to express a psychosomatic picture of humankind, and we have to be content with language which is evocative rather than adequate. In this respect, the view of human nature that we are presently pursuing does not differ from its reductionist or dualist competitors. We are all groping in the dark. Yet Christian discourse on salvation which can lay claim to serious attention in the context of a contemporary understanding of humankind will have to be prepared to speak in terms which are not exclusively those of a soul–body dualism.

There is a second scientific problem which such discourse must also address. It arises from the perception that present physical process is condemned to eventual futility. Cosmologists not only discuss the very early universe. They can also peer into its future. They tell us that it will end badly, either in a collapse back into the cosmic melting pot of the big crunch, or in the low-grade radiation of a cooling, ever-expanding universe. These prognostications are to be taken with the utmost seriousness. One way or the other, the ultimate prospects are bleak. Of course, the futility of this fate is not just around the corner. Tens of billions of years are expected to elapse before these things come to pass. But it is as certain as it can be that within the unfolding history of the present universe, humanity will ultimately prove to have been a transient episode.

It is possible to speculate that intelligence will nevertheless continue. It will have to engineer for itself new forms of embodiment, 'computers' taking more and more bizarre forms as the circumstances of the universe change. In the dying phase of an endlessly expanding universe, one might suppose that 'thinking' entities would come into being which were extended systems capable of processing information ever more slowly as energy runs out. In the hectic final stage of a collapsing universe, the whole cosmos might become an ever faster racing computer. Ingenious as these speculations of a 'physical eschatology' may be, they are subject to a variety of objections. They are framed in reductionist terms which equate fulfilment with unlimited processing of information. They suppose a persistent purpose for survival to be present in intelligent being, despite the possibility for self-destructiveness perceptible in human sinfulness. They do not meet the hope of individual destiny and fulfilment which belief in the God of Abraham, Isaac and Jacob encourages (Mark 12.24–7).

The final futility of the universe puts in question any ultimate recourse to evolutionary optimism. The unfolding of the present process will end either in collapse or decay, so that those who trust in a true and everlasting hope will have to look elsewhere for its ground and guarantee. Only God could release the universe from its 'bondage to decay' (Rom. 8.21).

On a much shorter time–scale, scientific knowledge already poses problems in relation to human significance and destiny. Culture's power to transmit information from one generation to another has profoundly modified evolutionary history, which previously had relied for such transmission on the limited resource of DNA. In the past the average life of a species was of the order of a few million years. It is not clear whether *Homo sapiens* may be expected to give way to an evolutionary successor in the same way that earlier hominids gave way to us, but claims of an ultimacy for humanity are problematic from a scientific point of view.

We are gaining the possibility of interfering with life by manipulating human genetic material. This ambiguous gift not only raises hopes of curing genetic disease but also the spectre of a eugenic programme reminiscent of Aldous Huxley's *Brave New World*. The more we are successful at biochemical manipulation, the greater will be the temptation to think of human beings as complicated biochemical machines. At the same time, the advance of technology increases the divorce between humanity and nature and, by the provision of greater leisure time, poses the question of what are the activities which truly enhance human value. These developments affect human self-perception and so impinge upon how the need and nature of salvation may be conceived. Scientific advance of itself is neutral; it simply extends the range of human choice for either good or ill. Yet its great success encourages the expectation that every problem will have its prompt and full solution, produced by a suitable research programme. Even in medicine this hope is illusory (the elixir of life will always elude us) and the pursuit of the good life requires much more than technological facility. Science is too external to our deepest nature ever to present the ground of a salvific programme. To suppose the contrary would be the grossest scientism, making the processes of the natural order as science has disclosed it the basis of religious belief.

Feminist challenges

If our intellectual environment has been changed out of all recognition by the advances in scientific knowledge, the social environment in which faith is professed and lived out has changed just as dramatically. While there is, of course, much political debate about how egalitarian society should seek to become, there is no question that previous generations were ready to assume a far more hierarchical ordering of the life of the community than would be at all acceptable today. The rise of the welfare state, our enhanced sensitivity to all forms of discrimination, and the widespread emphasis on human rights all affect at a deep level the way in which we now see the world. A particular example of such a change of consciousness, and one which has affected Christians most strongly in recent years, has been the widely dispersed awareness that the relations between the sexes have changed to an enormous degree.

The aspiration to change the relationship between women and men in a direction that remedies the political, social and economic disadvantage which has been suffered by women presses upon us in nearly every part of our lives. The action that is increasingly being taken to secure equality of opportunity in the workplace is probably where most people experience the pressure for change; the economic and political power of women and the possibilities which that power gives for influencing political and social structures is something which is recognised not only by women themselves, but by those who seek their money or their votes.

It is no exaggeration to say that all movements which seek political or economic justice, whether or not they seem initially to concern the relationship of women and men, have at some point, and now increasingly early in their development, to address the contribution of women to their programme, their ambitions and their strategy. It has not always been expected that women would play such a key role in determining the course and the outcome of campaigns for racial justice or industrial disputes; now that is largely taken for granted, and male protesters, campaigners, politicians and social activists find that they ignore the role of women at their peril.

Such a change of consciousness is not confined to women who see themselves, or are seen, as 'oppressed' though its form may vary according to the particular situations of particular communities. There is no single set of policies or ideas called 'feminism'; hence we speak of 'feminist challenges' rather than speaking in the singular. The implications of this change of consciousness cannot be avoided by simply noticing (quite accurately) that there is no single 'women's movement' or pointing out (equally accurately) that there are many women in positions of power and prestige. Neither of these observations takes away the force of an immensely important change of moral, social and political consciousness that belongs particularly to this century.

In such a context, it is hardly surprising that the contribution of women to the prayer, life and thought of the churches is far nearer the surface of Christians' awareness than has been the case in the past. The decades of debate about the place of women within the ordained ministry were in that sense inevitable, even though many denominations made a much more rapid adjustment. One result of that debate has been that most Christians, not least in the Church of England, can be expected to have formed an opinion on the matter, and those supporting and those opposing the admission of women to the priesthood find it equally necessary to demonstrate that in coming to the view which they hold they have taken seriously the social context of women's liberation.

That these social and ecclesiastical developments were bound to affect the conduct of all sorts of theological discussions was to be expected. All the major branches of theology evolved in a context in which the dominant role of men passed for the most part unquestioned and indeed unnoticed. The question therefore was bound to be raised, how the major theological disciplines should develop at a time when the influence of patriarchal assumptions is increasingly being suspected and a wide range of proposals is being canvassed for countering those assumptions in the present day. These proposals in their turn constantly raise the question how far and in which ways the authority of biblical and doctrinal statements can be questioned in the changed climate brought about by the rise of feminist thinking.

In considering the effect of feminist challenges within the life of the Church two particular points need also to be borne in mind: first, as in the case of secular thinking, theologians who regard themselves as speaking from a feminist perspective are engaged in vigorous debate among themselves about the scope and nature of feminist challenges to traditional theological thinking. There is a burgeoning literature expressing varied points of view and covering different aspects of Christian witness, much though not all of it concerned with very fundamental issues. Secondly, while theologians may differ on the detail and in their response, there would be widespread agreement that much of the Bible and of the later tradition of the Church contains material which assumes male supremacy, and that therefore any attempt to take feminist issues seriously is bound to involve discovering criteria for discriminating among different parts of the tradition.

While the emergence of feminist critiques of traditional expressions of Christian faith is a general issue in Christian doctrine, it has some very particular points of contact with the Church's witness to God's salvation of the world. It is important to note that we speak here of 'critiques' in the plural; for not surprisingly in the case of new and developing thinking, the arena is one of considerable debate. But the two main points which have to be addressed in a climate of which feminism is so important a part are the description of the human situation – the nature of the human peril as we have denoted it – and the divine response.

If sin is that from which humankind is to be saved, to what extent has the definition of sin been affected by the male-dominated cultures in which the doctrinal tradition has developed? There has been much debate about the core of human sin, so often represented as overweening pride, and also about the role of male domination in the development of the story of Adam's and Eve's disobedience in the Garden of Eden. From the earliest days of feminist theology, there has been a questioning of whether the character of human sin

17

was traditionally understood as pride because men had seen it that way. If women had been allowed to play a fuller part in the development of the concept of sin, might they not have wished to place a greater emphasis on sin as the failure to assert and take responsibility for oneself? If that is so, then while it might be very appropriate to exalt the virtues of gentleness and sacrificial vulnerability when you have a male audience in mind, to describe sin in that way to women might simply compound their negative self-image and encourage them to collude in a position of abiding weakness.

The tendency of traditional understandings of sin – and therefore of the human peril – to be drawn from 'a man's world' is very pervasive. Among the Ten Commandments are some clearly aimed at discouraging the people of Israel from adopting some of the oppressive features of the slave-owning culture from which they had emerged; even so women appear in the tenth commandment simply as adjuncts of the male audience to which the words are predominantly addressed. This will not pass unnoticed in our day; for to continue to speak in the same way about sin, without a good deal of interpretation and even, some would say, adaptation is bound to compound the situation of women: it conveys the message, whether intentionally or not, that for women rescue from the human peril consists in their accepting a highly negative self-image. In a society seeking to be sensitive to the place of women we have to take seriously the use to which concepts of sin have been put in the past and might be put in the present.

If the understanding of the human peril we can hold is affected by changes in male and female consciousness and the relationship between the sexes, so equally will be our understanding of how God has responded to human need. The statement that God in Christ responded to human violence, to hatred and the abuse of power, by absorbing on the cross the worst that humanity could do raises this question in an acute form. Was Christ responding to, and absorbing, primarily the sins of men? And was God's saving response of willing and meek self-sacrifice not simply an acting out of the role in which women have tended to find themselves, though in their case not willingly but as the result of the coercion and socialisation to which they have been subject? And if the self-sacrifice of a man is indeed a healing and saving response to the sins of men, what would be the response of a saving God to sins of collusion and of failure to act with an appropriate self-assertiveness and responsibility?

These questions go uncomfortably near to the heart of the gospel. For the doctrine of sacrifice has, as will necessarily appear throughout this report, been a central theme of the Church's preaching of salvation; and many statements about sacrifice within the Christian tradition are quite distant in their assumptions from modern understandings of what it is to make sacrifices or to display self-sacrifice. Such modern understandings are bound to affect the way in which Christian witness is heard in our time. That being so, the Church's witness to a God who saves by sacrifice is open to being suspected of being an attempt to exalt an alleged virtue which women have been obliged to practise in order to show that they knew their place. Such a witness is hardly likely to be experienced as saving, and whether a version of the doctrine of sacrifice can be expressed in terms which meet this objection is a matter to which we shall have cause to return.

The changing consciousness of women and men about their relationship goes to the heart of the doctrine of salvation in another way also. For the question is now bound to be asked whether a male saviour can save women. As has been evident in many of the debates about the ordination of women, this may be the sharpest form human beings have encountered yet of the paradox of Christ as both particular human being and universal saviour. It is true that the maleness of Christ has not been given much emphasis in traditional teaching about the incarnation; but recent debates have made clear that God's incarnation as a man is held by some to be a crucial dimension of our salvation.

That raises the issue of equality and difference which is so central to the quest for justice between women and men in a central matter of Christian belief. On the one hand equal treatment for women is being expected (for example in the workplace) and on the other proper consideration is demanded for differences of biological function, and whatever social and psychological differences they are thought to entail, if any.

Thus the rise of feminist consciousness is a very important part of the context of whatever we say about salvation. In any church or community there may be debate about this or that item of the feminist agenda; but such disagreements are dwarfed by the immense gap that separates our generation from those that have gone before; what makes us different is that for us these questions, whatever we think about them, are unavoidable. In the realm of Christian faith, that is particularly true when we consider how it is that we shall continue to say that God has saved the world through the cross.

Other faiths

The other major world faiths present a further challenge in any Christian reflection about salvation. Hinduism, Buddhism and Judaism predated Christianity; Islam and Sikhism have coexisted with the Christian faith for hundreds of years. Countless generations of believers have lived their lives within these religious frameworks, and passed on their faith. They have largely resisted the appeal of the Christian gospel, and found seemingly satisfactory answers to life's questions where they are. What is the place of these religions in a Christian understanding of salvation? Is their inclusion ruled out a priori? Or can they be salvific, in any sense of that word? And if we consider they can be, within a Christian understanding of the content of salvation, then are we imposing our content on something that these religions would define in various different ways? What is their doctrine of salvation, if they have one at all? Whom would they include within this, and under what criteria?

These questions now seem imperative to us, because of the presence of large numbers of adherents of other faiths in Britain, a development largely in the last thirty years, except in the case of Jews. This context is elaborated later in chapter 7.

However, the theological issue of the relation between other faiths and the Christian understanding of salvation is there, regardless of whether a single Sikh or Muslim actually lives in Britain. The fact that Christianity was born out of Judaism presented this issue from the beginning, as is highlighted in Romans 9–11. Questions have always been there for those in the so-called mission field. The difference now is that the challenge presents itself much nearer to home.

The Second Vatican Council's constitution on the relationship of the Church to non-Christian religions (*Nostra Aetate*) lists questions it considers always to have stirred the human heart:

> What is a human being? What is the meaning and purpose of our life? What is goodness and what is sin? What gives rise to our sorrows and to what intent? Where lies the path to true happiness? What is the truth about death, judgement and retribution beyond the grave? What, finally, is that ultimate and unutterable mystery which engulfs our being, and whence we take our rise, and whither our journey leads?

It then takes a revolutionary way for a Church which had affirmed for so long that outside the Church, by this meaning the Roman Catholic Church, there was no salvation: it speaks of salvific possibilities in other religions, as they try to answer in their own way these fundamental questions.

Even if the questions are the same, the answers they give vary greatly. This applies to what we need to be saved from, to what we are to be saved for, and to the means by which we are saved. They may not even use the world 'salvation'.

As we look at the self-understanding of various faiths, we can distinguish between the religions of the Book, Judaism, Islam and Christianity, on the one hand, and eastern religions on the other: these last are concerned primarily with how to be saved from the negativity of this world; in the former, on the other hand, this world is important for its own sake; history is where the events of the salvation story are determined, both within this world and in the 'not yet' of what is beyond history. In what follows we are inevitably summarising, both for lack of space and because within each religion, as indeed within Christianity, understandings vary greatly.

For classical Hinduism, salvation is a central concept; Hindus use the word *moksha* or *mukti*, which can be translated 'liberation'. This is the liberation of the soul from *karma*, from the chains of previous deeds, and from *samsara*, the endless cycle of birth and rebirth. The soul is liberated by being absorbed into God, or entering into total communion with God. This liberation may be by deeds, by devotion or by knowledge. Grace plays a varying part in different traditions. In general, the source of wrongdoing is seen to lie predominantly in ignorance, *avidya*; hence the well-known prayer from the Upanishads: 'From the unreal, lead me to the real, from darkness lead me to light, from death lead me to immortality.' On such a view there might be various ways to truth; and the Christian way may be one of them. Buddhism began as a protest movement within Hindu Brahminism; it largely shares the Hindu world-view. The central concept to describe salvation is *nirvana*. This is not annihilation in a metaphysical sense, but elimination of desire and clinging to self. It centres on liberation from attachment, from aversion and from ignorance about our true nature. It is clinging that causes suffering; the aim of the teaching of the Buddha is to be saved, not from suffering itself, which is universal, but from the mastery of suffering over us. Salvation is not brought by God – even if God exists; rather it is the responsibility of each to gain it for ourselves, with the help of teaching and meditation. We are responsible, too, for the salvation of the whole of creation; hence the centrality of compassion in Buddhist practice. There is no exclusivity here.

Sikhism also has an inclusive understanding of salvation. We are all dependent on the grace of God. Guru Nanak wrote:

> If a man goes one step towards him, the Lord comes a thousand steps towards man.

> Good actions may procure a good life, but liberation comes only from his grace.

Salvation can be described as union with God, and from this flow deeds of service to others. Heaven can be now, where God's praise is sung.

In Islamic understanding, Allah accepts whom He wills and condemns whom He wills: 'Allah leaves in error whom He will and guides whom He pleases' (Qur'an, 14.4). We can only throw ourselves on His mercy and do our best to do His will. It matters what we and our community do now, within history. We will be judged after death: 'To us they shall return, and we will bring them to account' (88.26). Heaven will be the reward for the faithful, which is graphically described in the Qur'an; this is what Muslims believe is going to be the reality, and includes being in the closer presence of God. Punishment is being cut off from Him. The best insurance for the moment is to do our religious duties, and those include our social duties, including caring for the poor. As regards those from outside the Muslim community, the Qur'an may not appear fully clear, but peoples of the Book at least, Jews and Christians, seem to have a chance of salvation too: 'Believers, Jews, Christians, and Sabaeans – whoever believes in Allah and the Last Day and does what is right – shall be rewarded by their Lord; they have nothing to fear or regret' (2.62).

Judaism generally prefers the word redemption to salvation. Repentance and returning to God are centrally linked. At times concentration is on individual repentance, at times on the corporate. In some traditions, the emphasis is on spiritual redemption, in others on the concrete experience of a return to the promised land and Jerusalem; at times, it is in the hands of the individual or the people of Israel, at other times it depends largely on the intervention of God from beyond history. The whole world must now be mended, because the whole world has been implicated. In general, Judaism is concerned with redemption within Jewish tradition; it respects the integrity of other faiths, and tends towards universalist possibilities, resting this on obedience to the covenant with Noah, which is available to all.

In dialogues about salvation, clearly it will matter greatly which faiths we are involved with. With a Hindu or a Buddhist, the nature of humanity will be central: what is it to be saved? For a Hindu, Jesus as the incarnation of God will not be a problem, but Jesus as the only incarnate one will be. For what does that make of Rama and Krishna and other incarnations? Jesus on the cross as a moral example will not be a problem; exclusive salvation through the cross will be. Most Buddhists will be able to affirm the example of Jesus enduring suffering in compassion for the whole world; but this can only be an example; we are accountable for our response to this example, or that of any other teacher. Sikhism will respond to Jesus as the Guru, teacher of a salvific way; Sikhs cannot see him as the only way. The Muslim and the Jew will be able to affirm much of our world-view; but not the place of Jesus, nor, above all, the cross. What is central is the almightiness of God, and total dependence on him; and for them Jesus is not God.

In general, it is the person of Christ, and the cross, which remain stumbling-blocks. The more these are central to our understanding of salvation, the harder it will be to find common ground. If we concentrate on concepts such as the kingdom of God, and the liberation, righteousness and peace that lie at the centre of the kingdom, if we look at the central teachings of the Sermon on the Mount, and if we are content to see the cross as primarily an example of the ultimate sacrifice of selfless love, then dialogue about salvation becomes much easier. But given that we profess that God became incarnate for us and 'for our salvation', there can be no escape from the way in which the life, death and resurrection of Jesus Christ are seen as decisive for human history and the fulfilment of God's purposes. There is no alternative, therefore, to the facing of these matters as they arise in dialogue between the faith communities.

These are the theological issues. In practical, day-to-day questions, people of all religious faiths may feel they have more in common than that which divides them, within an increasingly secular Britain which does not see any religious response as relevant. Is what we have in common a concern with similar questions, as the Vatican II declaration suggests? There will be many issues of individual and social concern, not least concern for the poor and weak within our competitive society, that may unite us. This is related to questions of healing and wholeness on which different communities of faith can work together now. Should this not be of central concern in any study of salvation?

By living and working with people of other faiths, and by recognising their integrity and faithfulness as well as, in many cases, their goodness and love, questions of salvation arise. Can the God of love, revealed in Christ, reject such people whom we admire? They follow a way of life based upon religious discipline, prayer and reading of Scriptures. Can the quality of their lives be separated from their religious belief? If not, how can we find an adequate way of speaking of salvation, one that both affirms the significance of the biblical witness to Christ and at the same time can take account of what we see before us? We return to these questions later in chapter 7.

Conclusion

We have sought to do no more in this opening chapter than sketch an agenda which indicates why witnessing to the salvation God offers in Christ is both vitally important and especially challenging: we are brought face to face with some of the most pressing questions of our age. Whatever the Church says in proclaiming the gospel will be judged by the extent to which we show awareness of the profound challenge which our culture presents to us. The Church is called to witness from its own experience and on the basis of the charge which the Scriptures lay upon it, to the truth that God is one who saves.

Yet to speak of the challenges of our 'culture' runs the risk of suggesting a range of somewhat abstract issues, matters which concern the particularly thoughtful or literate. This would be a quite inappropriate message for a discussion of salvation, a theme which has to embrace the whole range of human concerns and be offered to all, particularly to those to whom life appears to offer little, who are excluded from the adequate meeting of their material needs as well as participation in the range of human culture.

It is of the essence of all human communication, and has been a central feature of witness to the gospel of salvation, that as much attention is given to the message that is heard as to the message that is spoken. To speak of God saving humankind from the peril in which it stands, requires that we take seriously our context in a society in which there is no clarity, let alone agreement, about the peril in which we stand, and in which religious language has no natural and agreed reference point among our contemporaries. That is not to say, and the evidence of our quotations from contemporary literature supports this, that there are not seekers after salvation outside the churches: there are, and discerning the nature of the predicament they describe is an essential first step to sharing the Christian message of salvation.

We live also in a time when the universe has expanded dramatically through what modern science has revealed. That means that some of the language of Christian witness, even language that has appeared to stand the test of time, can well appear naive and even obscurantist if we speak as if only human history were the arena of salvation, and as though hope were a self-evident response to what we see around us in the material world. Profound questions about the nature of persons and the universe they inhabit present themselves to us.

As well as the new perspective presented by scientific cosmology, we have sketched two other major concerns of our time: the changed consciousness of women and men about what justice between the sexes requires, and which images of God and accounts of the work of Christ would be truly liberating for both; and the issues raised for the preaching of the gospel by the dialogue with members of other world faith communities, now much closer at hand in a smaller world and a nation of many peoples.

It is against such a background that what we have written will be read, and by its response to our contemporary situation that its truthfulness and not just its effectiveness will be judged. We are convinced that the gospel of Christ contains the resources we need when it comes to facing such questions, and the following chapters seek to present those resources. We do so while keeping in mind the questions contained in this chapter; they are not just those of our hearers and readers: they are ours also.

2

The giver and the gift

Salvation: a flexible concept?

The previous chapter explored the context to which the Christian message of salvation today must speak. But in order to clarify what that message is in our contemporary context, we need to explore the notion of salvation itself. What do we Christians mean by salvation? A sampling either of the history of Christian thought or of Christian opinions today could easily suggest that the term is an extremely slippery one, by which Christians in different times and places have meant a wide variety of different things. Is salvation going to heaven when we die or something experienced here and now? Is it deliverance from guilt and the threat of divine punishment or from the transience and mortality of earthly life or from demonic forces which tyrannise over human life or from oppressive political and economic conditions? Is it a matter of knowing God or of living a better life? Is it the salvation of individual souls from a corrupt world or the creation of an alternative society in contrast to the world or a means of transforming society into the kingdom of God? Does it make people divine or truly human? Differing answers to such questions about what salvation is relate very closely to differences on other important issues, such as whether what Christians mean by salvation is also available through other religions or to those who have no religious faith.

One response to the questions could be that many of the alternatives posed are false alternatives. Salvation need not be this *or* that; it can be *both* this *and* that. For example, salvation may be both something enjoyed in this life and also a destiny beyond death. Probably most Christians have thought so. But although not all of the alternatives need be exclusive alternatives, they do represent wide variations of emphasis in Christian understandings of salvation. Moreover it looks as though such differences of emphasis have a lot to do with the different social and cultural contexts in which the Christian message is presented and believed: the different ways in which people identify what is wrong with the human condition and the correspondingly different aspirations for deliverance or improvement.

For example, in the second and third centuries there was a widespread sense of human mortality and a corresponding aspiration to escape this mortal life and to share the immortal life of the gods. There was also a fatalistic sense of the domination of human life by demonic forces. The Christian gospel therefore appealed in part because it promised immortal life beyond death, which was often called deification: God's gift to humans of participation in God's own divine, immortal life, of which there can be a foretaste in the present. The fearlessness of the Christian martyrs in the face of death testified to Christ's conquest of death. Similarly, his conquest of the demons, demonstrated by exorcisms in the name of Christ, offered a kind of liberation for which many people were looking. By contrast, in the twentieth-century West, across the whole spectrum of types of Christianity, there seems to be a fairly consistent emphasis on salvation here and now rather than after death, which must be partly related to increased life expectancy and to the way modern western society has tended to push death to the margins of its consciousness. Humanisation rather than deification is naturally the theme in a society whose general sense of the divine is weak. Only a minority now sees present salvation as liberation from the demonic, though in the different cultural circumstances of some parts of Africa this theme does come into its own. In the affluent West, the typical existential ills of modern urban culture – lack of meaning and purpose in life, loneliness and quiet desperation, satiation with a materialistic lifestyle – have often been the plight from which Christ delivers, although pursuit of the kingdom of God through overcoming social deprivation has also had a place. But an emphasis on salvation as liberation from political and economic oppression is more characteristic of some types of Christianity in the

Third World (more accurately called the Two-Thirds World). It is no accident that other agencies or movements beside the Church – such as psychotherapy or the New Age movement in the West, political liberation movements in the Two-Thirds World – often parallel both the diagnosis of the need of salvation and to some extent the kind of salvation offered by the Church in particular contexts.

We need not be too disturbed by these contextually varying inter-pretations of Christian salvation. Certainly the Church should be in the business of criticising and correcting the way people perceive the human situation, but it must also make connections with its cultural context. Varying emphases may be justifiable so long as it is not the case that just any concept of salvation will do. Other examples can show that this is in fact not the case. To return to the second and third centuries, one way in which the culture of that period differed so radically from ours was in its sense, not only that mortality was an evil, but that the physical and material world is a place in which the human spirit does not belong. Liberation from the body and the physical world into a purely spiritual existence was therefore the most culturally appropriate form for salvation to take, and it was the form offered by the Gnostics. But the Church rejected this Gnostic understanding of salvation because of its conviction that the material world and the human body are God's good creation. Salvation is not liberation from them, but redemption of them. Thus one way of viewing the human plight and salvation from it, highly appealing in its cultural context, was found not to be an adequately Christian understanding of salvation.

So it is not the case that anything goes, but emphases do vary, and, up to a point, rightly so. But in that case, two issues arise. First, is there anything that provides continuity within the varying emphases? Second, does Christian salvation really differ from other claims to remedy human ills? In a pluralistic society like our own (which, in this respect, it is worth noting resembles the Roman world of the first three centuries AD) one cannot avoid asking whether the Church's understanding of salvation simply puts Christian packaging on a product essentially the same as that offered by others too.

The argument of this chapter will be that answers to both these questions can be found by thinking about the relationship of salvation to God. Salvation is not *only* the various good things that God gives us – forgiveness or eternal life or liberation from oppression or healing of relationships or finding our true identity. It is all these things – almost as many of these things as Christians have ever supposed it to be. Because it is all these things, emphases may vary, as the human situation and people's perception of it vary. Because it is all these things, what Christians experience as salvation always overlaps with experiences of liberation and greater fulfilment and enhancement of life that others experience in all kinds of ways. But what we mean by salvation is not only all these things. It is receiving these things from God in an experienced relationship with God as the source and the goal of them all. In Christian talk of salvation there is always an absolutely necessary reference to God. Moreover, this God who is both our saviour and our salvation is the triune God. In the next section we shall see why, as Christians, we cannot talk about salvation without talking about God. In the following section we shall see why, when talking of salvation, Christians find they need to talk not simply of God, but of the trinitarian God. The doctrine of the Trinity, we shall see, stands in the closest possible relationship to what we Christians mean by salvation.

God and salvation

Christians cannot talk about salvation without talking about God. For us in contemporary Britain this means talking about God and salvation in the kind of society described in the previous chapter – a pluralist society which, even to the extent that it is religious, is by no means exclusively Christian. In this chapter we leave aside the question of salvation in other faiths, and how this may relate to the Christian understanding of salvation. Another chapter is devoted to that question. For the moment we shall focus on the fact that ours is a society in which many people live their lives without reference to God. This will enable us to pose the question: what is it that distinguishes the Christian understanding of salvation from parallel notions of human fulfilment which make no reference to God?

The point is not at all to show that there is nothing in common between the two. The point is rather that, given that there may be a great deal in common, we are seeking what distinguishes the Christian understanding of salvation from notions of human fulfilment which make no reference to God. We shall use the term 'fulfilment' to describe what secular people seek when they aim (as all people do in some way or another) at some form of greater human well-being, but seek this without reference to God. The very use of this term shows that what they seek is in many ways comparable with what those of us who are Christians call salvation. The word 'fulfilment' could very appropriately be used to describe the experience of Christian salvation, and some theologians have so used it. Christians believe that true and complete human fulfilment can be found only in relation to God. The word 'fulfilment' puts the emphasis on what we, from our side, attain, while the word 'salvation' puts the emphasis on what God, from his side, gives. But this is no antithesis. The human search for fulfilment and the divine gift of salvation could appropriately be seen as two sides of the same coin. So it is only for convenience in the present context that we shall use 'fulfilment' to refer to the secular quest for fulfilment *without* God, and 'salvation' to refer to the religious concept to which God is essential. Because we wish to focus on the presence or absence of reference to God, 'fulfilment' is the more appropriate term for non-religious aspirations.

In our contemporary society it is increasingly the case that secular people seek *autonomous* forms of self-fulfilment envisaged in *individualistic* terms. We shall speak here of this dominant cultural trend, which can easily be observed in such indices of dominant culture as soap operas and advertisements. Of course, there are many people without religious faith whose understanding of their lives is quite different from this dominant culture's. There are many, for example, who hold to the highest ideals of a humanist vision of the world, strongly committed to moral norms. Nor are we here in the least concerned to pass judgement on people. It is not the moral or spiritual quality of people's lives that is at issue, but the kind of understanding of human fulfilment which is most characteristic of our secular culture at present. Various sectors of society may be more or less influenced by it. Reactions against it may even be gaining ground. But we shall certainly all be living with its influence for some time to come.

This dominant cultural trend is part of the transition, in which our society is currently caught up, from a modern to a postmodern culture. The term 'postmodern' is a useful means of signalling the idea that contemporary western culture is undergoing a major shift from the culture of modernity, which dates from the eighteenth-century Enlightenment, into a new phase. Postmodernity is more easily characterised negatively, as marked by the discrediting and disintegration of the major features of the culture of modernity, than it is positively. But autonomous individualism, which we have suggested is a keynote of contemporary aspirations to self-fulfilment, is certainly a significant feature of postmodernity. The emergence of this radically individualistic concept of self-fulfilment has accompanied the demise of the idea of human progress, which was so characteristic of the modern period and still retained some vitality until quite recently. This nineteenth-century idea of progress envisaged the progress of the whole of society towards goals which were perceived in moral and spiritual as well as material terms. It depended on some sense of normative values and ideals which defined the greater good of all people. But the only remnant of this notion which survives in any strength is the still widespread belief in the importance of technological advance, with which is closely associated the absolute imperative of economic growth. Ecological considerations have not yet significantly qualified the latter. Ever-increasing affluence is the only form of progress in which as a society we still believe, clinging to it with almost desperate devotion. It is widely assumed to be the essential prerequisite for most possibilities of self-fulfilment, but it scarcely constitutes in itself a form of self-fulfilment.

In our postmodern culture self-fulfilment has become a matter of individually self-chosen goals. Freedom – in the sense of the absolute autonomy of the individual – has become the single, overarching ideal to which all other goals are subordinated. I must be free to be whoever I choose to be and to pursue whatever good I define for myself. There must be no normative goals, models or ideals for which I *should* aim. The point is not simply that there *are* no such normative goals, but that there *must* be none, if I am to be truly free to be myself – to be the self I choose to make myself. Needless to say this contentless freedom is much more of an ideology than a reality. Most of us in fact seek fulfilment in goals presented enticingly to us by society, not least by commercial interests, as those normally thought desirable – especially in sexual relationships, work and an affluent lifestyle. But these are ideologically packaged as means to a freely chosen, non-normative path of self-creation. This ideological packaging is seductive. It leads people to set great value on, for example, freedom to buy things (consumer choice) and freedom from long-term commitments in relationships – understanding these things as important to their self-fulfilment. Such notions of self-fulfilment have all the potent allure of the ideal of freedom. They also have their victims: people impoverished by debt and children thrown out of a parental home to live on the streets are just some of the more obvious of these.

The roots of this particular ideology of self-fulfilment lie in the rejection of God, and it requires the rejection of God. This is because it envisages freedom as absolute autonomy. The freedom it desires is not freedom to discover and to embrace truth and goodness for oneself, but freedom to create one's own truth and goodness for oneself. 'God' is only conceivable as a kind of function of one's freedom, and in some debased forms of contemporary religion 'God' becomes a mere means to the religious person's self-fulfilment – a genie in their lamp. In a culture which has lost the sense of what it could mean really to believe in God, this is not surprising. But it illustrates how carefully Christians need to distinguish the Christian understanding of salvation from the culturally dominant notions of self-fulfilment.

Fulfilment as the pursuit of absolute autonomy has freedom from God as its presupposition. By contrast, salvation – in the Christian sense – is what people seek when they know that God is the reality to be reckoned with from first to last. For people who seek salvation, whatever else they may think they can know about God, it is self-evident that God is the source and goal of all things, never a means to an end. God is the source and the goal of my freedom, never its function. I do not know what Christians mean by salvation until I realise I can be fully myself only in receiving myself from God and in giving myself utterly to God. Salvation is to experience as the source and the goal of my own being and living the one who is the source and the goal of all things.

The point of drawing so sharply the contrast between postmodern secular self-fulfilment and Christian salvation is not at all to deny that many of the particular things in which people seek self-fulfilment – self-integration, healing of relationships, finding a purpose in life, and so on – are also aspects of Christian salvation. The point is that, beyond all such correspondences between secular fulfilment and Christian salvation, God makes all the difference. Fulfilment is sought axiomatically without God, whereas salvation is nothing at all without God. From one point of view the various aspects of salvation which can be sought and even attained by secular people without reference to God are good things. Their value should certainly not be denigrated. Christians themselves are constantly, rightly, engaged in pointing people to them and helping people find them. But nevertheless from the point of view of the Christian desire to see human life attain its fullest meaning and destiny, consciously integrated into its ultimate source and goal, these good things, had without reference to God, lack the one thing necessary. They are Hamlet without the Prince. From this point of view, we can see what Augustine of Hippo meant when he said that 'whatever God promises is worth nothing without God himself'.

In insisting on salvation's essential reference to God, we are not just saying that salvation comes from God. If salvation were just the various gifts which God gives us, then to have the gifts without recognising the giver, without even recognising them as gifts which come from a giver, would not be to miss anything essential. If this were the case, then we might well be able to say that, from a Christian point of view, the human attainment of a chosen self-fulfilment is in fact the divine gift of salvation, though not recognized as such. This is more or less how every twentieth-century Christian attempt to disguise the loss of God by putting a Christian gloss on secular experience sees it. There is a real element of truth in this perspective, for various human goods – all that genuinely contributes to healing and wholeness and life-enhancement – are recognisably aspects of what Christians call salvation. But still they are not salvation itself, because salvation itself is not only gifts from God, but God's gift of God's own self to us in his gifts and as himself.

This point can be easily understood by analogy with gifts in human life and relationships. Suppose I receive something valuable, gratu-itously but not as a gift from someone who meant me to have it. It may fall off the back of a lorry or I may win it in a competition. It is worth having; I shall be pleased with it; it will be useful to me or enhance my life. But this experience is quite different from receiving the same object as a gift from someone who loves me. In this case the object has not only the same value in itself as it would have if I had won it in a raffle; it also mediates a relationship between myself and the person who has given me it as a gift. It will have the added value of an expression of the giver's love, and the more my relationship with the giver matters to me the more this value will surpass the value of the gift in itself. Valuable or useful as the object is in itself, the greater difference to my life is made by the discovery or assur-ance that someone loves me. Because the gift expresses the giver's love, the giver, in giving the gift, also gives herself or himself to me. In receiving the gift as a gift, I receive at the same time the giver's gift of himself or herself. In the same way, God gives himself to us in all his gifts of salvation. If we have any of them without recognising them as gifts of God, we have something valuable. But to experience them as gifts, to recognise the giver in the gifts, is to know God. This is what Christians call salvation.

The point is always implicit and frequently explicit in the biblical account of salvation. In the Old Testament salvation is experienced in a wide variety of concrete human goods: deliverance from political oppression, economic want and threatened death, healing of disease, protection from war, wild animals and natural disaster. But the heart of these is always Israel's relationship with Yahweh, repeatedly expressed in the covenant formula: 'You shall be my people and I shall be your God.' Psalm 85, for example, beautifully illustrates how inseparable for Old Testament thought are, on the one hand, the identification of salvation with the political and economic well-being of the nation, and, on the other hand, the experience of God, known in God's steadfast love, God's faithfulness, God's righteousness and God's peace precisely in this very tangible gift of salvation. This experience of God in God's gift of salvation is the depth-dimension of the gift itself, without which it would not truly be salvation.

Similarly, in the gospels, the salvation Jesus initiates in his ministry takes many concrete forms in relation to a variety of human needs, but comprehensively it is the kingdom of God – the inclusion of all human life in the fully realised purpose of God – and at its heart it is the experience of God as Father. The terminology of salvation is used most frequently with reference to Jesus' acts of healing, but the regular association of these healings with faith on the part of the recipients shows that salvation is more than bodily health. For faith – which is not simply the will to live but the entrusting of oneself to God the source of life – the gift is inseparable from its giver. This is especially clear in Luke's story of the healing of the ten Samaritan lepers (Luke 17.12–19). Only to the one leper who returns, praising God, to give thanks for his cleansing does Jesus say, 'Your faith has made you well (saved you).' The point is not that God, like some patronising benefactor of the poor, requires us to be grateful. The point is that gratitude is a response to personal love. The thankful leper has experienced not only something, as the other nine have, but also someone. His thankfulness shows that for him his healing has been a new experience of God the giver in God's gift.

This essential relationship of faith to salvation receives its fullest exposition in Paul. Its significance needs to be appropriated in different ways in different periods. In the sixteenth century, the Reformers thought it important to stress that salvation is received from God as gift, against the misunderstanding that it could be merited as reward from God. Emphasis on faith made this point because faith is the appropriate attitude to what is received from God as gift. In our context, in which the issue of salvation must be subordinate to the issue of God, the New Testament's correlation of faith and salvation as gift makes an additional point. For those who receive the gift of salvation in faith, the fundamental human act is not the reception of the gift but the entrusting of themselves to God the giver of the gift. Where the Reformation emphasis was on the correlation between faith and the gift of God the giver, ours must be on the correlation between faith and God the giver of the gift. Where the Reformers insisted that salvation, by its nature, can only be received as gift, we need to insist that salvation, by its nature, can only be received as the gift of the God who gives himself in his gift.

The New Testament never dissociates salvation from the variety of specific ways in which God heals and enhances human life now and brings it to ultimate fulfilment beyond this mortal life. These are often comprehensively expressed by the term 'life', in its fullest sense of life in eternal union with God as the source of life. But alongside this positive emphasis on the gift of God fulfilling human aspirations, there is also a demand for self-denial and self-renunciation. The two are paradoxically combined in Jesus' teasing aphorism: 'Those who try to make their life secure will lose it, but those who lose their life will keep it' (Luke 17.33; cf. Mark 8.35 and other parallels).[1] It is important to address this paradox, because the secular quest for self-fulfilment can today so easily become self-seeking individualism, and a claimed duty to be oneself and to fulfil oneself can be used to justify disregarding one's responsibilities for others. The gospel demand for self-renunciation can sound quite contradictory to the quest for self-fulfilment. Of course, Jesus' aphorism deliberately exploits this contradiction, but affirms instead the paradox that self-renunciation and self-fulfilment are not in contradiction. The possibility of this paradox lies once again in our funda-mental distinction between autonomous self-fulfilment without God, and the salvation which is sought in relation to God through faith. As we have seen, even when salvation means receiving concrete benefits from God here and now, its human heart is the entrusting of oneself to God as the source and goal of one's life. Because salvation is found in God, who gives us himself and can be trusted to give us all things in himself, there is no need for anxious preoccupation with the task of fulfilling oneself. One is free to give oneself for others and for God – even in death, which the aphorism certainly envisages. While self-renunciation seems to contradict autonomous self-fulfilment, it is consistent with God's fulfilment of one's self.

Throughout the history of Christian thought about God and salva-tion run two themes, which are all too easily set against each other. The first is the thought that all aspects of human wholeness and well-being, all that heals, enhances and fulfils human life, is included in the experience of God which is salvation. To know God and, indeed, to live God as the source and goal of one's self, as of all things, emphatically affirms, while also surpassing, all other aspects of human fulfilment. False oppositions between the spiritual and the material, the individual and the communal, the this-worldly and the other-worldly have no place in this vision of the all-encompassing good encompassed only by God. But the second thought, from which the ascetic impulse in Christian spirituality springs, is that for the sake of finding God, in whom alone is salvation, everything else can and may have to be given up. In its authentically Christian form, this thought also has nothing to do with the false opposition between the spiritual and the material (although this Gnostic opposition has in fact had an unfortunate influence on Christian asceticism). In the dark night of the soul even spiritual goods have to be renounced for the sake of God himself. The point is not to distinguish among God's gifts, but to distinguish the giver from the gifts. And the aim is not to lose the gifts, but to find the giver who is infinitely more than the gifts. The two themes are not in the end logically incompatible, but their reconciliation in life is only found existentially and contextu-ally.

In this section we have seen that Christian salvation encompasses all that heals and enhances human life. This gives it its continuity with much that takes place in human life outside an explicitly religious context. We have also seen that at the heart of the Christian understanding of salvation is a transforming relationship with God. This both distinguishes it from secular aspirations to human fulfilment and provides the common thread by which all the varying ways in which Christians have talked about salvation are united. But in speaking of God we have not yet considered God as Trinity. God as Christians know God through Jesus Christ is the trinitarian God: the Father, the Son and the Holy Spirit. So we have not understood salvation in fully Christian terms until we have understood its relationship to the trinitarian being of God. In the next section, we shall see how the approach to salvation we have outlined so far can be spelt out more fully in trinitarian terms.

The Trinity and salvation

Just as Christians cannot talk about salvation without talking about God, so they cannot talk adequately about salvation in Christian terms without talking about God as Trinity. The God to whom salvation is necessarily related is the God of Jesus Christ: God the Father, God the Son and God the Holy Spirit.[2] We can see this at once if we put in trinitarian terms the main point we have been making about salvation: that God does not just give us various gifts such as forgiveness or immortality, but gives us, in and with these gifts, the gift of himself. This point is most emphatically made in the New Testament when it is said that God gave his Son (e.g. John 3.16; Rom. 8.32) and gives his Spirit (e.g. John 14.16; Acts 11.17; Rom. 5.5). These phrases mean, of course, that God gives himself to us in self-giving love. In the incarnation and death of Jesus the Son, God *gave* himself *for us* in the once-for-all historical event which constitutes our salvation, and as the indwelling presence of the Spirit in our lives God continually *gives* himself *to us* in our present experience of salvation. To use the fully trinitarian terms, the Father gave his Son for us (e.g. John 3.16; Rom. 8.32; Eph. 1.22), the Son gave himself for us (e.g. Mark 10.45; John 6.51; Gal. 1.4; 2.20; Eph. 5.25; Tit. 2.14), the Father has given us the Spirit (e.g. Acts 5.32; 1 Thess. 4.8; 1 John 3.24), and the Son has given us the Spirit (cf. Acts 2.33). With this divine self-giving all other specific aspects of salvation can be taken for granted: 'He who did not withhold his own Son, but gave him up for all of us, will he not with him also give us everything else?' (Rom. 8.32).

The formulation of the doctrine of the Trinity in its classical form as a result of the debates of the patristic period took place in close continuity with this New Testament emphasis. The doctrine insisted that all three trinitarian persons are truly and equally God, because it is as these three that God gives himself to us in salvation. If the incarnate Son Jesus were less than truly God or if the indwelling Spirit were less than truly God, salvation would be jeopardised. It would not be God's gift of himself. The gift of the Son would be a gift of something less than God himself, and the gift of the Spirit would be a gift of something less than God himself. The divine activity in salvation – the gift of the Son and the gift of the Spirit – would not be the activity of divine *self*-giving that the New Testament witness sees in it. Salvation would be only the receiving of certain good things from God – forgiveness, immortality, and so on – not the experience of the self-giving love of God. This argument from the nature of salvation was the really decisive argument for Nicene orthodoxy against all of the more or less Arian positions in the fourth-century controversies.

The doctrine of the Trinity, which states that the one God exists as three truly divine persons, Father, Son and Holy Spirit, is a statement of who God is, both essentially in himself and historically in God's self-giving for our salvation. It is vital to recognise that this statement of the divine being was never intended to *replace* the story of what God has done and is doing for our salvation in history. This is why the terms it uses (the Father, the Son and the Holy Spirit) are those which the New Testament uses, not in trinitarian statements of God's being as such, but in trinitarian *narratives* of God's self-involvement in human history. The New Testament statements of

God's self-giving which we have quoted – God gave his own Son, the Son gave himself for us, God has given us the Spirit – are examples of brief trinitarian narrative summaries. They summarise the much more diffuse and extended narratives of the gospels and Acts, which themselves are the climactic continuation of all the Old Testament narratives of God's activity in the world and in the history of God's people Israel. In fact, the gospels and Acts are also trinitarian in the way that they speak of the acts and involvement of God in the human historical story they tell; they too speak of God as Father, Son and Holy Spirit, and narrate the relations between these three in God's activity in history for our salvation. But the summaries, by crystallising the theological essence of the stories, also succeed in bringing their trinitarian shape into particularly sharp relief.

The summaries are still narratives of divine action and passion. The doctrine of the Trinity takes a further step away from the primary narratives. It derives from the narratives a statement, not in narrative form, of who the God is who acts and suffers in this story. If we ask whether it is legitimate to derive such a statement about the divine being from the story of God's activity, the answer is that it is legitimate precisely because the story narrates God's *self-giving* in history. If God really gives himself, then who God is in the story of God's self-giving is who God really is. In God's own eternity God is none other than who he is for us in the story of our salvation. In this way, the doctrine of the Trinity is an understanding of God's being derived from the narrative, while at the same time it serves to safeguard the theological reality of the narrative as the story of God's self-giving. Because God is Father, Son and Holy Spirit, because the Son and the Spirit are as truly God as the Father is, therefore the self-giving which the story narrates is a real giving of God's own self for us and to us. The doctrine of the Trinity assures us that what happens in the biblical story of salvation really is salvation in the fully biblical sense. It is not that we can ever do without the narrative. The doctrine of the Trinity does not replace the narrative, but it crystallises an insight conveyed by the narrative itself in order to help us read the narrative aright. We can see how appropriate it is that both of the creeds we regularly use – the Apostles' and the

Nicene – tell the story of salvation within the framework of a *trinitarian* confession.

The doctrine of the Trinity, properly understood, is not a speculative prying into the eternal mystery of God. But it does affirm that God in his own divine self really is such that God *can share himself* with his creation. God is not only the utterly other, who infinitely transcends creation; God can also be deeply and intimately present within creation, as the Spirit, and God can also be one of us, a genuinely human person, as Jesus Christ the Son. Therefore God can and does open his own life for his creation to share. Moreover, because God is Trinity God can share his life even with those created beings, ourselves, who are alienated from God and opposed to God. As incarnate Son and indwelling Spirit, God enters our situation of evil, suffering and mortality, shares with us the pain of our alienation, bears for us the pain of overcoming our enmity and healing our estrangement, sustains us in the struggle to be truly human, redirects our lives towards the Father as the source and goal of our being. The New Testament summary narratives of trinitarian self-giving imply all this. It is as Father, Son and Holy Spirit that God can and does save us.

The intimate connection between the trinitarian being of God and the nature of Christian salvation can be explored a little further by way of comment on two major themes in the biblical and Christian understanding of salvation: life and love. In the biblical tradition that which, more than anything else, characterises God in distinction from creation is God's essential and eternal livingness. Only God has life inalienably as his nature. All other life is received as God's gift. It is God's Spirit, the breath of life from God, which animates all living things and without which they cannot live. To be alienated from God, the source of all life, is to die. To be saved from mortality is possible only through permanent union with the undying source of all life.

This essential and eternal divine livingness is trinitarian life. It is the common life of the Father, the Son and the Holy Spirit. This is why it can be shared with mortal creatures. As the Fourth Gospel puts it, the Father communicates to his Son the intrinsic divine livingness ('life in himself') so that the Son – meaning the divine Son become human as Jesus Christ – may give life to other human beings (John 5.21, 26). But this is not a straightforward mediation of eternal life from God to mortals. The incarnate Son participates in the eternal divine life in an extraordinary form: the form of a mortal life taken through death into eternal life. Because of his uniquely unbreakable union with his Father, Jesus received life from God even in death. Death is the loss of that life which comes from God, but in Jesus' case not even death could put an end to his eternal participation in the common life of the Trinity. Thus by entering our experience of death his divine life overcame death. In the book of Revelation, therefore, the risen Christ can claim the uniquely divine titles of eternal livingness: 'I am the first and the last, and the living one' (Rev. 1.17–18). But he claims them in his own way, not in the way the Father claims them. He claims them as the one who participates *through death* in the indestructible divine life: 'I was dead, and behold, I am alive forever and ever; and I have the keys of Death and Hades' (Rev. 1.18). This then makes a difference also to the way the Spirit communicates life to created beings. The Spirit of life is now the Spirit of the risen Christ and is therefore now the Spirit of life-from-the-dead, the Spirit of resurrection life for the dead (e.g. Rom. 8.11).

Thus God does not give us eternal life as something other than and separable from himself. God gives us life by giving us himself: by giving us God's Son to share our mortality and thereby to transcend it, and by giving us God's Spirit to unite us with the Son and to share his resurrection life with us. To have eternal life is to know God as Trinity: to experience the Spirit of Jesus Christ who unites us with Jesus Christ the Son of the Father. It is to share, through the Spirit, that unbreakable union of Jesus Christ with the Father which has broken the power of death. It is to experience the trinitarian life as our own life, within and beyond the conditions of this mortal life.

When the New Testament and later Christian tradition use 'life' as a term for salvation, the term is an appropriately comprehensive one. Life is a word which stretches from a minimal to a maximal sense. In the minimal sense life is that without which human persons do not exist. Even though we nowadays find it difficult to define the minimum (is it breathing or brain activity?), it remains an essential distinction between inanimate things, which exist without life, and human persons which can exist only by living. However, life in the maximal sense is much more than mere existence: it is real life, all that it is to be fully alive, all that makes for a life worth living. In this maximal sense, life is an open-ended concept. The maximum of life transcends description and imagination. Thus life as a term for salvation is, on the one hand, rooted in our creaturely dependence on God for sheer existence, which in salvation God gives back to us, out of death, but on the other hand it also extends to the prospect of unlimited abundance of life which eternal union with God opens up for us.

Because life as a term for salvation means much more than mere existence, we can also complement it with other terms, of which perhaps the most important is love. For human persons life and love are inseparable. Real life is living with others, for others, through others, from others, in others. It is the reciprocal giving and receiving of life in love. But it is this for us because it is in the first place this for God. God's eternal livingness is no merely abstract existence, but consists in the loving communion of the Trinity. It is the life which exists in the reciprocity of the Father, the Son and the Holy Spirit. Therefore the sharing of the divine life with us, which is possible for God because God is Trinity, is equally a sharing of the divine love with us, possible because God is trinitarian loving communion. This does not mean only that we are objects of God's love, but that we are drawn into and included in the divine life of love. The Father's love reaches us in the Son who identifies with us in love. Drawn out of lovelessness by God's love, we experience the Spirit as our own power to love God and others.

One of the most revealingly trinitarian statements in the New Testament is Paul's claim that 'God has sent the Spirit of his Son into our hearts, crying, "Abba! Father!"' (Gal. 4.6). If we ask how it is that we may know God as Father, the answer is twofold. In the first place, it is because there is already in God's eternal being the loving reciprocity of Father and Son, and from eternity the Spirit is God's openness to sharing that reciprocity. In the second place, it is because the eternal communion of the Father and the Son has been actually incarnated as human possibility in Jesus of Nazareth and actually opened by the Spirit who indwells us to enable us to share it. Therefore the Christian relationship to God is defined by the characteristic, first-century Aramaic term used by Jesus of Nazareth – Abba! – while at the same time it is included in the open circle of the divine love. Finding ourselves within the story of salvation, we find ourselves also within the love that God eternally is.

God, language and gender

One way in which the feminist challenges, discussed in chapter 1, have impinged on Christian theology has been in relation to traditional language about God. Traditionally Christians have used, almost exclusively, masculine pronouns for God (he, him, his, himself), along with a variety of masculine images such as Lord and King. Trinitarian language about God has used two masculine images – Father and Son – as the normative terms for the 'first' and 'second' persons of the Trinity, though the normative term for the 'third' person – the Holy Spirit – is not inherently masculine. Occasionally feminine language has been used for the Spirit,[3] and striking examples of feminine imagery for God as such and even for Jesus the incarnate Word can be found in the Bible and the tradition. But these have been no more than variations from the standard pattern of masculine language. Such language has come into serious question only in recent years, when the reasons for questioning it have been, broadly two. In the first place there is the strictly theological consideration that God is beyond gender. Christian theology has never supposed that God actually is male. Moreover, it is not only male human beings who are created in the image of God. This is equally true of women (Gen. 1.27). It is therefore difficult to see how, when our language refers to God in terms otherwise used for human persons, these should be exclusively or even predominantly masculine. Such language can be felt to exclude women from participation in the image of God. But secondly, feminist critics point out that this is a far from narrowly theological issue. The use of masculine language for God has functioned to legitimate male dominance and the oppression of women. The masculine God is the heavenly counterpart of patriarchy on earth. Even if, in a society where there was no discrimination on grounds of gender, the use of masculine language for God might be treated as an arbitrary linguistic convention, this is not how it has actually functioned and feminists cannot be expected to see it as harmless.

The reason for addressing this issue briefly at this point is that readers sensitive to it will have had ample opportunity to observe our own linguistic practice in the earlier sections of this chapter. Some may have concluded by now that we are not taking the issue seriously, because we continue to use some masculine language for God.

The practice we have adopted is no more than a provisional solution to the problem of language about God at a time when the issue is only beginning to be widely appreciated in the churches in Britain, and is no more than a practice we have thought appropriate for our present purpose in writing this report. Addressing first the issue of the use of pronouns with reference to the noun 'God', the problem, of course, is that English lacks common-gender third-person singular pronouns (which some languages have). There are therefore currently three practices. There is the traditional practice which treats 'God' as a masculine noun and uses masculine pronouns. There is a new practice of alternating the use of masculine and feminine pronouns, implying that 'she' and 'he' are equally appropriate with reference to God. Finally, another new practice which is gaining ground in theological writing is that which avoids pronouns altogether. The word 'God' itself is repeated where traditional language used 'he' and 'him', 'God's' is used in place of 'his', and 'Godself' substituted for 'himself.' This practice has the advantage that for much of the time it is unobtrusive, and so can avoid offence to those who feel deeply either that exclusively masculine language should not be used or that traditional usage should not be changed. However, at times, especially when God is the subject of discussion, as in this chapter, this practice inevitably does become obtrusive, and those whose ears have not become attuned to it find the repetition of 'God' and the use of the neologism 'Godself' awkward. Some also hear it as a retreat from personal language, though this is far from the intention of those who use it. The practice which we have adopted is a compromise. We recognise that the constant use of masculine pronouns can give a misleading impression of divine maleness. We have therefore avoided pronouns wherever this can be done without linguistic awkwardness, but have retained the occasional masculine pronoun where natural English necessitates a pronoun. In other words, we have greatly reduced, but not eliminated the use of masculine pronouns.

With the question of masculine images for the persons of the Trinity, we are in deeper theological water. In this chapter we have deliberately continued to use the terms Father and Son for the 'first' and 'second' persons of the Trinity, despite the criticism of this usage by some feminist theologians. There are important reasons for retaining these terms, while also ensuring that they are understood neither as attributing gender to God nor as in any sense privileging the male over the female. In the first place, the terms Father and Son, as terms of reciprocal relationship, point to a loving reciprocity already within God which is the source of God's relationship with us. Proposed alternative series of terms, such as Source, Word and Spirit, are not adequate substitutes for Father, Son and Spirit, because they do not indicate the relationship within God. As ways of indicating how God as Trinity relates to us, such terms can certainly be helpful enrichments of the classic trinitarian terminology, but they cannot replace it. The use of Creator, Redeemer and Sanctifier, on the other hand, may well be misleading, if it is understood as dividing the work of creation and salvation between the trinitarian persons.

The substitution of the terms Parent and Child for Father and Son would indicate reciprocal relationship in non-gendered terms. But the second reason for retaining the terms Father and Son becomes relevant here. These terms not only refer to an eternal reciprocity within God, but refer to it in the terms in which Jesus of Nazareth perceived and expressed his own relationship with God. They keep us aware that the way we glimpse the loving reciprocity within God is by seeing its human historical form in the life of Jesus. They make it clear that the Trinity is not an abstract definition of God, but a summary of how God is known in the biblical story of salvation which climaxes in the history of Jesus. And so perhaps the most important means of ensuring that the doctrine of the Trinity does not exclude or subordinate women is to tell the trinitarian story of salvation in such a way that those disciples of Jesus whom he calls his sisters and mothers (Mark 3.35) are no less prominent than those he calls his brothers. But in addition it needs to be said that, while the trinitarian terms Father and Son cannot be replaced by others, they can certainly be supplemented by others. They do not say all that Christians want to say about the 'first' and 'second' persons of the Trinity, and they have never been the only terms used. The Book of Revelation, for example, develops a rich trinitarian doctrine of God with only occasional, though significant, use of Father and Son. Where terminology is misunderstood and misused, it can often be rescued by the use of other terminology alongside it, which prevents misunderstanding. Patriarchal misunderstandings of the terms Father and Son can be corrected by the use of both other traditional images and appropriate new ones, such as mother and child, lover and beloved, friend and friend, but the terms Father and Son remain theologically normative in Christian trinitarian discourse.

Creation and salvation

So far in this chapter we have been concerned with God as saviour. But God is also creator. In the context of a global crisis due to disastrous distortions of the human relationship to the rest of God's creation on this planet, it hardly needs to be said that a renewed sense of God as creator is urgently needed. It is needed for its own sake. But it is also needed for the sake of putting the Christian understanding of salvation in its proper relation to the doctrine of creation. Some recent critics have charged the Christian tradition

49

with emphasising the need for salvation in such as way as to denigrate creation, leading to the neglect and abuse of the created world. The Christian tradition is alleged to have encouraged people to think of themselves as essentially distinct from the rest of creation and metaphysically superior to it. Preoccupation with the material world is a temptation and a distraction because our true destiny is to be saved from this world. The creation is no more than a transient environment for spiritual beings like ourselves, and its only valid function is to serve our needs. This kind of caricature of the Christian tradition warrants, for some contemporary thinkers, the charge that Christianity itself is the ideological source of the ecological crisis.

The charge does rest on a caricature, but we should recognise the elements of truth in it. We can confine ourselves at this point to the medieval and early modern periods, which are the most relevant to current debate about the intellectual origins of the modern project of technological domination and exploitation of nature. In these periods we can identify two relevant ways in which the Christian tradition was not entirely faithful to its biblical roots and its fundamental insights. Firstly, some forms of medieval Christian spirituality inherited, and continued to be influenced by, a kind of matter–spirit dualism which is Greek in origin and encouraged people to think of salvation as the liberation of the human spirit, which is akin to God, from the material world, which is the source of temptation. This kind of thinking has had a considerable legacy in western Christianity. However, it is an aberration which the Christian tradition, in the medieval period as in others, has continually corrected from its biblical and traditional resources. The authentic Christian view of the world has a strong sense of the essential goodness of God's creation, which is nowhere more emphatically expressed than in the creation narrative of Genesis 1. As far as human destiny is concerned, the insistence on bodily resurrection throughout the Christian tradition makes clear that salvation is not the salvation of the spiritual from the material, but the redemption of human nature in its essential solidarity with the rest of God's material creation. But, secondly, the interpretation of the passage in Genesis (1.26, 28) which gives humanity dominion over other living creatures has been problematic. In the medieval period this belief in a special role for humanity within creation was usually balanced by the sense that human beings are themselves creatures who belong within creation. Even when misinterpreted to mean that other creatures exist for the sake of human beings, it coexisted with the strong sense that all creatures, human and non-human, exist for the glory of God. It was in the Renaissance that the sense of human creatureliness began to be lost. The Genesis dominion then took the form of a view of humanity's relation to creation which set human beings intrinsically above creation, exercising godlike power and creativity on it. It was this development which coincided with the modern development of science and technology. It therefore fed into that modern ideology which conceived of science and technology as the means of remaking the world to our own design and to serve our own needs. In effect, this was a secularisation of the Genesis text which disastrously removed the idea of dominion from its context in a doctrine of creation.

It may be debatable how far aberrations in the Christian tradition are implicated in the roots of the ecological crisis. This is a difficult issue of historical interpretation. More relevant now is the fact that in the modern period the Church's message has tended to take creation for granted, concentrating on the plight from which people need to be rescued. This coincided with the way that people in modern western society lost that sense of createdness (of being creatures of God, part of a created world, and as creatures dependent on God) which was much more common in pre-industrial society. Living in a world which could easily appear to be mostly a human creation, alienated from natural relationships with the rest of creation, understanding their relationship to the world in terms of mastery and exploitation rather than reciprocity and appreciation, modern urban people have generally lost an existential sense of creation and of God as creator. They can and do experience it, but not with the easy availability of pre-modern people. To the extent that the Church has responded to this situation by accepting it and focusing its message exclusively on God as saviour, it has made a serious mistake, since it is dubious whether belief in God as saviour can long retain its existential reality where belief in God as creator is weak.

If creation has been neglected in favour of salvation, the remedy is not to neglect salvation in favour of creation, but to explore the essential connection between salvation and creation. Salvation is not the rejection or replacement of creation, but its renewal and completion. Indeed, it is helpful to realise that there are ways of talking of God's relationship with the world which do not obviously require the distinction between God's creative and God's saving activity. We could say, for example, that the God from whom all things derive is continuously active, enabling all things to reach their goal of perfection and fulfilment in God. Is the distinction we habitually make between creation and salvation therefore perhaps a case of misleadingly dualistic thinking?

The distinction between creation and salvation should not be absolutised. It makes a distinction within a continuity. But it does serve two important purposes. In the first place, it acknowledges that God's good creation has been disrupted by evil, which is not inherent in the nature of creation. Damage has been done which needs to be repaired. Because this point has often been misunderstood in recent criticism of the traditional Christian emphasis on salvation, it needs to be said very clearly that this emphasis, so far from contradicting the fundamental goodness of creation, including human nature, actually entails it. Only a fundamentally good creation could be redeemed. Not even God could redeem a creation fundamentally corrupted by evil; such a creation God could only replace. The doctrine of salvation itself means that human beings are not trash, to be thrown away, but the good creation of God which God can and does rescue from evil. The doctrine of salvation does not contradict, but presupposes the doctrine that God created human beings in God's own image.

Belief in a fundamentally good creation which God rescues from evil requires a doctrine of the fall. Essentially this means that human beings, originating as morally innocent creatures, chose evil. The story in Genesis 3 is a picture of this, not a literal account of how it happened. At one level of interpretation, the story of Adam and Eve represents the choice which confronts all human beings, and the disobedience to God into which all of us fall. However, when we repeat the disobedience of Adam and Eve, we do so in a context in which sin is already endemic and from which innocence has already vanished. The story in Genesis 2–3 depicts a state of human innocence which existed before any human sin. Given that this primal innocence is represented for us imaginatively, not literally, in Genesis 2–3, there is no conflict with our modern awareness of evolution and pre-history. Traditional elaborations of Genesis 2–3 are much more problematic, for they have depicted a state of paradisal perfection before the incursion of evil. This is not required by a doctrine of the fall as such. Such a doctrine entails only that our first genuinely human ancestors, when moral awareness first dawned in their experience, faced moral choices, not with an inclination to evil, but in innocence. They might have chosen only good, but in fact chose evil. The mystery of this primal choice belongs to the insoluble mystery of evil itself, but it was a real choice, not determined by the created nature of human beings themselves or of their natural environment.

Traditional doctrines of the fall sometimes claimed that physical death and all other forms of what we call physical evil resulted from – and so only appeared in the world subsequently to – the sin of our first human ancestors. What we now know of the physical and biological world and its history makes this impossible. Since death occurred in the animal world for hundreds of millions of years before human beings appeared, death cannot be the wages of sin in the sense that physical death would not have happened apart from human sin. But we can still maintain that death as sinful human beings experience it, as the fate of the godless and the godforsaken, is given its fatal and fateful character by the fact that human beings have turned away from God the source of life. Similarly, the evils that come upon us purely as a result of the physical nature of our world – earthquakes, floods, some forms of disease, and so on – cannot as such result from the fall. But we can say not only that the experience of them in a world of moral innocence would have been different, but also that their destructiveness is in fact greatly increased by human negligence and malice. So the distinction between physical evil (disasters which happen to us) and moral evil (evil we choose to do) is vital. To some degree the former are inevitable in a physical creation like that of which we are a part, though we cannot fully tell how they would have affected us had we not turned from God. Moral evil, on the other hand, is not inherent in the nature of the created world. It is a corruption from which we can be healed.

Of course, the inherent goodness of our created nature was marred but not eradicated by the fall. It is true that some parts of the Christian tradition, especially the Augustinian and Reformed theological traditions, have placed much emphasis on the corruption of human nature. But this emphasis was polemically directed against Pelagianism. It was intended to make the point that human beings are not able to achieve their own salvation without saving grace. When these same theological traditions have been faced with Manichean dualism, which treats the material world as the source of moral evil and irredeemable, they have made the opposite polemical point: that the material world, including human bodies, is God's good creation and remains so. Such emphases – either on the inherent goodness of creation, despite the fall, or on the plight of creation, subject to the ravages and corruption of evil because of the fall – are relative. They are always contextual and often polemical. The important point is that all Christian traditions have held both that evil is serious and that creation is redeemable. Without a distinction between creation and salvation it is difficult to maintain both.

One possible result of eliminating this distinction is that moral evil is reduced to a necessary stage in the development of creation. Creation develops from the less good to the better; it does not need redemption from evil. But then the nature of evil as what is not merely less good but radically opposed to good cannot be recognised. Alternatively, the seriousness of evil can be recognised but treated as integral to the nature of creation. Evil is how creation had to be. But in that case it is hard to see how evil can be overcome without the abolition of creation. Avoiding either of these unsatisfactory conclusions, the distinction between creation and salvation takes evil seriously without attributing it to creation.

The second important function of the distinction between creation and salvation is that it makes it possible to see the future of creation, in the purpose of God, as more than the realisation of potential already inherent in creation. Salvation is often portrayed in the Bible as new creation. Raising the dead, to take a key example, is not literally the same as creation out of nothing, but it is comparable, because resurrection is not a possibility the dead have within their created nature. It is a new possibility given them out of the creative transcendence of God. It is not surprising that a theological tendency to collapse salvation into creation often results in confining the scope of Christian hope within the limits of this mortal existence. Again we must guard against a current misunderstanding. What we are suggesting has nothing to do with the picture of salvation as God's intervention from 'outside' in a creation he had previously left to manage itself. Language of divine intervention, like all such language of divine action in the world, is metaphorical, and has usually been used, not to imply that God was not present and active apart from his intervention, but that at this point he did something different and distinctive. Miracles were called divine interventions, not because God was thought to be usually inactive in the world, but simply because God does not usually work miracles. Much modern theological polemic against an interventionist God has misunderstood a relatively useful metaphor and attacked an Aunt Sally. However, the more important point is that God is, of course, unceasingly involved in God's creation. But God is involved as the transcendent God of infinite possibility, who in the work of healing and perfecting the world transcends not only its negative corruption by evil, but also its positive potential. In particular, God promises to take creation beyond transience and mortality into permanent union with God's own everlasting aliveness.

Alongside the essential distinction between creation and salvation, the Christian tradition has frequently emphasised also the continuity.

For example, our Anglican tradition has often emphasised the connection between creation and the incarnation, in a way that has precedents in the Fathers and in Duns Scotus and his school in the late medieval period. It is the same divine Word who was active in the work of creation who then becomes incarnate within creation. The incarnation thereby brings to perfection the relationship of creation to God. The Scotist view was that incarnation would for this reason have been necessary even apart from sin and evil. Those who have detected a danger that this emphasis plays down the reality of sin and evil have often countered an emphasis on incarnation as such with an emphasis on the cross. The latter connects with our first reason why the distinction between creation and salvation is important. The Son of God did not come into a good world simply to make it better. As incarnate in this fallen world, he bore the full brunt of its sin and evil in order to rescue it from that sin and evil. It would also be possible to counter an emphasis on incarnation as such with an emphasis on the resurrection. This would connect with our second reason why the distinction between creation and salvation is important. The Son of God did not simply fulfil the inherent potentiality of this creation. When God raised him from the dead, God gave creation a new possibility of life beyond its otherwise natural end in death. But these various emphases are precisely a matter of emphasis. Both the continuity of creation and salvation, which an emphasis on incarnation highlights, and the discontinuity, which is emphasised by attention to the cross and the resurrection, are important. The Christian view of the world makes sense only if neither is absolutised.

Thus the essential distinction between creation and salvation needs to be held within a broader sense of the one God's consistent purpose for the same created world to which God remains faithful to eternity. This means that to know God as saviour is necessarily to know God also as creator. Those who experience the gift of God's self in Christian salvation – God's Son given for them in the incarnation, death and resurrection of Christ, God's Spirit given to them in indwelling power to live for God and for others – also discover or rediscover the gift of God's self in creation and all its blessings. And they know these not as two gifts but as one: the self-giving of the same God giving himself to us and giving himself back to us in all things. Those who find God in word and sacrament are often those who love God's creation most and find God, differently but equally, in their fellow-creatures, human and non-human. For salvation, as we said in the second section of this chapter, is experiencing the one who is the source and goal of all things as the source and goal of our own being and living.

Notes

1   On this saying, see also the discussion in chapter 4 below.

2   This section takes further the discussions of the Trinity in the two earlier Doctrine Commission reports in the present series: see *We Believe in God* (Morehouse Publishing 1987) especially chapter 7; *We Believe in the Holy Spirit* (Church House Publishing 1991) especially chapter 4.

3   See *We Believe in the Holy Spirit*, pp. 4–5.

3
Saving history

Introduction

We have now argued that 'salvation' is the work of the one true, triune God. This inescapably points us to the question of salvation within history. The triune God who saves is known as such supremely in Jesus Christ. It is thus a direct implication of the doctrine of the Trinity that this salvation is somehow planned, effected, and offered within history.

But how? What is the relation between 'salvation' and history? This question lies near the heart of a good many issues that have troubled Christian people throughout the history of the Church. It has many facets and dimensions. This chapter cannot address all of them; it offers some guidelines as to how they may be approached.

To begin with, some comments about the two key terms 'salvation' and 'history', and how they are used here.

The word 'salvation' is a shorthand way of referring to quite an elaborate set of ideas. When we say 'the Christian doctrine of salvation', we call quickly to mind a set of stories about the plight of the world and the action of its creator to rescue it from this plight. Within non-Christian systems of thought, the word can evoke quite different stories. They may, for instance, speak of the solution to the plight of the world, and of humans, as coming from the humans themselves, unaided, or from some other force already within the world, rather than from a transcendent god. Thus Marxism (for instance) would see the solution to the world's problems as lying within the range of this-worldly possibilities. Or it may speak of salvation coming from a force outside and beyond the world entirely – that is, a force other than the God revealed, precisely within the world and history, in Jesus and the Holy Spirit. They may offer different diagnoses of the ills of the world, and prescribe different solutions. Part of the task of exploring the meaning of the word 'salvation' is therefore to unpack and examine the implicit stories which the word evokes. The role of the present chapter, within this larger task, is to see just what sort of stories make sense, within Christian understanding, of the relation between salvation and history.

Most people who think of 'salvation' today, be they Christian or not, think in one of two apparently watertight worlds. Many Christians think of 'salvation' in exclusively 'religious' or 'other-worldly' terms, assuming that the word 'salvation' itself, not least when it occurs in the Bible, refers to a state of bliss outside our present space and time. Many non-Christians, however, are happy to use the language of 'salvation' to denote political and social events of processes. We shall need to keep in mind the question of how the 'religious' and 'secular' salvations relate to each other. Are we justified in separating them out so neatly? Does 'salvation' in the Christian sense have anything to do with actual history? If so, what? Is 'salvation' (and its opposite) to be found within socio-political processes, or outside them altogether? Or is there a more complex relationship between them, and if so what can be said about it?

A further level of questioning has to do with where salvation may be found. Does it have one point of origin, or is it available and find-able in many places? The Judaeo-Christian tradition speaks of the one God acting decisively within history; it is therefore bound to stress the uniqueness, particularity, or specialness of this action. In consequence, it has seen itself (in various ways) as having a respon-sibility to share what it has with the rest of the world, who, by implication, do not have it. 'Salvation is from the Jews', as Jesus in John's Gospel said to the woman at the well (John 4.22). Others, including some Christians, find it simply incredible that one small tradition within world history should be the carrier of salvation for all the other vast tracts of human and cosmic history. All, or at least most, must find their own way. This has the effect, of course, of moving 'salvation' away from direct correlation with specific events. Between these two extreme positions there are, predictably, many others which seek to combine in some way the specialness of Judaism and Christianity and the availability of salvation in and through other traditions.

The second term in our puzzle is 'history'. There are four ways in which this word may be used, and it is important to distinguish them from the start.

First, 'history' can refer to 'events taking place in sequence'. History here is simply the events themselves. When we say 'Did that really happen in history?' we are not asking whether somebody wrote about it, but whether the event in question simply took place. 'History' can then come to mean simply the sum total of all the events which have in fact taken place. In principle at least, this ought of course to include the entire history of the cosmos; in practice, it usually refers to the history of *Homo sapiens*. Earlier events are sometimes, understandably though perhaps somewhat illogically, referred to as 'prehistoric'.

Second, 'history' can often mean 'human writing about things which took place'. Indeed, many would say that it is a vital part of being human that we tell the story of what has taken place, interpreting it and commenting upon it (inevitably and rightly) as we do so. It is perhaps because of this second meaning that the phrase 'pre-history' regularly refers to human events prior to the writing of history.

Third, there is a more abstract meaning. This is 'history' as the *fact of* events occurring in sequence within the space-time world. To say 'God is at work in history' does not necessarily mean 'God is at work, always and equally, in all events that have ever taken place' (meaning 1); nor does it mean 'God is at work in the writing and reading of history books' (meaning 2) (though that might be true as well). It means 'God is at work *within* the connected sequence of events in the world'. 'History' here denotes the process, the *fact* of a connected series of space-time events, rather than the events themselves.

Closely connected with this, there is a fourth meaning of 'history' which draws attention to the *space-time location* of events as opposed to their occurrence within the world of thought and ideas. To say 'God is at work in history' in this sense stresses that God is at work within the space-time world, rather than simply within some 'religious' world which only intersects with the space-time world at a tangent.

How then, within Christianity, might 'salvation' and 'history' be related to one another?

Obviously, all will depend on which meanings of the two words we are choosing. Fortunately, we do not have to labour the point, since the reason for talking about salvation and history in the first place within the Christian tradition grows out of the central Christian emphasis that in Jesus Christ the one true and living God has revealed himself fully, finally and above all savingly within history. This means that we are talking about 'history' more specifically in senses 3 and 4: (3) God has acted savingly in Christ at a specific point within the ongoing sequence of events; (4) God has acted savingly in Christ within the world of space and time, not merely in an abstract, non-historical, non-physical way. And this in turn means that we are claiming that 'salvation', within Christianity, cannot belong purely in a 'religious' world, removed entirely from space and time, from the flow and flux of historical causation.

This conclusion would be acceptable to most Christians. But it does not, of itself, answer the questions we raised a moment ago. These questions are vital; according to the answers we give to them, the entire character of our perception and practice of Christianity will differ quite radically. This has been so from quite early on in the history of the Church. Professor Henry Chadwick, in his well-known book *The Early Church,* described the great divide at the start of the Middle Ages as the cleavage between those who wanted to rule the world and those who wanted to renounce it: in other words, the papacy and the monastic movement. But it is not only popes and monks who have taken these routes. They are well travelled highways, and most Christians live somewhere near one or the other.

In order to understand these routes, and to make (perhaps) some intelligent choices in relation to them, what we need is of course a map. That is what this chapter seeks to provide. As with all maps, much is hidden and much distorted, in order that key elements of information may be highlighted. (Consider how accurate, and yet how inaccurate, is the map of the London Underground.) We cannot hope, in a single chapter, to indicate and name every stream of thought, every contour of opinion. What we can offer is a description of the two broad highways of theological thought, each of which takes its own route through the landscape of theological questions. We shall then be in a position to stand back and see what the strengths and weaknesses of each position may be, and to ask the further question: can we learn from these two routes? Is it possible to find a route in which the good points of both are retained, and the weaknesses and dangers eliminated?

In each case, there is of course a further spectrum of opinion. Among the distortions of the mapping process is an inevitable element of caricature; not all popes actually wanted to rule the world, not all monks sought to renounce it. Not all theologians who seem to be travelling along the first route, or the second, take exactly the same turns and twists as one another. The description will be broad-brush, risking caricature for the sake of clarity of line. Numerous possible variations within each position will be quietly ignored. This makes it all the more important that we distinguish, within each position, two alternatives: in each case, (a) a more extreme and (b) a more nuanced and subtle version of the route in question. And, just as theologians, and ordinary Christians, may well combine in themselves some aspects of the two main routes, so some may exhibit now the more extreme, now the more nuanced, version. We are, after all, not the first people to see the shape of the problem and to attempt to find ways through it. Others have laboured; and, though our solutions may not resemble theirs in all particulars, we are attempting to enter in a fresh way into their labour.

The two main routes, then, are ways of putting together the great concepts of salvation and history. To caricature by way of introduction: The first route ('ruling the world'), seeks to affirm the world, the created order, and history, and to find salvation through working with, and within, history. The second route ('renouncing the world') seeks to escape history, as it seeks to escape the created order. If we are to do justice to the whole history of Christian tradition (that is, the history of what Christians have said and done as they have read Scripture and thought seriously about it), we must be sure that the strong points of the rulers and the renouncers are contained in any fresh suggestion that we may make.

One final comment by way of introduction. The question of salvation and history has sometimes been marginalised in theological discussion. The approach taken in this chapter demonstrates that the question is in fact intricately interwoven with the many other great questions that the word 'salvation' generates. 'Salvation-history' is not a category that can be shunted to one side, dealt with as a curious oddity or aberration, and then forgotten. Whatever we say about salvation is bound to include a position of some sort on the question of history.

Route 1: Salvation within history

The first Route through the landscape of Christian theology recognises from the beginning that the world is God's world. Creation is his handiwork; history (the flow of events within the world) was his idea. God reveals himself through both; and he saves through both.

For this Route, the historical process is a story which will all come right in the end. It is the means through which salvation will be accomplished. The role of grace is to complete nature. Sometimes, in this view, it may even look as though grace simply *is* what-is-going-on-in-nature. On the broadest canvas, some have suggested that the entire cosmos is evolving towards its Omega point, spiritually as well as physically. Process theologians have attempted to discover God, not just directing this process, but actually within it. This might be classified as 'salvation within *cosmic* history'.

A second version of this Route shares the same outline, but with a much more political slant. This is seen in certain forms of liberation theology, which offer a salvation *for* the world, *within* its history, with the Church (ideally) as the agent of this salvation through its prayer and action. God is at work in movements of liberation; the Church must not be shy of recognising this and putting its shoulder to the wheel. As in the Marxist theory with which this is sometimes allied, it is by no means clear whether the process of liberation is driven by some inner determinism (in which case it might be better to let it go on its way without interference), or whether it can only come by human aid (in which case the argument that it is predetermined looks very shaky). At any rate, at least some liberation theology clearly follows this Route: it stresses the saving nature of the divine acts in the Old Testament, especially the Exodus, and asserts the continuity between such acts of God within socio-political history and the saving acts of liberation which God desires to effect in the present and future, still within space and time.

On a smaller scale, thirdly, the story of Israel in the Old Testament, and of the Church in the age after Pentecost, is often seen as a progressive unfolding of salvation, in which, within history itself, God's purpose is steadily accomplished:

> God is working his purpose out,
> as year succeeds to year . . .
>
> Nearer and nearer draws the time,
> the time that shall surely be,
> when the earth shall be filled with the glory of God
> as the waters cover the sea.

This view – 'salvation within *ecclesial* history' – has had a solid foothold in the sub- or semi-conscious mind of British culture ever since Handel's *Messiah*, and is further reinforced by the traditional Christmas service of Nine Lessons and Carols. In the former, the Church preaches the gospel to every creature ('Their sound is gone out into all lands') after the resurrection of Jesus, and at the end of this mission there comes the Hallelujah Chorus, celebrating the fact that 'the kingdom of this world is become the kingdom of our God, and of his Christ'. It is only *after* this that the final resurrection of the dead takes place. In the traditional Carol Service, the sequence of carefully chosen prophetic readings gives an impression of smooth historical process, of prophecy steadily working towards fulfilment. If we were to examine the whole books from which the passages are selected we might well find this idea called into question.

Sundry varieties of salvation-within-ecclesial-history may be found within some Catholic thought, in a view of the Church as simply marching forward through time towards its historical salvation. This, of course, is quite compatible with a negative view of non-ecclesial history; though, as debates in former days between missionaries would indicate, the 'Protestant' missions tended to be deeply suspicious of all 'non-Christian' culture, while the 'Catholic' missions, though sure that salvation was to be had within the fold of the Church, tended, true to Route 1, to affirm all that they possibly could within a local culture. Again, the Protestant rejection of Catholic salvation-within-*ecclesial*-history has, in our own century, gone hand in hand with a more general rejection of Route 1 as a whole. This happens, for instance, in the rejection (by Barth and others) of 'natural theology', the attempt to see the creation as a revelation of the true God, and of its political equivalent, the attempt to see what God is doing within history and then simply join in. At this point, and at many others in the discussion, one might want to enquire whether there are other factors involved: whether, for instance, some people incline, for psychological reasons, towards a form of self-hatred which inclines them towards Route 2, and whether others incline towards a form of self-assertion which inclines them towards Route 1. The basic, unadorned, version of Route 1 underestimates the seriousness of sin. Sin, in fact, may well be seen merely as human consciousness of problems within God's good, albeit developing, world. In the same way, there will not be much need for a strong theology of the cross; it may sometimes be seen simply as the preliminary to the resurrection, the birth of renewed creation. This means that followers of Route 1 are unlikely to have a strong critique of human sinfulness; they are more likely to seek things to affirm wherever they can. In particular, they are very likely to affirm the goodness and perhaps the saving power of religions other than Christianity.

There are, of course, more nuanced versions of Route 1. Many Christians whose basic stance has been world-affirming have nevertheless been conscious of evil as a real and potent force, and have seen the need to show how God deals with it. They have emphasised the presence of salvation within history, while allowing at least some weight to the serious problem of evil. This version of the Route would be eager to affirm the presence of salvation in various places where Route 2, as we shall see, would be unlikely to recognise it at all: in various forms of social, political or psychological change, for instance, and in various religious beliefs and experiences with no connection to the Judaeo-Christian tradition. The excesses of the naive Route 1 can be avoided: 'salvation' does not come about simply by some immanent process in which the world is automatically moving towards its goal. Evil is a reality: in particular, evil is found in 'exclusive' systems (including various forms of fundamentalism) which oppress, judge and condemn other forms of religion and experience. A nuanced version of Route 1 might thus affirm 'history' in the sense of 'the fact of events taking place in the world', while being deeply critical of 'history' in the sense of 'the *actual* events that are taking place'. Salvation comes about by the activity of God, and also by the activity of human beings, working to rescue people and situations from the evil into which they have fallen. Salvation is thus at work within history, even though not identical with the historical process itself. It is much wider than the Christian tradition, though the Christian tradition also bears witness to it. Salvation, in other words, is very much a this-worldly matter, but without the naive optimism of the more basic type of Route 1.

The great strength of all forms of Route 1 is that they take creation very seriously indeed. They refuse to see evil as an equal and opposite force to the creator God and his providential working. They refuse, likewise, to write off the social and political dimensions of human existence as irrelevant to the processes of salvation, and try to include them within its overall theological compass. The Route 1 theologian takes the story of Israel in the Old Testament seriously as part of the saving work of God, which is arguably (in those general terms at least) something which the New Testament also stresses; and tries in various ways to understand the whole of church history under the rubric of the continuing saving work of God. To these extents this Route is clearly crossing some terrain which must be included within any fully Christian proposal.

The weaknesses of all forms of Route 1 have to do with a refusal to take seriously two features which are central to biblical and main-stream Christian theology. First, this Route blurs the *ontological* distinction between the creator and the cosmos: pantheism and process theology are the most obvious culprits, but the tendency is, perhaps, present in other forms as well. Second, it is always in danger of losing sight of the moral distinction between good and evil. For Route 1, particularly in its more naive form, Evil is, if anything, simply not quite as good as Good. It is not a radical, dark power, threatening the world and humans. Over the whole of Route 1 stands the charge of Anselm: you have not yet considered the seriousness of sin.

As a result, the work of God and the processes of the world are not as clearly distinguished as they should be. The radical newness of salvation, bursting upon the world with the force of an apocalyptic revelation, is lost sight of behind a smooth, steadily developing historical process. If the cross does very much towards the achieving of salvation, it is held within this steady process, rather than being the abrupt, shocking scandal and folly of which Paul speaks. Though the more nuanced versions of Route 1 do their best to avoid these weaknesses, all sorts of questions remain. That, in part, accounts for the popularity of Route 2, to which we now turn.

Route 2: Salvation *from* history

The second Route to be mapped here is perhaps the more familiar. In some well-known varieties of Christian theology, world history is regarded as simply the strange and somewhat alien environment where human souls are prepared for a non-historical 'eternity'. Attaining to this non-historical goal is what is meant by 'salvation'.

Examples of this viewpoint can be found all over the history of Christian thought. A modern, popular one is provided at one point by John Betjeman (though in other ways he belongs in Route 1; poets, like theologians, are allowed to be inconsistent), according to whom Jesus taught that

> This world is just an ante-chamber where
> We for His Father's house prepare.

The only value of history, in this scheme, is that it is the place where the all-important decisions of faith and morals have to be made, according to which the non-historical salvation will either be granted or denied. History is seen as one aspect of the world of sin, corruption, decay and death; salvation consists in humans being rescued from history, set free from its endless cycles of futility, and liberated into a non-historical world. This, broadly, has been the belief of millions of Christians, for whom phrases such as 'eternal life' have meant, basically, non-historical life, a dimension of 'eternity' in which time as we know it, part of the present created order, will be no more. Several other religions, too, would agree that a 'salvation' of this sort is the ultimate goal; disagreement between them would then focus, not on the meaning of 'salvation', but on the route by which one might attain it. Many, too, who do not profess any religion understand the term 'salvation' in this way. That is part of what they disbelieve in when they disbelieve in Christianity, or other religions which teach it.

Route 2 has had a strong influence on certain aspects of biblical scholarship, especially when it comes to interpreting St Paul. It has often been thought that Paul was expounding just such a view of salvation when he set forth his doctrine of justification. Rudolf Bultmann, alluding to Romans 10.4, wrote that 'Christ is the end of history as he is the end of the law'. The second-century heretic Marcion, who believed that the God of Jesus Christ was different from the God of Israel, claimed to be expounding Paul. He has had many followers.

The history of theology suggests that this Route can branch off quite easily into various forms of Gnosticism. For the serious Gnostic, the world of space, time and matter, and hence of history, is simply evil; salvation consists of rescue from the world, history, time and space altogether. There are, of course, various half-way stages on the route to this extreme position. Most serious Christian theologians would reject the full-blown Gnostic position on sight. Yet, as we have seen, the view persists, not least at a popular level, that salvation and history simply do not belong together. History, including our own history, is a chaotic muddle; God's answer is to save us from it.

Within the naive versions of Route 2, all history, including the history of Israel before the coming of Jesus Christ, is seen in a very negative light. It is, at best, the dark backcloth for the bright jewel of the gospel. Jesus is the one who comes from the non-historical world, to rescue those trapped in history and free them for a non-historical salvation. So, too, the life of the Church is compromised as soon as, and to the extent that, it becomes an 'institution' within history, whether in its own life or as an agent of social and political change. Tinkering with society, i.e. acting to affect the course of history, is simply a distraction. The Church's task is to present to humans the timeless call to decision, to conversion, which is ultimately aimed at snatching people out of history and into eternity.

When it comes to other religions, Route 2 takes a very negative line. (This is actually a little odd, since the escape from history is something it seems to share with Hinduism and Buddhism [see p. 21].) Christians who travel by Route 2 will probably regard all other religions, and indeed many other versions of Christianity (especially Route 1 in all its variations), as delusory and dangerous. They are human attempts to find a salvation which is, in fact, uniquely offered in Jesus Christ. The scandal of particularity becomes, on this view, the scandal of divine action which judges the entire world, including all human religion.

There are, of course, several far more nuanced versions of Route 2. The main and most interesting one, which does its best to build into Route 2 some of the strengths of Route 1, allows that, though salvation is ultimately *from* history, salvation may nevertheless be reflected, or foreshadowed, *within* history.

In this more nuanced version of the Route, it is recognised that there is, within history, something that can properly be called 'salvation'. At the same time, one must insist that the full meaning of that term be reserved for something which lies beyond history altogether. The Exodus, the Return from Exile, and the acts of healing in Jesus' ministry are in some sense 'salvation', but they are not the thing in itself; rather, they are reflections, examples of the saving action of God, designed to lead the eye up to the reality of spiritual salvation. In terms of the map, this nuanced Route attempts to retain the direct line of Route 2 while wanting at least some of the view one might get from Route 1. In theological terms, 'salvation' remains beyond history; but God is the Lord of History, and God effects within history events which share something of the character of that non-historical salvation. In terms of grace and nature, grace works in parallel to God's actions in nature, and is reflected there, but remains ultimately in a different sphere altogether. This way of travelling across the terrain allows for foreshadowings of salvation: it gives rise, in particular, to allegory (seeing hidden meanings about eternal issues within the space-time events) and to typology (seeing an earlier saving event as a foreshadowing of a later one).

In both cases, one might debate whether it really matters that the original event actually happened. This is actually a significant and recurring question whenever Christians discuss salvation and history: how important is it that, for instance, the Exodus actually took place? Logically, one might expect those travelling on Route 1 to insist that the saving events must have taken place, and those travelling by Route 2 to sit light to such a necessity. In fact, however (this is another example of the way in which these categories are more simplistic than most real theologians), many Route 2 thinkers come from a very conservative background, and many Route 1 thinkers from a more radical background; so that Route 2 often finds itself asserting the importance of the historical events, if only to 'prove the Bible true', while Route 1 often asserts their unimportance, even if only to show that salvation is found far more widely within history than in a few selected and unprovable occurrences in the past.

This more nuanced version of Route 2 encourages a particular form of the promise-fulfilment scheme. This consists of isolated texts in the Old Testament, taken out of context, and supposedly fulfilled piecemeal by Jesus and/or the early Church. This attempt to discover 'fulfilment' in the atomistic accomplishment of contextless prophecies has often given the whole idea a bad name. Those who have tried to 'love' the truth of Christianity through listing such supposed fulfilments, as though their apparently miraculous nature provided sufficient evidence of divine intervention, have courted their own nemesis in the retort (made often enough in the last two centuries) that the early Church made up 'events' in the life of Jesus to show such fulfilment. Since this is what many people at once think of when 'promise and fulfilment' is mentioned, we should not be surprised that the concept is often rejected.

What would this more nuanced version of Route 2 say about other religions? The 'biblical theology' movement which exemplified the more nuanced version of Route 2 a few decades ago was not particularly sympathetic to non-Christian religions, with the important exception of Judaism (since it shares the biblical salvation-history). Route 2 would not normally regard events in other religions' histories as examples of 'salvation', despite texts such as Amos 9.7, which speak of saving events within the history of nations other than Israel.

The main strength of Route 2 is the seriousness with which it takes the fallenness of the world and the sinfulness of sin. It feeds on the observable dangers of its mirror opposite (Route 1), which insists on the goodness of the historical process. It claims support from Paul, though arguably at the cost of some central Pauline emphases (such as the renewal of creation of Romans 8). It recognises, in classic Protestant fashion, that any self-congratulation on the part of the Church is hollow and pretentious. It sees very clearly that historical process by itself, and even historical process somehow invisibly steered along by providence, will never bring salvation in all its fullness. The symbol of this strength is of course the cross, which stands as the great God-given 'No' across all attempts to find a straightforward equation between salvation and history. Indeed, this view often stresses the cross as a decisively new event, bringing divine judgement on the old world as well as the promise of salvation. In all these ways Route 2 strikes what may be thought a necessary note.

A second strength of this Route, related to the first, is the fact that it allows fully for the transitoriness of the present world. Evening and morning, built into the present creation, witness to its impermanence. This is not simply a matter of the fallenness of humankind or the world. The creation was made, it seems, to point beyond itself. Birth, growth, decay and death all indicate that, even apart from sin, the present creation was not intended to be the creator's last word. How much more, then, when it has been corrupted by sin? Salvation must then be more than simply a matter of historical process. God, we are told, will make new heavens and a new earth; Route 2 emphasises the word *new*, and focuses on heaven rather than earth.

The weaknesses of this Route are as easy to point out as its strengths. First, despite the impression given at first glance, it is unbiblical. As we shall see, the New Testament writers regularly link the 'mighty acts of God', in saving his people in the pre-Christian era, to the events of Jesus' death and resurrection in a far more organic and interlocking way than this view can possibly allow. The notion of time fulfilled, which Jesus preached and Paul echoed, indicates a positive attitude towards that time.

Second, it is dualistic. Creation may be transitory, but it was and remains good – and that includes its history. The view we have been expounding has at best a shaky grip on the first article of the creed, and hence on the presupposition of all biblical thought. As the orthodox writers of the second century saw, and as some even within the Bultmannian tradition have come to see, the line of thought that runs from Genesis through the Psalms and Isaiah to Jesus, Paul and the author of Revelation envisages a good creation, and hence a salvation which will involve, not the abandonment of creation to its corruption and decay, but the elimination of that corruption and hence the renewal of creation itself. This finds classic expression in Romans 8.18–30.

Route 2, in fact, can only be sustained in practice by operating a 'canon within the canon'. Obvious examples are the treatment of Romans and Revelation. The first eight chapters of Romans are much beloved by adherents of a strong version of Route 2, since they are read as setting out the eternal message of salvation; chapters 9–11 are regularly marginalised. Equally, within chapter 8 itself, verses 1–11 are favoured, as speaking (apparently) of an individual and 'spiritual' salvation, along with verses 28–30 and 31–9; but the vital passage, 8.18–27, is often played down, since its message – a salvation which offers the Exodus hope to the whole cosmos – cannot so easily be fitted into the scheme.

The book of Revelation, where it is not treated simply as a rag-bag of proof-texts, is normally regarded as a book 'about heaven', conceived as non-spatio-temporal. But this, in fact, represents a thorough misreading of the apocalyptic genre on the one hand, which certainly intends a reference to this-worldly events, and a marginalising on the other hand of the vital and climactic chapter 21, in which heaven and earth are not separated, but are finally married. This seems clearly to indicate a salvation that consists in the total transformation of the space-time world. We are therefore driven forwards in the quest of a more satisfactory solution.

The salvation *of* history?

We began our consideration of the two main types of Christian approach to salvation and history by quoting Chadwick's dictum about those who would rule the world and those who would renounce it. But is there not a middle position? Might not salvation be God's means of redeeming history? Might there not be a way of combining the strengths of both Routes and eliminating at least some of their weaknesses?

This possibility, like the two Routes just outlined, can itself only be outlined here. In any case, it would be silly to suppose that we can solve, in one chapter or even in one report, a problem which has taxed the greatest minds of Christianity for two thousand years. Equally, we should not imagine that we are breaking completely new ground in moving cautiously forward towards a position which does more justice to the data than either of the basic Routes have done. One of the main characteristics of all truly great Christian theologians is that they have seen beyond the confines of the basic structure of thought within which they were working. For us, then, hindsight has certain advantages. It is at least possible to note certain boundary-markers, certain points which must be included in any eventual solution and certain other points which must be avoided. Within the framework that this offers, there may be further things that can be said, pointing forward to other parts of this report where some of the details are followed up more fully.

The category of 'redeeming' (as opposed to 'ruling' and 'renouncing') has this great virtue: that it takes with full and equal seriousness both the God-givenness of the whole created order and the reality and awfulness of sin. There is no hint of Route 2's incipient dualism, or of Route 1's glossing over of the problem of evil. The notion of redemption, on the contrary, implies a threefold story about the world, and hence about history: (a) that it is basically good, (b) that it is in deep and serious trouble, and (c) that the aim is neither to jettison it, nor to offer a less radical diagnosis, but to deal with the problem at the root and so to reclaim and restore the created order. This, it seems, is what the more nuanced versions of both Routes have been struggling, not always successfully, to say.

What might a Route look like which took seriously the strengths of both those we have examined? For a start, it would have to say that the world, and history, are the good creation of the good God, though not in themselves complete. They are made for the further purposes of the creator, and he will one day be 'all in all' in relation to them. The analysis of evil, within such a Route, would stress that the plight of the world, and of humans, is that they are dislocated from their intended order, in relation to the creator, to themselves and to each other. Sin and death, as they now appear, do not represent the creator's best and final intention, and both will at the last be done away.

The story of the salvation, or redemption, of history would have to give a large place to the story of Israel. The history of Israel, and the Old Testament as it both records that history and interprets it as the story of the creator God with his covenant people, would be seen as the God-given narrative of how the creator set in motion his plan to deal with the plight of the world, and of humans. It is, strictly in its own terms (i.e. not merely with Christian hindsight), a story in search of an ending. As things stood in the first century BC, no Jew would have retold the story of Israel in such a way as to claim that this story had reached its complete fulfilment; all retellings at that time pointed forward to a great act yet to come within history. This act, which would liberate Israel from her enemies, would also be the time when God's justice, and hence salvation, would in some sense or other spread to the rest of the world.

If the story had come to a stop at that point, it would have been a tragedy. That is, it would have spoken of a remarkable plan for the world, which ran out of steam because of Israel's failure and exile, and her bondage to the very pagan nations to whom she was supposed to be shining with God's true light. However, Christian hindsight from the very beginning saw Israel's ambiguous and recalcitrant character as itself a part of the divine purpose. The line of covenant history was not, and was not intended to be, a smooth unfolding path to glory. The prophets had seen this already. The covenant history reached its goal, not in the smooth triumph of Israel over paganism, but in the crucified and risen Jewish Messiah who was to redeem the world. That was, from the beginning, the point of Israel's vocation.

This is where a very different scheme of 'promise and fulfilment' may be found to that which formed part of Route 2 above, and which, as we saw, has come in for a good deal of justified criticism. The Old Testament as a whole moves towards a great climactic act of redemption, with '*all* the Scriptures' – not merely a collection of obvious 'proof-texts' – leading towards the great Return from Exile, the Coming of the Kingdom. It is important to recognise that the events of Jesus' life, death and resurrection were manifestly not what Jews in the first century were expecting. Further, the way in which scriptural prophecies were used in the early Church was not to 'prove' the truth of Christianity, but to demonstrate to Jews who already believed in the Old Testament as a story in search of an ending that this ending, this climax, had in fact, however surprisingly, been reached in the events of Jesus and the Spirit. These events were, to the eye of Christian faith, the real 'return from exile', the coming of the kingdom.

How might we tell the story of Jesus, within a Route that was attempting to do justice to the best of the two standard ones? It might, perhaps, follow this fourfold outline, in which this history (Israel's history, as the focal point of the world's history) comes to its intended fulfilment. We may here anticipate, and perhaps set in context, some features of what will be said in chapter 4 below.

(a) The *incarnation* was not a tangential intrusion of the creator into his world, an invasion from outside followed by a return to the beyond. It was the completion of the long divine plan, which, with hindsight, Christians see to have been all along a plan devised for God's own use. It is *completion*, not merely fulfilment: that is, it brings the continuous (and highly ambiguous and potentially tragic) story of Israel and the world to its critical and climactic point, rather than merely 'fulfilling' various predictions and types scattered at random in earlier sayings and events.

At the same time, it brings a decisively new element into the story, namely the living presence of Israel's God, the creator. According to some texts (e.g. Isaiah 40–55; Zechariah 2), Israel longed for her God to return to her in person, to liberate her from her sins and their effects. The early Christians were unanimous that this had happened in Jesus of Nazareth. The story of Israel, *and* the story of Israel's God, both reached their fulfilment in Jesus; but in both cases there is a vital element of subversion as well as of completion. In neither case does the story exhibit a smooth, simple line. The story of Jesus offers itself both as the climax of what went before and as something decisively new. The stone which cannot be fitted in to the regular building now turns out to be ideal as the head of the corner. History is the sphere in which fresh divine action takes place.

(b) Jesus' *proclamation of the kingdom* was the prophetic announcement to Israel that her story was reaching its long-awaited crucial moment, and that this story possessed, like many good stories, a vital twist in its tail. Jesus, in the prophetic tradition, announces that divine judgement must fall on Israel herself, and that only those who join his renewal movement will constitute the new people of God who will be the beneficiaries, and thus the agents, of the kingdom. Jesus' announcement puts himself, as the announcer, fair and square at the centre of the kingdom's in-breaking presence, with the totally unexpected corollary that he will be, in himself, the place where Israel's judgement is borne and Israel's new life comes into being. As the bearer of salvation, he himself belongs firmly within the history of salvation. He is not simply announcing a message about something else. He is, in his own actions, words and personal story, the focal point of his message.

(c) The *cross*, from this point of view, was not the mere negation of history, nor simply the fulfilment of types, shadows and predictions. Nor was it simply the tangentially historical outworking of an abstract 'spiritual' or 'theological' theory or mechanism of atonement. It was the completion of Israel's covenant history, that is, the story of the creator, the world and the covenant people. In going to the cross, Jesus acted out his own version of the total story, according to which Israel, represented by himself, must be the people in and through whom the creator God would deal with the evil of the world and of humankind. The cross, as the execution of Israel's Messiah outside Jerusalem at the hands of the pagans, was thus the great summation of Israel's exile, which was itself the fulfilment and completion of the ambiguous and tragic story of Israel as a whole. At the same time, the cross was the supreme achievement of Israel's God, returning to Zion as he had promised (e.g. Isa. 52.7–12; Zech. 14.5; Mal. 3.1; etc.;

picked up by e.g. Luke 19.11–48) to deal with his people's sins and their consequences. This view seeks to take evil totally seriously, while the goodness of creation – and of Israel as the covenant people – is at the same time reaffirmed.

(d) The *resurrection*, from this point of view, was not (of course) the mere resuscitation of Jesus, as though history were simply continuing without change. Nor, however, was it merely the coming to faith of the first disciples, as though it were not itself an event within history. Rather, it was the event (presupposing incarnation, kingdom and cross) through which history itself was and is redeemed; through which, that is, the return from exile finally takes place, and the story of Israel comes to its fruition in the birth of the new cosmic order. The story of Jesus thus takes on its full colouring as the climactic moment in the story of Israel, which offers itself as the focal, and redeeming, point of the story of the world.

Proceeding to think through the story of the salvation, or redemption, of history, we come to Pentecost. The Holy Spirit was not given merely to provide humans with a new sort of religious experience, as though their happy subjectivity were the aim of the whole business. Rather, it was the creation of a community of renewed human beings, still subject to sin and death, but with the sure hope of sharing the resurrection of Jesus Christ. They are not required to repeat the story of Israel over and over again in an endless cycle. Rather, they are to live at its new leading edge, as history moves forward into uncharted territory. Tragedy has been turned to victory, and the returned-from-exile Israel goes on its way, charged at last with its proper mission of bringing God's justice and salvation to the world. If Christ is the goal/end of the covenant history that had begun with Abraham, this can only result in his being also the start, the launching-pad, for the movement – still within history! – whereby the creator now completes the purpose for which Abraham was called in the first place.

The story of the Church is therefore neither a sorry tale of mistake, and of declining away from a true vision, nor a triumphant story of marching from glory to glory. Church history matters; that is, it matters that the story of the creator and the creation has not come to a full stop with the Christ-event. But the post-Pentecost chapter of this story must be told both as the story of what the creator has done and is doing by way of inaugurating his kingdom and as the story of human distortion of vocation – *and*, further, as the story of how even that distortion is taken up into the continuing divine purposes.

In this light, the task of the Church cannot be conceived simply as the summoning of men and women to a non-historical salvation. The Church is to be the agent of a salvation that transforms history; and it can only be this as it implements the work of Calvary, by living and praying at the place of pain in the world, so that the apparently automatic entail of sin, violence and degradation may be stopped in its tracks and replaced, however partially and fitfully, with actual historical forgiveness and reconciliation. The movement which flows from the Messiah, to implement the salvation for the world which he accomplished, is thus itself ambiguous, involving the call of sinful human beings to become disciples, followers, preachers and teachers. Yet this ambiguity is not simply identical with the ambiguity which characterised the people of God between Abraham and Christ. It would be misleading, not to say ironic, if, under the blanket rubric of 'salvation history', we were to lump together the people of God BC and AD as if they were but two manifestations of the same non-historical phenomenon – 'salvation history'! Rather, we must allow fully for two different modes of historical life, contained within the one complete divine plan.

The place of 'other religions' within this combination of Routes 1 and 2 raises one of the largest questions of all. How can it be that the salvation of the world should hinge on one incident within one small historical strand within one tiny segment (the history of the earth) of total cosmic history? Despite Route 1's coyness about it, this scandal of particularity is a non-negotiable part of Christian tradition. The whole point of the Judaeo-Christian world-view is that the creator of the whole cosmos is in covenant with Israel; this always was ridiculous, seen in terms of the scale of near eastern empires, let alone in terms of the aeons of cosmic history. It always was something visible only to the eye of faith. But to abandon it because it makes such an extraordinary claim is tantamount to abandoning the equally extraordinary claim that a first-century Jewish man executed by the pagan authorities is the Lord of the entire cosmos. One cannot abandon the essential oddness of the particularity of God's choice of Israel – and of Jesus – without dismantling the very centre of Christianity.

At the same time, precisely because in this rethought Route history itself is redeemed, it would be wrong to assume that the exclusiveness which characterises most versions of Route 2 will necessarily be retained. On the contrary, we might come to insist that salvation, precisely as the redemption of history, can never remain merely God's gift to the Church, but must also be, at least, God's gift *through* the Church; and not necessarily 'through' in the sense of conscious mission. If it is true that there now exists a body of men and women indwelt by the Spirit of the crucified and risen Jesus, their very existence, irrespective of their activity, might be supposed to make a difference. Down some such path, perhaps, we may wish to say more of a positive nature about those who have stood, and who still stand, outside the Christian tradition. How might this be done?

We need to take a step backwards to get our bearings. According to the controlling Jewish story which the New Testament writers saw as having been fulfilled in Christ, Israel was to be saved *in order that,* through that event, salvation might come to the Gentiles. To elevate Israel's separation from the Gentiles into an absolute principle for all time was therefore to nullify the purpose for which that separation had been commanded in the first place. This, more or less, is what Paul argues in Galatians 3. But, according to John 20, Acts 1 and the whole letter to the Romans, the purpose for which the Church has itself been saved is that, through the Church, the sovereign and saving rule of Israel's God might reach to the ends of the world. Within this controlling story, the salvation of those who have faith cannot be the end of the matter.

The New Testament's retelling of the Jewish story, after all, looks back to the divine purpose in creation, where humankind was created to bear the divine image before the whole created world. For the Church, as the redeemed humanity, to clutch at salvation as a private possession, or (in traditionalist terms) to clutch at the private spiritual salvation of one's own soul as of the essence of the gospel, might just be to make the same mistake that Paul and Luke saw the Pharisees making. By speaking of the redemption of history, we might perhaps point towards new ways of articulating an alternative to the exclusivity of Route 2 or the casual inclusivity of Route 1. We will have more to say on this matter in chapter 6 below.

The hope for the future, within this rethought Route, is for a history which will be fulfilled in God's new creation. Just as Jesus was both the culmination of the history of Israel and the world, and yet marked a decisively and qualitatively different stage in both those stories, so the final kingdom will be the true culmination of the story of salvation from Abraham onwards, and yet will remain the fresh gift of God, the stone that will go nowhere else in the building yet will finally take its place at the top of the corner. The New Testament holds out the pictures of birth (Romans 8) and marriage (Revelation 21) as major images of the coming new age. Both speak of continuity with the past and yet also of a decisive moment in which all things become new. When God liberates the whole cosmos from its bondage to decay, consequent upon the resurrection of his people; when heaven and earth are joined together in God's new order, the fulfilment of his purpose from the beginning; then *of course* the story will reach its ultimate goal in Christ himself. Whether the *phrase* 'second coming' does justice to this reality may be doubted; that there is a reality to which that phrase attempts to point seems an essential part of the entire narrative.

How much strength does this middle way possess? We have aimed to take with full seriousness both the fact of sin and wickedness and the God-givenness of creation and history. We have tried, that is, to do justice to the central insights of the two main Routes, while not falling victim to their inadequacies. Within such a reading of salvation in history, history itself is redeemed and transformed. Transformation does not mean abandonment. If we were to allow for a moment the Route 2 assertion that 'Christ is the end of history as he is the end of the law', we would have to assert equally strongly that, in the resurrection, Christ is the rebirth of history, a redeemed history, just as in Pauline language those who are 'not under the law' are nevertheless under 'the law of Christ' (1 Cor. 9.21). The world of space and time, along with the material world, are reclaimed in the resurrection of Jesus, and are to be fulfilled in the resurrection of Jesus' people and the consequent transformation of the whole cosmos (Rom. 8.18–27). *The one saving plan always was cruciform;* that is the point that ties together the continuity and discontinuity, the affirmation and the negation, the emphases of Routes 1 and 2.

From this perspective, it is not sufficient to see the Old Testament as merely a book of types and shadows. That cannot be the full story of how salvation and history work together. Types and shadows there are in plenty, of course; but the Old Testament is far more. It is the story of the people of God, chosen by the creator to be the bearers of his salvation for the cosmos, the world of space, time, matter and hence of history. Equally, it will not do to see the New Testament as a book which merely offers 'individual salvation'. To be sure, there can be no corporate or cosmic salvation that does not call each human person, as a responsible being, to the obedience of faith. But the New Testament is the charter document for a people, living still within history, chosen by the same creator to be his agents in putting that salvation into effect. The more nuanced readings of Routes 1 and 2 do not go far enough. What is required, if we are to do justice to the biblical record – that is, to the overarching story of creator, cosmos, covenant and Christ – is a scheme of thought that catches up the other two Routes and holds them in a new creative scheme.

Conclusion

What then may we say about salvation and history, about the questions with which we began?

The relation of 'sacred' to 'secular' turns out to be more complex by far than has been supposed by the would-be 'secular' thought, and for that matter the would-be 'religious' thought, of the last three centuries. From the Christian point of view, nothing is 'secular' in the sense of being outside the order of things created, and claimed in love, by the one creator God. The question of the this-worldly 'salvation' of people, nations and races cannot therefore be either highlighted (by secularists) or marginalised (by Route 2 Christians) as though it had no 'religious' (or, better, 'God-oriented') dimension. If we are to take seriously the possibility of a more integrated soteriology such as the nuanced versions of the two main Routes are striving towards, Christian missiology must address the task, which faces the whole world in this post-Cold War and post-Apartheid period, of grasping the full dimensions of that salvation for which the world cries out, and of finding ways to bring it to birth.

But that raises all the more acutely the second question. By what right does any nation, any group, any person suppose that he or she has the answer, or an answer, to someone else's problem? 'Secular' analogies are ready to hand. Western aid in the Two-Thirds World, it is sometimes alleged, has made things worse, not least because it has been self-serving. Might the same be true of Christian mission? Is it not better to let all peoples find their own way to salvation?

The Christian remains committed to the belief that Jesus Christ is the Lord of the whole cosmos. This belief is non-negotiable; it looks the charge of particularity in the face, and answers it by speaking first and foremost of the cross and resurrection, which rule out arrogance or triumphalism by highlighting the vocation of the suffering servant on the one hand, and the renewal of creation on the other. It is the events to do with Jesus, at the heart of the whole matter, which claim the undivided allegiance of the Christian. Either they are the unique, definitive self-disclosure of the one God of all the world, or Christianity from first to last is a horrible mistake.

At the same time, those very events warn Christians against being arrogant, patronising or self-serving in their mission. The scandal of particularity is meant to generate the vocation of service. If history is to be redeemed, that must mean that the course of events in the present world can be changed; can be changed by God; can be changed by God acting in various ways, including action through human agents. This, indeed, is part of the Church's own agenda and vocation. One crucial part of the Church's service to the world is that it should be the agent of healing and salvation within history itself. The sorrows and pains of the world will not be healed finally, to be sure, until the creation of the new heavens and the new earth. But the cross and resurrection indicate that healing and salvation can and do begin in the here and now; that is, within history itself. To work for this is to work for the coming of God's kingdom in earth as it is in heaven; in other words, for salvation and history ultimately to meet and merge. That, after all, is at the heart of the prayer that Jesus taught his followers to pray.

4

The story of the saviour

We shall now look more closely at what the New Testament says about salvation, both how it continues Old Testament emphases on the physical reality and corporate dimension of salvation; and also how it introduces a new note of completedness and finality – of salvation achieved through the atoning work of Christ. And we shall explore some of the ways the rich imagery of atonement in Scripture has been reflected upon and developed in Christian tradition.

Continuity with the Old Testament

The various words in the Hebrew and Greek Bible which we translate 'save' and 'salvation', along with related terms like redeem, restore and deliver, have an originally material connotation: they refer to rescue from dangers, both those that afflict individuals like sickness and private feuds, and those that involve the whole of society like war, famine and plague. To be saved is to escape from anything that threatens to damage or destroy life, and conversely to enjoy health, peace, prosperity and blessing. The religious connotations of the English noun 'salvation' and the verb 'save' when used with persons as its object, are much less material; to be saved and to attain salvation, is to be assured of sins forgiven, to escape eternal punishment, to go to heaven and glorify God for ever. In English one can be saved in the religious sense at the same time as remaining unsaved in the physical sense without any hint of contradiction or even tension. In the Bible, religious and material salvation are much more closely related; and when one is claimed in the absence of the other, there is always an element of tension and paradox involved.

The vocabulary of salvation cannot be considered in isolation from the basic biblical paradigms for salvation from which it takes its distinctive colouring. For Israel this was the Exodus; for the Church the death and resurrection of Jesus Christ. The Exodus, with its themes of election and covenant takes precedence even over the creation stories, both as a matter of historical reconstruction of the development of Israel's faith and in terms of its literary presentation in the final form of the Pentateuch. The early chapters of Genesis function as an introduction to the history of salvation, and anticipate many of its major themes: election, rebellion, wrath and redemption. While later Christian systematics has tended to move from creation to salvation, Old Testament theology develops backwards from salvation to creation. For the New Testament also there is a movement backwards from the death and resurrection of Jesus 'according to the Scriptures', from the saving event to a reinterpretation of the history of salvation, beginning with creation in which Christ is already active as the agent of God (John 1.2; Col. 1.15). The parallel with the Exodus is sometimes made even more explicit: Jesus' death is compared to the offering of the Passover Lamb (1 Cor. 5.7) which protected Israel from divine retribution on its enemies; Jesus is to accomplish a new Exodus (Luke 9.31) bringing victory and release from slavery. One effect of this common biblical pattern of movement back from salvation to creation, from history to cosmology, is to make the Fall less pivotal for biblical theology as a whole than it was to become in later Christian thought. It is not contemplation of the human plight as such which gives rise to soteriology, but particular historical experiences of the saving power of God.

The Law of Moses sealed the Covenant with the elect People and provided a juridical and cultic system of atonement for sins committed against that covenant. The People experienced God's judgement and mercy, not only within the pattern of salvation history, but also through the outworkings of the Law and the offering of sacrifice. In the latter we can glimpse a more mysterious insight into the enduring effect of human sin and disobedience – a glimpse into the sphere beyond time where relationship with the eternal God is, as it were, suspended in the timelessness of liturgy. In this context, we encounter those images of sin offering, unblemished victim, and the cleansing, life-giving power of blood, which will be taken up so powerfully in Christian reflection on the meaning of Christ's death.

These two approaches to atonement, the historical and the cultic, already begin to converge in the prophets of the Exile. If the cult were to become a purely ritual way of dealing with sin, it would imply a mechanical, external operation, and an evasion of the human responsibility to live with the consequences of our actions; but conversely, a purely historical concept of judgement, that failure to keep the Covenant is punished by historical disaster, would have great difficulty explaining the problem of innocent suffering. The great prophets of the Exile, Second Isaiah, Jeremiah and Ezekiel, saw their role and that of faithful Israelites as bearing the consequences of the sins of others and purging the guilt of their disloyalty to God by means of suffering. This theme is then reapplied in later crises of Israel's history, notably in the Maccabean period (see 2 Macc. 7.14). The cultic idea of sacrifice is thus merged with a moral notion of self-offering and this forms the essential background as we shall see for the understanding of the death of Christ. He both fulfils the vocation of the prophets to innocent, vicarious suffering and is also offered as the one unblemished substitute and sacrifice for sin.

For most of the Old Testament period, Israel had no concept of personal survival after death: the body returned to the dust of the earth or continued a shadowy existence in Sheol (the underworld) and the life force returned to God who gave it; only the People lived on. But in order to defend belief in the justice of God in the face of the experience of injustice, torture and martyrdom in the second century BC, and partly also under the influence of neighbouring religious systems founded on beliefs concerning life after death, this concept began to enter Israel's tradition. However, its introduction did not, surprisingly perhaps, displace the older view of salvation as having a primarily this-worldly reference. There was no radical restructuring of traditional soteriology; the new belief was simply placed alongside it. God would save his People, both in this world, by political and even military means, and in the world to come, mysteriously by resurrection. The two were seen as complementary moments of salvation; belief in the latter was not a compensation for loss of belief in the former. The book of Daniel combines an immediate, earthly hope of freedom and human victory, with a longer vision of ultimate and universal divine victory. This apocalyptic vision represents not the breakdown of traditional Israelite historical theodicy, but its reaffirmation and extension.

In the New Testament period there was still in Judaism a variety of beliefs about the after-life, ranging from the outright rejection of the doctrine by the Sadducees to a rather individualist and spiritualised hope of survival after death in Hellenised varieties of Judaism, but the form which was to become orthodoxy was the Pharisaic/Rabbinic doctrine of the final judgement and resurrection of the dead, which retained the corporate and physical emphases of the older soteriology. Early Christian belief in the resurrection of Jesus must be interpreted against this eschatological horizon. It was not the resuscitation of one individual to continued earthly existence, but the anticipation in one special instance of the future hope for the general resurrection of all God's People. Belief in Jesus' resurrection was the partial realisation of a future hope; it allowed early Christians to see salvation, in continuity with Old Testament tradition, not just as something to be hoped for at the end of time, but as something to be experienced here and now insofar as they were incorporated into the body of the Risen Christ, the Church. In other words, the Church was enabled to resist the possible disintegration and divergence of the different ideas of salvation that existed alongside each other in inter-testamental Judaism. The death and resurrection of Jesus became the new centre around which the various strands to which we have referred, the Exodus and Covenant, sacrifice and atonement, the Exile and Return, prophetic suffering, and vindication beyond death, could be integrated into a consistent and comprehensive soteriology.

Salvation in the ministry of Jesus

An examination of the use of the word 'save' in the gospel accounts of the ministry of Jesus confirms the observation already made that there is a strong continuity between the testaments in their physical and corporate understanding of salvation. The themes of Jewish apocalyptic, deliverance from famine, pestilence and earthquake, civil war, betrayal and persecution are reproduced in the Synoptic apocalypse (Mark 13 and parallels in other Gospels) with its typical mixing of this-worldly political concern and hope for the ultimate victory of God. Jesus' words here assume that such threats are real and pressing; they have not therefore receded with the appearance of the Pax Romana and the Emperor as 'saviour of the world'. On the contrary the rhetoric of the self-divinising State and its false claim to have ushered in the age of universal peace constitute a blasphemy, which recalls that ancient prophecy in Daniel of 'the desolating sacrilege' (Mark 13.14). Jesus expects salvation to come not from armed rebellion but through the perseverance under present oppression of the politically helpless and by the imminently future and dramatic intervention of God: 'The one who endures to the end will be saved' (Mark 13.13); and 'If the Lord had not cut short those days, no one would be saved' (Mark 13.20).

Along with the meaning of 'to save' as rescue from the turbulence of the end time, we find the meaning to heal, to regain health. Almost half of the references in the ministry of Jesus to salvation are of this therapeutic kind. The opposite of being saved in this sense is not to be judged or condemned eternally, but to be maimed or die. To take just two examples: the ruler of the synagogue asks Jesus to heal his daughter, 'that she may be saved and live' (Mark 5.23), and the woman with the haemorrhage is commended for her persistence and will to live, with the words, 'Daughter, your faith has saved you' (Mark 5.34). It is no doubt true that this formula 'saved by faith' was retained in the tradition because it echoed the post-Easter doctrinal principle of salvation by faith developed in the Church's controversy with Pharisaic Judaism. What the Church ultimately came to mean by the phrase was that we receive ultimate 'religious' salvation from sin and eternal death through the cross and resurrection; but in the original context of Jesus' ministry it would have had a broader, simpler, more material meaning.

Even references to the future hope of resurrection and entry to life beyond death are expressed with physical analogies in the New Testament and in continuity with the materialist understanding of salvation. This may be illustrated by Jesus' humorous warning against the rich: 'It is easier for a camel to go through the eye of a needle than for someone who is rich to enter the Kingdom of God' (Mark 10.25). The disciples' astonished reply is 'Then who can be saved?' And their logic seems to be: 'If not the rich, then what chance is there for the poor? The rich are blessed, their wealth allows them to give alms and not cheat their neighbours!' In his reply, Jesus does not dispute this line of reasoning; what he says, rather, is that entry into the kingdom is hard but not impossible, for nothing is impossible with God.

As if to reinforce this reluctance to retreat into a private, spiritual realm of salvation, the key term in Jesus' preaching, the kingdom of God, holds together at least three ideas. As we have just seen, the kingdom may be synonymous with eternal life, entered at death by any individual (Luke 23.42–3) or experienced by all at the moment of resurrection (Luke 20.34–6). But equally, the kingdom of God is a reality present wherever healing and freedom from the forces of evil are attained (Matt.12.28). And again, the coming of the kingdom is that universal, public vindication of the elect poor, for which the disciples are to pray as a future earthly hope (Luke 11.20; cf. Luke 6.20). The kingdom image is remarkably varied and combines all these facets together.

In stark contrast to the life-affirming attitude to salvation in the references we have looked at so far, there is in the teaching of Jesus what appears to be a life-denying ascetic strand. The best example is the saying in Mark 8.35: 'Those who want to save their life will lose it, and those who lose their life for my sake, and for the sake of the gospel, will save it.' This saying puts a question mark against the natural human instinct for survival, health and prosperity, and recommends instead the path of self-sacrifice and martyrdom. While elsewhere in the Gospels to be saved means not to die, here it means willingly to die. The saying has often been interpreted in a non-literal sense, referring to inward detachment from worldly concerns or self-denying service to others. Such interpretations depend on a sudden switch in mid-sentence in the meaning of either 'life' or 'save'; but we ought to hesitate to collapse a sparkling paradox into a linguistic ambiguity, in this way. At Mark 8.35, the first clause is a common-place: 'Those who save their life will lost it', i.e. those who are preoccupied with their own safety are the ones most at risk of acci-dent. But such traditional wisdom, if so, is immediately confronted by the challenge of the antithetic parallel: 'If you lose your life, you will save it.' So, the first and primary meaning of 'save', even in this saying, is the physical, life-affirming sense outlined earlier. It is then confronted sharply with the opposite sense, as a deliberate paradox designed to jolt the listener.

This discussion of paradoxical references to salvation in the gospel tradition leads us naturally into a consideration of Jesus' attitude towards his own death. This topic is a very controversial one in New Testament study; the authenticity and interpretation of the relevant material is hotly disputed. It may be as well, therefore, simply to list the main data and outline some of the options. Jesus predicts his own passion in a series of references to the necessary suffering of the Son of Man (Mark 8.31; 9.31; 10.33, 45 etc. with parallels in other Gospels). Depending on one's interpretation of the Son of Man designation, the necessity referred to here could be that of the human race generally born to suffer, with the case of the speaker as its immediate instance, or the pattern of prophetic suffering, or the end-time suffering of the faithful remnant, or the unique and vicari-ous suffering of the Servant of the Lord of Isaiah combined with the Danielic image of future vindication as an alternative Messianic title to Son of David. What we may safely say is that the necessity ('The Son of Man must suffer') is scriptural, even though the precise textual background may be elusive. A scriptural pattern of suffering also lies just beneath the surface of the Parable of the Wicked Tenants (Mark 12.1–9 and parallels). The servants represent the prophets, and the death of the son represents the rejection of the vineyard owner's final appeal. The result of that rejection is unmitigated tragedy and loss. No hint is given of any positive meaning in the son's death; his father's patience, so sorely tried, is now exhausted. The parable is, therefore, not explanatory but exhortatory. Jesus' parable itself functions as God's final exhortation to repentance.

In the passion narrative there are three other sayings directly relevant which probably go back in essence to the historical Jesus, for they display a similar understanding of his death. The words at the Last Supper (Mark 14.22–5) acted out in the breaking of bread and pouring of wine, imply at the very least acceptance of imminent death as within God's purposes of salvation for many. The more explicit interpretative details which appear in Matthew's version, 'for the forgiveness of sins' and ' the new covenant' (Matt. 26.28), may be his own additions. Without them, the Last Supper scene is consistent with the prayer of anguished self-dedication in Gethsemane (Mark 14.36). Jesus does not presume to know the reasons behind the death he sees rapidly approaching, but he accepts it in obedience to the Father's will. The cry from the cross in Matthew (27.46) and Mark (15.34), quoting Psalm 22, again offers no theoretical explanation of atonement, but rather conforms to the scriptural pattern of obedient submission to the will of God.

Thus, even staying within the strict limits of what can be said with some historical certainty about Jesus, and resisting the imaginative speculations offered by popular apologists or hostile critics, we are nevertheless in a position to claim that the atonement has its basis and ground in what Jesus actually said and did. But this conclusion also means that it is legitimate, and indeed necessary, to go beyond the evidence of Jesus' ministry, and in the light of Easter and Christian experience to begin to offer explanations of how atonement through Christ was achieved. The New Testament after all contains many examples of this, to some of which we shall return later. It is important for Christian doctrine to be able to trace the fact and work of atonement to Jesus himself; but elaborate theories of the atonement are secondary, necessarily diverse and all to some extent inadequate to the reality of their subject and to the profundity of its meaning. The Apostles' Creed seems to sense this in its remarkably plain statement: 'He suffered under Pontius Pilate, was crucified, dead and buried.' And that plain, hard realism is preserved for Christians in the gospel passion narratives, as they are read in devotion, recalled at every Eucharist and recited dramatically in the liturgy of Holy Week. It is to these that we now turn.

Narratives of the passion

The origin of the passion narratives is to be found in the forms of earliest preaching. The first Christians preached a scandalous message of the crucifixion of Israel's Messiah. They did not hide the scandal but paraded it. The way of salvation through Christ was preached, both within the community (1 Cor. 11.26) and for those outside it (1 Cor. 1.23 and Gal. 3.1), in the form of a rehearsal of the story of his Passion. The one constant element of theological interpretation was the connection by quotation and allusion of the events with the predictions of Scripture. This layer of interpretation did not interfere with the dynamic of the story or distract the hearers' attention from its often brutal actuality. This is why the passion narratives in the Gospels remain the best examples from ancient literature of utterly realistic narrative.

The passion narratives all tell recognisably the same story. This may be due in part to their literary interdependence, but it is also because they arise from similar settings in communal life and are in touch with the same basic facts of history. There are, however, several discrepancies between them in detail: the chronology of events, the nature of the Jewish trial, the motivation and fate of Judas, the words from the cross, the number of visitors to the empty tomb and so forth. These have long been noticed as a problem and explained away by different means: allegory, harmonisation and (in modern critical study) by tradition-history. The differences between the accounts not only pose a problem, they also provide insights into the intentions of the different evangelists. The method of gospel study known as Redaction Criticism has been developed to illuminate, by comparison of the accounts, the distinctive theological stance and purpose of the individual gospel writers and the peculiar situation of their communities. So, for example, it is possible to detect in Matthew's Gospel a series of small but significant changes in wording which build up into an emphasis on Jewish culpability for the death of the Messiah and its dreadful consequences (e.g. 22.7; 27.25), and then to explain this anti-Judaic tendency by reference to the memories and present experiences of the Matthean Church.

Using Form and Redaction Criticism, scholars of the previous generation attempted to divide gospel material sharply into what was tradition and what was Evangelist's interpretation. But these methods have in recent times been called into question. They are sometimes too blunt and uncertain to deliver the precision their analysis requires. The processes of oral tradition are not easily reduced to laws of transmission. Wildly varying explanations are offered for the distinctive features of a particular Gospel, which depend on speculative reconstructions of its date, setting and purpose. And further, to emphasise redaction at the expense of those features of the story which all the narratives have in common is to distort the reading of the text, so that what is distinctive, in comparison with others, is taken to be disproportionately significant.

For these reasons, New Testament scholars have begun to adopt what is known as a 'holistic', or 'narrative-critical' reading of the Gospels, where every part of the narrative is treated seriously within the overall literary dynamic. Clearly it is impossible here to do more than illustrate the approach. The last words of Jesus may serve as an example. In Matthew and Mark they are the cry of dereliction which we have already discussed. By contrast in Luke's Gospel, Jesus utters three sayings: forgiving his persecutors, reassuring a fellow sufferer and delivering his spirit into the hands of his Father. In John, he makes provision for his mother to be taken to the home of the Beloved Disciple, fulfils Scripture by crying out 'I am thirsty' and dies with the words 'It is finished'. Abstracted like this from their surrounding narratives, these divergences have seemed to constitute a major historical problem, and to call for explanation in terms of the different and even contradictory theologies of the Evangelists. Thus, for example, Mark's view of the atonement could be seen as substitutionary, with the sinless one becoming sin and experiencing alienation from God for our sake. Luke on the other hand appears to portray Jesus as an inspiring example of forgiveness and quiet serenity; while John's doctrine of incarnation and his high Christology have, it is claimed, all but eclipsed Jesus' human suffering. But seen in the context of their respective narratives, these explanations become much less convincing. Mark quotes Psalm 22.1 in Aramaic before giving its translation and he is more concerned with the crowd's mishearing of it as an appeal to Elijah than with its theological content. It is typical of Mark, especially in this part of the passion, to emphasise irony and misunderstanding. The second loud cry which tears through the veil of the Temple and convinces the Gentile centurion that Jesus is truly the Son of God may tell us more about Mark's own particular view of the atoning death of Christ. In Luke's account there is no agony in the words from the cross; but this is because he has already covered the theme in the special material of his Gethsemane story (22.44), in which Jesus also confronts the powers of darkness (22.53). Nor should we forget that his final self-commendation into the hands of God is not quiet resignation; even in Luke, it is accompanied by a loud cry (23.46). Similarly, in John's narrative taken as a whole, the reality of the human suffering of Jesus cannot be in any doubt. Peculiarly the Evangelist emphasises that Pilate brought Jesus humiliated out in front of the crowd wearing the crown of thorns and purple robe, and presented him with the words: 'Here is the man' (19.5).

The deficiency of narrative criticism, as currently practised, is its tendency to dismiss those questions of history and tradition that the older methods were designed to address; but its great value is that it has restated an obvious truth which scholarship had managed somehow to ignore, namely that the gospel narratives are story. Although they are rich in theological meaning, they cannot be replaced by a series of abstract propositions or by conjectural historical reconstructions. And as story they are appropriated in the first instance by the listener through sympathetic imagination, in the manner of tragic drama. The desertion, betrayal, denial, mockery, scourging and execution move the audience to pity and to that sympathy which searches the memory for parallels in their own experience. The story carries the reader beyond the crucifixion to the denouement of the resurrection, with the implication that Jesus' claim to bring the kingdom of God was here vindicated. As a consequence Jesus is able to grant to his disciples access here and now to the banquet of the kingdom, uniting in a fellowship of forgiveness and new life all who follow him in simplicity of heart.

Images of the atonement

The resurrection is the presupposition in the light of which faith in Jesus was preached and the documents of the New Testament written. The resurrection implies that in Jesus God has already acted to open the kingdom to all. Many who might have expected to have been excluded, or to have had great difficulty in qualifying themselves for participation, will be included. The judgement will reverse expectations. Those proud of their righteousness, like the Pharisees, will make way for publicans, the humble in heart, the poor and the outcast. Even those who fulfil their religious obligations will need to say: 'We are worthless slaves'(Luke 17.10).

Traditions such as these drove Paul to formulate the view that Christ died for us while we were helpless, and still in our sins (Rom. 5.8). God's action in sending Jesus is pure grace, not the result of what we have deserved or merited. So our being put right with God (our 'justification') is an act beginning with God's grace, to which we can only respond with the full commitment of faith. This God-given faith brings us out of a life of sin and death in which we are trapped, into the new life of resurrection, a life of love in the Spirit of Christ. Thus justification by grace alone to be received by faith alone is the fundamental resurrection message. Jesus Christ was betrayed to his death for our sins and was raised for our justification (Rom. 4.25).

Those who have by faith participated in Christ's death and resurrection are now joined inseparably to his love (Rom. 8.39).

Yet this message, which lies at the heart of the gospel, raises numerous consequential questions. The most obvious of these is why the death of Christ should have this astonishing result. In the New Testament writings a great variety of scriptural images is called upon to illuminate some facet or other of the central mystery of the faith. They are pressed only as far as they are helpful and then the believing imagination moves on to feed elsewhere, with no sense of obligation to restrict the interpretation to one standard form. In the Fourth Gospel, for example, Jesus is the Lamb of God who takes away the sin of the world (1.29); he dies at the same time as the Passover sacrifices (19.31f); he is silent (19.9), like a sheep dumb before the shearer; but at the same time he is the Good Shepherd who lays his life down of his own accord (10.11), whose own recognise his voice (10.4) and who silences his enemies (18.6).

Christian tradition taken as a whole has seemed intuitively to recognise this fact of the diversity of images for atonement in the New Testament and has not tried to impose one particular theory as an agreed dogma. Some interpretations bear very centrally upon valued understandings of the sacraments and ministry, for example the death of Christ as perfect sacrifice for sin. It may even be possible to speak of a consistent teaching in the New Testament on the 'sacrifice' of Christ, as long as it is recognised that, when the term is used in this way, it is being refined and redefined by the atoning work of Christ. But sacrificial imagery in the stricter, cultic sense, is only one among many images that are used. When New Testament writers refer to Christ dying for us, or for our sins, or to Christ's blood, they do not necessarily imply that they have this image of sacrifice in mind; they could be referring more generally to the benefits of his passion and the violent manner of his death.

We should remember that, before the disappearance of the Temple cultus with the destruction of the Temple in AD 70, the word sacrifice would normally have had straightforward, literal reference, usually to the offering of a ritually slaughtered animal. After this time, of course, both in Christianity and in Judaism, non-literal understandings of sacrifice become the norm. But to appreciate its earliest uses in the New Testament, we need to recall this literal sense, in order to see just how daring, and indeed subversive, it is to describe an event like the crucifixion as a sacrifice. Paul may be alluding to this imagery in several places, but the clearest instance is Romans 3.25. Nowhere else does Paul use the term he uses here, variously translated as 'expiation', 'propitiation', or 'mercy seat'; his Gentile readers may not have been so concerned with the technicalities of Jewish sacrifices. In the context, Paul wants to emphasise the importance of faith and the present justifying activity of God, but Paul was probably borrowing the language of sacrifice from a lively tradition in Jewish Christianity.

The Epistle to the Hebrews, more than any other document in the New Testament, sets out to explore the richness and depth of the cultic image of sacrifice. It is used as the key to understanding not only the death of Christ, but also his person as high priest and mediator, and the whole of his work, his earthly testing and consecration as well as his final ascension and continuing role as intercessor. From the vividness of its references to the actual circumstances of Jesus' crucifixion, it is clear that Hebrews is fully aware of the metaphorical character of the language of sacrifice. The horrific and intrinsically defiling public execution of a condemned criminal is very far from being the serene self-offering of the perfect priest and unblemished victim. But when the two images come together, they interpret each other. The sordid realism of a crucifixion becomes the occasion for discovering the forgiveness and reconciling power of God.

The sacrificial metaphor is therefore a deliberate paradox. Although it has been developed and extended into an overarching motif in the Epistle to the Hebrews, there is no doctrinal statement anywhere of how precisely the death of Christ atones for sin. Many different types of Old Testament sacrifice – the Day of Atonement, covenant, purificatory rites, communion offerings and so forth – are all conflated into one composite idea, the principal purpose of which is to assist a moment of disclosure concerning the meaning of Jesus' historic death: that it was not merely what it appeared to be – tragic, coerced, shameful and unholy – but was in truth the freely chosen path of obedience and access into God's presence, effecting atonement and sanctification.

The sacrificial metaphor is prominent in Hebrews, and appears explicitly at other points in the New Testament. But it is by no means the only metaphor used in the New Testament to spell out the belief that 'Christ died for our sins'. Similar uses of striking images, deliberately superimposed over the story of Jesus' death, can be found. As we have seen, the Exodus was for Israel the classic saving event; and Exodus typology, the Passover Lamb, the testing in the wilderness, and the hope for freedom and deliverance, are used to illuminate aspects of Christian experience and relate it to the work of Christ. The Book of Revelation in particular exploits these images; and constructs its vision of heaven around the throne of God and the Lamb slain (5.6). In Colossians 2.11–15 are details from the institution of slavery, and the image of slave release is held up to reflect the event of the passion. The nails that fixed Christ to the cross in fact pinned up the notice of our liberation from slavery or 'manumission' in the technical sense. It was our old nature that was stripped and exposed to humiliation. It was the powers of this age that were led in public spectacle. When we recall that crucifixion in the Roman Empire was the punishment particularly reserved for runaway slaves and captured rebels, the full irony of this use of imagery comes home.

When in Paul's Epistles the death of Jesus is referred to as an act of acquittal or justification, the image again paradoxically reverses the remembered facts of Jesus' trials: as in the narrative presentations in the Gospels, those who presume to judge are themselves judged by their encounter with Jesus. It has often been claimed that, in his arguments in Galatians and Romans with some who wanted to impose the marks of Jewish identity on his Gentile converts, Paul interprets the condemnation of Jesus under the Law as the condemnation of the Law and the acquittal of those who live by faith. This metaphor works, like the others, only as long as the paradoxical tension between the language which it uses and the event to which it refers is constantly borne in mind.

One of the most significant images used by Paul to convey the meaning of the cross is that of reconciliation. This would have had a particular appropriateness to Gentile converts who formerly, viewed from the Jewish standpoint, had been enemies of God and idolaters, but who had now found peace and forgiveness. The image of peace negotiations and diplomacy, like that of the law court, slave-release and the sacrificial cultus, is surprisingly and daringly inverted. If a public execution is needed to keep the peace, that implies that all human diplomacy and humanly constructed peace have failed. God's diplomacy and peace are, however, revealed in the cross.

The common feature of all these uses is the way positive metaphorical images are held in conscious tension with the negativity of the remembered facts of the crucifixion. Realism and the imagination interact. The passion narratives in the Gospels are very stark; the story is allowed to speak for itself without gloss or technical explanation. And yet in the New Testament also, the imaginative creativity of early Christian reflection on the death of Christ is everywhere apparent. It seems that these opposing poles, realism and imagination, were deliberately kept apart in order to retain the full power of their mutual attraction. The writers of the New Testament have in common also the need to testify that in Christ they have encountered a salvific experience of freedom and transforming new life. So vivid is this conviction that they are driven to employ a variety of metaphors in order to try to articulate what has happened to them. It is like a new creation (2 Cor. 5.17) or new birth (John 3.3–8); a new covenant (Heb. 9.15) or life from the dead (Rom. 6.5–11). Salvation for them is not a theological concept but a present reality.

In this chapter we have looked at some of the New Testament evidence on salvation and the atoning work of Christ, and we have emphasised above all the primacy of the event of the passion with the cross as its central symbol. Story and symbol come first. They are worked out in images and metaphors, sometimes striking often paradoxical. Eventually doctrines of the atonement emerge, which are attempts to devise as coherent answers as possible to the questions raised by the narrative; and these doctrines have been many and varied in the history of Christian thought. To try to reduce this variety to a single agreed statement on the doctrine of the atonement would be untrue both to the New Testament and to our Anglican heritage. Far better, and more consistent with our rich Christian tradition, to provide a series of angles of vision, or reference points, to sketch the great mystery of the atonement. These are complementary insights and are not in competition with each other; they are facets of the central jewel of Christian faith, that in the cross and resurrection of Jesus God has won our salvation. In the next chapter, entitled 'Retelling the story', we provide modern restatements of some of the principal ways in which Christian people have understood that mystery of salvation, which is the subject of this report.

5

Retelling the story

Christ in our place

In its deepest dimensions what is wrong with human life is the lack of God. We could offer a threefold diagnosis. First, there is sin, that deeply rooted tendency to selfishness which in all of us taints even our best intentions and implicates us all in the web of human evil. In sin we turn our backs on God and find ourselves on the well-frequented highway that leads us ever further from God. In our consciousness of sin we know that God, the absolute good, must oppose and condemn our evil. As sinners we are the godless – in the real sense of that word: alienated from God. Second, there is the meaningless tragedy of life. This is not the evil for which we know we are responsible, but the incomprehensible suffering that comes upon us and may overwhelm us. In pointless suffering we feel that it is God who has turned his back on us. We are the godforsaken – for it seems that God has left us to suffer. Finally, there is death. Death may be seen as the end to which our culpable failure in life must lead. The fate of the godless is to perish. Death may also be seen as the final surd which threatens everything else in life with meaninglessness. Godforsakenness is to be left to die.

In all three experiences human beings sink to the depths and find the deepest horror of those depths to be the absence of God. In evil and tragedy and death – when we manage to face up to each without illusions – what we miss is the love at the heart of reality. This is why, in such extremities of life, the word 'God' comes to the lips even of those who have rarely used it seriously before. They cry out for God or they cry out against God. They recognise that in its deepest dimension the human plight is alienation from God.

The depth of our alienation is such that God is not to be found by us unless God enters that alienation and finds us there. This God did in the crucified Jesus. Jesus lived a life of loving identification with others, in all sorts and conditions of human life. In other words, he practised the kind of love which is not mere benevolence, wishing people well from a distance, but that love which enters people's situations and makes their plight sympathetically its own. Jesus identified especially with those who experienced the depths: healing the very sick and the destitute beggars, restoring the dying to life, touching the lepers, befriending the outcasts, freeing the demented from the demons of oppression and isolation, attracting the notorious sinners with his freely forgiving love. Finally, he ended up where any of these people could have ended up: a failure, condemned as a criminal, in agonising pain, deserted by his friends, forsaken by his God. He died the kind of death which symbolised God's verdict on sinful humanity: condemned to perish. He died expressing the tragic meaninglessness of the human fate: 'Why have you forsaken me?' As Jesus died he entered those depths where godless and godforsaken human beings can only cry out to God or for God or against God. But he did not enter them on his own account. He did so in consequence of the loving choice of identifying with others which he made in his life and sustained in his death. He died our death, sharing our failure, condemnation, despair and godforsakenness. So throughout Christian history the guilty and afflicted have recognised their own plight in his.

In doing so they have found God in their alienation from God. For the crucified Jesus was not just one more godless, godforsaken human being, dying as all of us must. He was the man who chose to identify himself in love with the godless and the godforsaken. It was his mission from God to do this. As the one who came from God, the incarnate Son of God, it was God's love he expressed and enacted in his identification with the godless and the godforsaken. Therefore the crucified Jesus brings the love of God into the depths where God's absence is known. Because he suffers that absence of God, no one else need do so.

103

For the guilty this is forgiveness. Because he bore their condemnation, they can face up to its truth without the hopeless alienation from God it otherwise creates. On the contrary, in the crucified Jesus God's love reaches them where they are, with forgiveness, enabling them to put sin behind them, initiating a life lived out of God's love instead of in flight from God's demands. For the godforsaken, who suffer life's meaningless tragedy, the cross does not, of course, remove the suffering, but it heals the heartless depth of that suffering: the lack of God. Even when incomprehensible tragedy overwhelms, the suffering may find God's love incomprehensibly greater. Because Jesus suffered their abandonment, in their affliction they are not abandoned.

Only because he died our death can his resurrection also be ours. We participate in his resurrection through the transformation of life which begins now, as God's love penetrates the depths of our human plight, and which culminates in the future in God's new creation of all things. Though this new creation also includes all rightings of wrongs and healings of hurts, it does so because it overcomes the last enemy: death. Because Jesus died our death, identified with us in death, God's love reaches even the dead and raises them to new life. Because Jesus died our death, death need not be the fate it otherwise is. The light of Jesus' resurrection dispels the shadow death casts over life.

Christ the friend betrayed

Anyone belonging to a political party knows well how much more acrimonious are the quarrels one has with one's friends than those with one's enemies. With friends and allies any disagreement quickly brings the sense of betrayal, and betrayal is one of the most difficult things ever to forgive. We hear it in the angry shouts directed at those who work during a strike, see it in the headlines that appear whenever a spy is discovered in high places, and can practically touch it in the atmosphere when a spouse feels the marriage covenant has been violated. It takes a miracle to find a way back into relationship when betrayal is in the air. Of all wars, civil war is the most devastating, as we have seen daily on our television screens in recent times; and it leaves wounds that are the hardest to heal.

So 'on the night of his betrayal' cannot just be another way of giving the date. It links every Eucharist with the most searing aspect of what the passion of Christ represents, and in a way which, if words do not simply become a habit to us, speak of something most of us know about at quite a deep level. We know, too, that it is not simply a matter of something Judas is supposed to have done: the story of God's dealings with humankind is a story of repeated betrayal, and Jesus is the climax and symbol of all those times when God comes to, and is rejected by, God's own.

So the God who is to be known as the one who saves from all that ruptures our relationships with one another has in particular to be known as the one who can even transform betrayal into a source of hope, so that the worst that has happened is transformed into the best that can happen. The mention of the 'night when he was betrayed' presents us with the character of God's constancy that can even confront and transcend betrayal. When we are in contact with human constancy that goes far beyond what could be expected we are most especially aware of seeing the character of God at work: when people stand by those who let them down badly, when parental love stands firm against every attempt of a child to bring about rejection, or when children retain their capacity for affection towards adults who betray their trust, when Muslim befriends Serb or when a community refuses to cast out those who let it down, then we are presented with the most powerful picture of what salvation is, and of the way in which God deals with humanity.

The gospel is about how the most death-dealing aspects of our life were and are transformed into what is most life-giving, through the fact of God's unwavering constancy. Through that constancy the one who was handed over becomes the life that is handed on, and through the retelling of the story of the passion we are made aware again and again of that holding on through rejection which is the way God saves us and the way we are to be with each other. That holding on is what could transform a meal in the presence of treachery into the first taste of the kingdom banquet.

Christ who justifies

Broken promises are amongst the most disappointing features of relationships: we hate letting someone else down, and feel even worse when our hopes are not fulfilled. Christ keeps the promises of God to us and for us so that God neither lets us down nor finds us lacking in keeping our promises. The whole framework in which to understand this is the covenant promises of God to Abraham that by him 'all the families of the earth shall be blessed' (Gen. 12.3). God makes repeated agreements or covenants with his people, and they are repeatedly aborted by the people's failure to keep their side of the bargain. God's intention to bless everyone through Abraham is thwarted. Human failure frustrates the purposes of God, in a way like a man's broken promise to marry his fiancée, makes it impossible for his fiancée to keep her promises to the man she loves. When human beings refuse to keep the covenant which God has made with them, they prevent the full relationship with God which had been his intention for them, and through them to others. God does not stop loving and caring any more than the fiancée does: we read about what that feels like in the story of Hosea which compares God to a husband whose wife has betrayed him; who knows that the 'sensible' thing to do is to divorce her, but whose love is so strong that he finds himself compelled to take her back and restore the relationship.

In Jesus Christ, God begins the relationship again with human beings on a new, but parallel, basis to the one offered in the old covenant. At the Last Supper, Jesus makes clear that the death, which he is about to die, initiates a new covenant between God and his people. This covenant is one which cannot be broken since God in Christ has kept both his part and ours. Because Jesus Christ is fully divine and fully human he is able, in his own person, to keep God's side of the agreement but what is new is that he keeps the other side too – he is able to keep our side, in perfect obedience to God, such as God asked of his people of old. We participate in this covenant in the same way as we could have participated in the old one, but there is a radical change as well. We participate by trusting God, as Abraham did, but we accept Christ's obedience on our behalf; so salvation is by grace and faith in a radically new way. Our obedience becomes an expression of our gratitude to the God who in Christ has done everything on our behalf and who calls us to welcome the blessing offered to all the families of the earth through this descendant of Abraham by whom God has kept his original promise.

There is no exact parallel to this unique event, but it is something like a parent who is playing chess with a child; they begin the game expectantly, each concentrating earnestly on the task, but the child gets into major difficulty and clearly cannot think of an appropriate strategy; body language signals that he is on the point of giving up, which will destroy the game for both of them. At that moment, mother walks round the table and gives careful thought to how it looks from the other side. She makes a splendid move, which neutralises the faults, and not only makes it possible for the contest to continue but makes it clear how the child's future strategy might develop. She resumes her place and the game progresses, since the child accepts this gracious act on his behalf. Mother's promise that she will play a game of chess with her son is fulfilled because the relationship does not end with the son's error; it continues because of the mother's adoption of his place and side.

This is called justification because it shows that God is just or right to keep his side of the covenant or agreement even though we have not kept our side, since God does not ignore human failure, but puts it right in Jesus Christ. The result of this is our justification or righteousness, since we are now in a right relationship with God again because of what Jesus Christ has done. This means that the only question which is left for us to decide is whether we will receive what God in Christ has done on our behalf, for us, and in our place so that we accept the proffered relationship of blessing. 'We do not presume to come to this your table, merciful Lord, trusting in our own righteousness, but in your manifold and great mercies' is our proper response to this new covenant of which we are reminded every time we come to the Lord's Supper.

Christ who makes amends

All of us feel at some time in our lives the need to give concrete expression to our feelings of regret for what we have done. A mere verbal apology seems inadequate: so we offer as well a bottle of wine or a bunch of flowers, or perhaps breakfast in bed! It is all part of our embodiedness, a fact upon which this report has laid much stress. To achieve reconciliation, we need not only to say something, but to express that penitence and desire for a renewed relationship also in the language of our bodies. This was something of which medieval society was acutely aware, and from this arose a system of 'satisfactions', embodied ways of making amends: sometimes token, sometimes substantial – depending on the nature of the offence – but always symbolic of a desire for restored fellowship and mutual interdependency.

It is from this background that at the end of the eleventh century St Anselm, Archbishop of Canterbury from 1093 to 1109, developed the so-called Latin theory of the atonement, traces of which can still be found in the Prayer Book, as also in some of the imagery of the Reformers. Anselm was the greatest philosopher of his age, and so it is important when considering his position not to confuse the dryness of his argument in *Cur Deus Homo* with its intended religious implications, which can be more clearly ascertained in his prayers, or in his much briefer *Meditation on Human Redemption*.

The latter work ends with the plea: 'O Lord, draw my whole self into your love . . . let your love seize my whole being; let it possess me completely.' This, Anselm holds, is the only possible response once we understand what God has done in Christ. For, had we properly understood our situation before his intervention in our world, we should have seen how desperate our situation really was. To give a modern parallel, it was rather like those who have done some dreadful deed from which they know no release. In anguish they cry:

'I shall never be able to forgive myself!' and search endlessly for forms of reparation, none of which seems quite to do the trick. Similarly, we owe everything to God as our creator, and so the more conscious we become of that debt, the more anything we offer as amends seems hopelessly inadequate to match the mess we have made of things. Such gifts are in any case only returning to God what we have already received from his own bountiful generosity towards us.

So how is the process of amends to begin? What if God himself became human and helped us to achieve reconciliation? To give a modern analogy, it is as though a group of vandals having ruined a pensioner's home – and unable to afford the tools and equipment and lacking the know-how to right the situation – are joined by the pensioner working alongside them. Instead of youths resentful at an externally imposed community service order, the pensioner has become the catalyst for a radically new situation: one in which by his 'mucking in' the guilty youths are transformed from those who feel themselves merely to have 'done their time' into human beings who both desire and know themselves to be forgiven.

What we have here thus is not some purely legal exchange nor the simple following of a moral example, but God taking with the maximum seriousness our embodied condition. Our longing to say 'sorry' becomes increasingly incapable of realisation, the more we understand how far we have departed from the plan God intended for our world. But with that realisation can also come not only the cry 'How can I ever be forgiven?' but also the certainty of forgiveness in the conviction that God the Son became one of us and stood in solidarity with the mess that is the human condition. Through his embodiedness he was able to offer a life of perfect obedience and thus make perfect amends, a life which can now empower our own feeble efforts at amends as they are transformed through his ever-present life in us as the head of his continuing embodiedness, the Church.

Christ our representative

Among the various models of the atonement to be found in Scripture and the Christian tradition, that of Christ as our representative has particularly commended itself to modern Anglican theologians. This model of the atonement links up with the insights of Peter Abelard in the early twelfth century. The Abelardian interpretation is also known as the 'exemplarist' view – not because it takes Jesus Christ as a mere example to Christians but because the death of Christ is held to set forth or exemplify in an unparalleled way the love of God for estranged humanity, and at the same time to set forth or exemplify uniquely the authentic response of humanity to God – the response of penitence, faith, gratitude and love.

This tradition of reflection on the atonement sees Jesus Christ not as a mere individual, a solitary saviour who on the cross accomplished a remote transaction with God from which we can benefit by a legal fiction, but as a representative or corporate figure in whom the whole of humanity is really embodied and involved by virtue of the incarnation.

Scriptural support for this interpretation rests on the Gospels and the Epistles. The Gospels present the representative character of Jesus Christ in three ways. First, as the Son of Man (the truly human one and plenipotentiary of God: cf. Dan. 7.14; Luke 22.69). Second, as the Suffering Servant – the embodiment of Israel for the fulfilment of God's purpose (Mark 10.45; cf. Isa. 52–53). And, third, as the True Vine – the remnant of Israel, God's husbandry (John 15; cf. Isa. 5.1–7). Paul portrays Jesus Christ as the Last Adam (Rom. 5.12–21; 1 Cor. 15.20–8) and other Pauline letters speak of the new humanity in Christ (Col. 3.10; Eph. 4.24). The Epistle to the Hebrews depicts Jesus as one who shared our human lot to the full, was tested to the uttermost yet did not fail. He was qualified by his sufferings to offer himself to God and thereby to lead his people, as their forerunner or pioneer, into the presence of God (Heb. 2.10, 14–18; 4.14–16; 5.7–10; 12.2).

As the mediator between God and humanity, Jesus Christ represents in his person, and especially in his death on the cross, both God's gracious approach to lost humanity and the appropriate human response. On the one hand, he perfectly displays the compassionate love of God for estranged humanity. On the other hand, his outpoured love on the cross awakens in us a corresponding penitence, faith, love and obedience.

The representative perspective enables us to do justice to the redemptive significance of the broader context of the death of Christ – above all the incarnation, followed by Christ's ministry, active obedience, solidarity with sinners and outcasts, compassion, confrontation with evil and judgement on corrupt ecclesiastical structures – together with the resurrection, the ascension and the heavenly intercession of the risen Christ. Clearly it is vital to be able to integrate the events of Jesus' life before the passion into his saving work.

The western Christian tradition has tended to concentrate in a one-sided manner on the death of Christ at the expense of the incarnation and his 'active obedience'. This emphasis is reflected in the Book of Common Prayer. But in modern Anglican theology the balance has been redressed. The incarnational strand of Anglican Catholic theology, which was deeply influenced by the Greek Fathers (notably in Charles Gore), converged with developments in biblical scholarship that brought out the true humanity of the figure of Jesus of Nazareth in the Gospels. This influential conjunction of incarnational theology and biblical criticism tended to eclipse the atonement in the narrow sense (regarded as a decisive act accomplished at Calvary) by the incarnation, 'the cross by the crib', so to speak. In one phase of modern Anglican theology (represented by the contributors to *Lux Mundi* in 1889, and Archbishop William Temple) this emphasis on the representative humanity of Jesus Christ culminated in a 'Christocentric metaphysic' that attempted to 'explain' the world, rather than a redemptive gospel that radically changed the world. This concern with rational explanation went too far, as even Temple recognised. But the emphasis on the incarnation and the real humanity of Jesus enabled theologians to affirm the salvific significance of the whole person and action of Jesus Christ. As Benjamin Jowett put it in the mid-nineteenth century: 'Christ died for us in no other sense than he lived or rose again for us.' The report of the 1922 Doctrine Commission, *Doctrine in the Church of England* (1938) rightly insisted that 'the cross is not to be separated from the person of him who died upon it or from the content of his whole life. It is the consummation of the earthly life of Jesus' (p. 92). We need to hold together the life and death, the incarnation and crucifixion, the person and work of Christ our representative before God.

Salvation and a suffering God

The twentieth century has seen a radical shift in our understanding of the nature of God. Classical Christian theology presupposed a God whose bliss could not be touched by the pain of God's creation. God was invulnerable or 'impassible'. It followed from this presupposition that Christ could only suffer in his human nature, not in his divine nature. This assumption, which owes more to Greek philosophy than to the biblical presentation of the God of Israel and the Father of our Lord Jesus Christ, has undergone widespread collapse in the face of our intensified awareness, in the present century, of the scale and depth of human suffering. The traditional theology has been challenged by Protestant theologians such as Bonhoeffer and Moltmann, and Roman Catholic theologians such as Schillebeeckx and Küng. This perception of a God who freely makes himself vulnerable to the suffering of his creation has converged with the strand of atonement theory stemming from Abelard to create a new emerging consensus that has as its central conviction the solidarity of God in Christ with our sin and suffering.

It seems that the interpretation of the atonement which sees Christ as the embodiment of God's solidarity with human suffering best reflects our (admittedly selective) contemporary moral sensitivities. The theology of a reconciliation of humanity to God through God's bearing of human pain (as well as of human sin) has emerged from the massive human experience of affliction in the twentieth century – from the trenches of the First World War to the extermination camps of Nazi Europe, and from our deeper awareness of the darkness of mental illness to our growing realisation of the innumerable ways in which women have been exploited and oppressed. The gathering conviction that 'only the suffering God can help' (as Bonhoeffer wrote from prison) has led to widespread questioning of the traditional assumption that the divine nature cannot enter into or share human experience, especially suffering (the traditional doctrine of divine impassibility). A strong connection has thus been forged between the doctrine of the atonement and the acute theological problem of theodicy – of reconciling the course of the world with the nature of God. The only ultimately satisfactory response to the problem of unmerited or disproportionate suffering is to believe that our creator, through a wonderful act – at once of self-limitation and of self-expression, is present in the darkest affliction, shares our pain, bears our sorrows, and sustains us through it all, creating good in spite of evil, so revealing the true nature of divine power as showing mercy and pity.

These insights have hardly penetrated the official liturgies of the churches. But there is little doubt that the traditional patriarchal images of God as king, lord, judge, warrior, etc. that belong to the traditional vocabulary of atonement with its central themes of law, wrath, guilt, punishment and acquittal, leave many Christians cold and signally fail to move many people, young and old, who wish to take steps towards faith. These images do not correspond to the spiritual search of many people today and therefore hamper the Church's mission. In responding, through liturgical revision, to contemporary aspirations of spirituality, we might take our cue from W. H. Vanstone's reflections on the cross of Christ as revealing the heart of a fellow-suffering God (*Loves's Endeavour, Love's Expense*)

These receive eloquent expression in his hymn which bears the title 'A Hymn to the Creator' and which may be found on the final two pages of his study *Love's Endeavour, Love's Expense*. We quote the last three verses of this hymn:

Drained is love in making full;
Bound in setting others free;
Poor in making many rich;
Weak in giving power to be.

Therefore He Who Thee reveals
Hangs, O Father, on that Tree
Helpless; and the nails and thorns
Tell of what Thy love must be.

Thou art God; no monarch Thou
Thron'd in easy state to reign;
Thou art God, Whose arms of love
Aching, spent, the world sustain.

Christ our sacrifice

Of all the biblical and traditional images of the atonement, that of
Christ's death as a sacrifice to God is particularly problematic today.
It is felt by many to be peculiarly open to abuse. A number of
modern theologians have alerted us to the danger of sacrificial
language being invoked to exploit and oppress the vulnerable.
Feminist theologians have protested that exhortations to sacrifice,
appealing to the sufferings of Christ, have hardly been distributed
evenly between men and women in the history of the Christian
Church. The example of Christ's sacrifice has been invoked to legitimate the burden of pain, drudgery, personal humiliation and social
inferiority borne by women in a tradition that is overwhelmingly
patriarchal, sexist and androcentric. The German theologian Jürgen
Moltmann, who served on the Eastern Front in the Second World
War, suggests that the rhetoric of totalitarian militarism has
rendered the language of sacrifice debased and unusable. Moltmann
therefore declines to employ traditional terms like 'atoning sacrifice'
to interpret the death of Christ. He does not believe that sacrifice
can be understood in a humane and personalist way. Similarly, Hans
Küng believes that sacrifice can only be used in connection with the
death of Christ if it is detached from its Old Testament connection

and pagan cultic background and used in an ethical and metaphorical sense for self-dedication in the face of suffering.

How should we respond to this veto on sacrificial imagery? To put a moratorium on all sacrificial language would be to cut ourselves off from one of the primary biblical images of salvation. A vital dimension of biblical revelation would be lost. Sacrifice is one of the most prominent images for the death of Christ in the New Testament. It is explicit in Ephesians 5.2 where Christ is described as 'an offering and a sacrifice to God'. There is a rich vocabulary of offering and sacrifice in Hebrews. The sacrificial motif is marked in the Johannine literature: the Lamb of God – probably the Passover lamb – (John 1.29, 36); the 'eucharistic' discourse in John 6; the 'High Priestly prayer' in John 17. Indeed, wherever in the New Testament we find the language of blood, covenant, expiation, cleansing, sanctifying, offering, eating and drinking, the sacrificial theme may not be far away.

So if we are to think in line with the Scriptures about the death of Christ, sacrifice must remain a normative model. However, we need constantly to be vigilant and sensitive to the unacceptable connotations and threatening reverberations that sacrificial language has for many thoughtful Christians today. Some of the difficulties and objections mentioned above can be defused if we bear in mind a number of points about the meaning of sacrifice.

To begin with, sacrifice is a fundamental sacred metaphor with a wide range of meanings and is not confined to cultic practice, to literal blood sacrifice. Etymologically it means to make holy. There is no 'orthodox' or received interpretation of sacrifice, either in Judaism or Christianity, to which we are bound. For Christians the sacrifice of Christ becomes definitive of all sacrifice and the criterion by which all invocations of 'sacrifice' are measured.

Sacrifice is not intrinsically violent. Even in the Old Testament sacrificial cultus, the death of the victim and any concomitant suffering was not a necessary aspect of sacrifice. Libations and cereal offerings were also sacrifices. Sacrifice is not necessarily propitiatory. Not all sacrifices in the Old Testament were of an atoning nature, intended to effect reconciliation between the people and their God. There were thanksgiving sacrifices and communion sacrifices as well as sin-offerings and guilt offerings. Old Testament sacrifice was far from dominated by expiation. Aquinas' view that 'a sacrifice, properly so called, is something done for that honour which is properly due to God, in order to appease him' is a one-sided restrictive interpretation of sacrifice.

Sacrifice is essentially about communion with God. While sacrifice is an image that is used in a variety of ways in the Bible and in Christian worship and theology, its central meaning is communication with God through an intermediate object that is both offered and received. Consistent with this is Augustine's classic definition that 'sacrifice is offered in every act which is designed to unite us with God in a holy fellowship'. Sacrifice seems to involve a transaction or exchange and this is taken up in the familiar New Testament equation 'the just for the unjust' (1 Pet. 3.18; cf. Rom. 5.6–21; 8.3f; 2 Cor. 5.21; Gal. 3.13 – all of which arguably imply a broadly sacrificial framework), sacrifice involves 'a pattern of interchange'.

Sacrifice is set within a gracious, God-given relationship. Sacrifice is given its effectiveness as communication with God through its setting in a covenant relationship – that mutual commitment and spiritual marriage graciously initiated by God and accepted by God's people – both in the Old Testament and in the New. Hence the trouble taken by the four Evangelists to link Christ's passion to the Passover season, when God's redemptive, covenant-giving act in the Exodus was celebrated. This connection becomes explicit in Paul's affirmation: 'Christ our Passover is sacrificed for us' (1 Cor. 5.7)

Finally, this interpretation of sacrifice is grounded in the Old Testament as well as in the New. There is already a critique of cultic sacrifice within the Old Testament: for example in the Psalms (Ps. 50.13f: 'Do I eat the flesh of bulls, or drink the blood of goats? Offer to God a sacrifice of thanksgiving, and pay your vows to the Most High') and in the prophets (Hos. 6.6: 'I desire steadfast love and not sacrifice, the knowledge of God rather than burnt offerings'). This prophetic interpretation of sacrifice points to the fundamental ethical and devotional meaning of the concept of sacrifice. In Hebrews, Christ's sacrificial death is interpreted in terms of his ethical obedience to the will of God. Christian sacrifice is primarily the dedication of our lives to the service of God in gratitude for all that we have received in Christ (Rom. 12.1) Rightly understood, it is subversive of all attempts by one group to exploit, abuse and oppress another.

Christ the victor

Although the biblical tradition repudiates any ultimate dualism, in a fallen and sinful world the forces of evil are powerful, dominating and deceiving. The God who creates the world and sees that it is very good is the righteous God who judges and condemns evil, working to liberate his children from the idolatry of false gods, enslavement to the principalities and powers of this world, and the ultimate denial of meaning in death. The powers of evil that dominate and destroy are seen as both the tyrannies of the political order in this world and superhuman forces. In the apocalyptic writings a cosmic battle between good and evil, the angelic hosts of heaven and the demonic forces which enslave humanity, provides a dramatic context for the ultimate triumph of God in the day of salvation, when God's will is perfectly done and God's Kingdom comes.

The New Testament writers see the redemption achieved by Jesus as the definitive victory of God over the power of sin and evil. In Jesus the rule of God is present and God's Kingdom comes. In the power of the Spirit Jesus casts out demons and heals the sick. One of the prominent themes of St John's Gospel is the understanding of Jesus' ministry as a conflict between light and darkness. In going to Jerusalem he engages in the last battle; he is judged by religious and political leaders, but in reality he is the Truth which judges them. In the end, nailed to the cross like a criminal, he nonetheless reigns as king. As the darkness over the land engulfs the one who claimed to be the Light of the World, Jesus dies, and death seems victorious, the powers of evil have triumphed. But although he enters the domain of death and darkness, sharing to the full our human mortal destiny, death is not the end. From death he is raised in triumph. New life is born in the grave, the powers of death and evil are defeated, the Day of the Lord comes, and, as the first-fruits of God's new creation, Christ is raised to new and endless life, and he bestows this Easter life as the eternal life he shares with his people in baptism.

In the icons of eastern Christendom the resurrection is portrayed as the 'harrowing of hell' (a theme dramatised in the apocryphal Gospel of Nicodemus and powerfully portrayed in medieval miracle plays). Christ defeats the powers of evil, Satan and his minions are bound, the imprisoning gates of hell are broken open, and Christ grasps the hands of Adam and Eve, the representative figures of all humanity, to lead them from death to life. Our Easter hymns echo this ancient understanding:

> From hell's devouring jaws the prey
> Alone our Leader bore.
> Earth's ransomed hosts pursue their way
> Where he hath gone before.

The cross is seen as the place where:

> Death and Life have contended
> In a conflict all stupendous;
> The Prince of Life who died
> Lives and reigns immortal.

In the Orthodox Liturgy, as Christ's resurrection is proclaimed, words from an Easter sermon of St John Chrysostom ring out: 'Christ is risen and the demons are fallen! Christ is risen and hell has lost its prey! Christ is risen and Life reigns!'

This vivid pictorial language has had a particular influence on liturgy, particularly the liturgy of Holy Week and Easter, where it is well adapted to depict the drama of salvation. Theologically it reflects the deeply rooted sense of the Christian Passover, which holds together Good Friday and Easter, the passion and the resurrection, a resurrection fulfilled in the ascension in which the principalities and powers are seen being led captive by the ascending Christ (Eph. 4.8; Col. 2.15) Of all the images of the atonement, the theme of the victory of Christ over sin, evil and death is the only one to hold the cross and resurrection closely together. The cosmic Christ, who fills all things, has destroyed all that imprisons. The liberation he offers is good news to the poor, and the hope of eternal life in the face of death. 'Death has been swallowed up in victory. Where, O death, is your victory? Where, O death, is your sting?' (1 Cor. 15.54f) In the victory of love won through sacrifice, the kingdoms of this world have indeed become the kingdom of our God and of his Christ (Rev. 11.15)

Christ's victory overcomes the world, and Christians are those who are called to live in the power of that victory. This Easter faith gives strength to the martyrs of this and every age, and underlies the Christian protest against tyranny and oppression. The reality of evil which engulfs and enslaves nations and peoples, known in this century in the Holocaust, the killing fields of Cambodia, and the tribal genocide of Rwanda, is countered by the victory of the love of God who in Christ freely chose to plumb the depths of hell and the darkness of death. The gospel of the resurrection gives to us a hope, that 'neither death, nor life, nor angels, nor rulers, nor things present, nor things to come, nor powers, nor height, nor depth, nor anything else in all creation, will be able to separate us from the love of God in Christ Jesus our Lord' (Rom. 8.38f).

6

Receiving the gift

A treasury of images

In previous chapters we have observed how both in the Bible and in the subsequent history of the Church writers ransacked, as it were, the treasure-house of metaphor in order to convey the full impact of our Lord upon their lives. Thus within the New Testament the image now is of ransom from slavery, now of victory over supernatural powers, now of sacrificial victim, here of deliverance from bondage in Egypt, there of restored health from blindness or some other debilitating infirmity, now of reconciliation with enemies, now of bringing to birth new life, and so the list might continue. It is a pattern which is then repeated in later centuries. For, though at times one image may seem to dominate, further investigation discloses others just bubbling beneath the surface. So, for instance, though the image of victory was most dominant in Christianity's first millennium and then seemed to decline, not only did it find a major place in Luther's theology, it continues to be reflected in some of the hymns we sing today (e.g. 'Sing my tongue the glorious battle'; 'The royal banners forward go'). Again, penal imagery, though it only becomes dominant at the Reformation, has clear antecedents as early as Athanasius in the fourth century. This is an argument which can be repeated for almost all the principal metaphors, and so, as we noted in the previous chapter in introducing the various 'angles of vision' with which that chapter ends, it would seem a mistake to search for a single 'theory' of the atonement and its appropriation. Instead, we should, so far as possible, draw on the whole range of this rich imagery, while fully acknowledging that now one, now another may have been proved more fruitful either in the wide range of historical circumstances with which the Church has been confronted

120

in its mission, or for particular Christians in their practice of discipleship even within the same historical period.

One key factor affecting choice of imagery concerns where the stress is put, on salvation as escape from something unpleasant or as the realisation of some good. It is a tension which one finds reflected in both the Greek and the Latin words for salvation, which depending on context can mean either being brought to safety from a position of peril, or a making whole and healthy, or both. Unfortunately in English the term is all but confined to theology, but the two senses are well illustrated by the French use of the ordinary word for safety (*salut*) and the German resort to a word (*Heil*) whose normal resonances are those of health. Other religions of course exhibit a similar tension, sometimes speaking of release from such things as ignorance, sin, death, punishment or suffering and at others more of an ultimate goal in fullness of being, though where this is held to involve loss of personal identity (as in some eastern religions) it clearly stands at a considerable remove from Christian understandings of what could be meant by such fullness of being. In what follows we shall seek to give due weight to both these aspects, but given the prominence of the former in the New Testament, it is appropriate that we should begin with the question of what it is from which we are saved.

Salvation as our deliverance: sin and forgiveness

In what is perhaps salvation's most familiar sense, Matthew opens his Gospel by explaining Jesus' very name in these terms: 'you are to name him Jesus, for he will save his people from their sins' (Matt. 1.21). A similar present stress is not uncommon elsewhere in the New Testament (e.g. Luke 1.77; John 1.29; Eph. 2.5). But also frequent (and perhaps predominant in Paul) is reference to a future rescue, from the forthcoming divine wrath. Jesus is the one 'who delivers us from the wrath to come' (1 Thess.1.10) and that is why we can talk of 'the hope of our salvation' (5.8). Such a stress was almost certainly conditioned in part by expectation of the imminence of the world's end ('salvation is nearer to us now than when we became believers', Rom. 13.11). This may explain why the theme is less prominent in later strands of the New Testament. But, whether or not there is such a change of perspective, this should not blind us to the permanent validity of the underlying issue, that as Christians we need not only to be delivered from the sins of our past but also from our continuing sins, including those that will remain clinging to us on the Day of Judgement. Such language thus highlights the Christian hope that not only now but on that day also forgiveness will be ours in Christ. So, though elsewhere in the book much consideration has already been given both to the work of Jesus on the cross and to his future role, here we ought not to omit how these two aspects impinge upon the present reality of our lives as Christians.

> Bearing shame and scoffing rude,
> In my place condemned he stood,
> Sealed my pardon with his blood.

So runs one verse of the familiar hymn 'Man of Sorrows', and dating from the nineteenth century its use of penal imagery is almost as predictable as was the battle metaphor we quote earlier from two sixth-century hymns. For many Christians today the notion of God offering himself as a substitute to be punished for our sins is deeply repellent. Morally they recoil from such a narrowly retributive conception of human justice, far less divine. But from that we should not infer that the image has lost all appropriateness, as we consider the impact of Christ's death upon ourselves. Far from it. Indeed, arguably in a world which has lost any deep consciousness of sin there remains a version which can speak very powerfully to our own day.

There is of course the characteristic New Testament imagery of cost, as in Paul's phrase 'bought with a price' (1 Cor. 6.20), that underlines the costliness to God of our salvation; behind it lies implicitly the recognition of how great our value is to God. One may also observe that even someone hostile to penal imagery might still find singing 'There was no other good enough to pay the price of sin' a powerful reminder of the way in which sin always has its innocent victims. They might also recall the way in which it is so often the case that it is the innocent who must take the costly initiative in correcting the consequences of others' sin, as with the bomb-disposal expert who risks life and limb to immobilise the device which threatens many lives. But among modern theologians it is perhaps Karl Barth who comes closest to giving a generally acceptable sense to penal imagery. Though excluding any necessity for punishment, he uses the metaphor to show how consciousness of judgement and forgiveness might be effected in the one and the same act. In his short work *Dogmatics in Outline* he writes that 'in the strict sense there is no consciousness of sin except in the light of Christ's Cross' (p. 119). Though, if taken literally, this must be an exaggeration (as the Old Testament's consciousness of sin amply illustrates), nonetheless there is an important sense in which reflection on the events surrounding Jesus' death can heighten our sense both of sin and of the forgiveness that comes with it. As we read the story of Jesus, what we discover is the wickedness and weakness in ourselves, the Judas who betrays his friend, the Caiaphas not open to new possibilities, the Pilate wanting the easy way out, the faltering Peter, and so on. This innocent man sent to his death was not sent there by the scum of humanity but by the humanity in each and every one of us that is all too capable of acting as scum, even ordinary English villagers as in Stanley Spencer's powerfully evocative paintings of the passion based on Cookham in Berkshire. Yet that same discovery of the depths of human wickedness also reveals its cure. For this innocent man was also God incarnate and yet that, so far from merely intensifying the crime, also provides its resolution as he offers forgiveness from the cross. We have discovered the worst that we are capable of doing both to our fellow human beings and to God; yet God forgives.

But what are we to understand by such forgiveness? Here it is important to be clear about the sense in which it is and the sense in which it is not a blotting out of the past. Sin is constituted by all the wrong deeds and thoughts which make us fail to hit the mark of the kind of people God intended us to be, all the badness in us that alienates us from his goodness and holiness. To suggest that at one fell swoop all that disappeared would be to reduce our faith to an implausible fairytale. Rather, what happens is that God assures us of a new status as we throw ourselves on his mercy, upon that offer of forgiveness from the cross. Not only does he make explicit the worth he has already assigned to us in creating us, he declares that worth to be absolute in his eyes, despite all the evidence we have created to the contrary. Thereby we are freed for a new future, one in which we can now be confident of our own worth, that value that has been accorded us by God, and so there ceases to be any need for self-justification, for in any sense proving to others or to God that we are indeed of some worth or importance. The result is not only a new status for us vis-à-vis God as accepted and forgiven in Christ but also a new status in respect of our relationships with fellow human beings. Indeed, these relationships are now profoundly altered. For one of the major occasions for sin is self-assertion, nagging doubts about our own worth leading us aggressively to prove it by gaining advantage over others. At a stroke, such a motivation is slain, and the Christian acquires a freedom and confidence unknown to unredeemed humanity.

But that this much can be instantaneous should not be allowed to conceal from us the more gradual character of much else. Anyone who has ever been faced with the possibility of forgiving a burglar knows how much more complicated the issue can be. In that case not only are there wider social issues – reporting the crime to the police, social expectations of punishment and so forth – there is the obvious practical point that ostentatiously to forgive would be to invite a spate of further burglaries! But the point is certainly of wider application. All of our actions carry with them consequences which may not admit of easy or immediate remedy. So it no more follows that the penitent burglar of today can escape all the consequences of his actions than could the penitent thief who continued to hang on his cross despite Jesus' gift of forgiveness.

This is a point which needs much stressing as there is a natural human desire for a totally new start, which is fine if it is possible, but so often it is achieved only at the cost of concealing from ourselves the continuing consequences in the present of our past bad actions. Take, for instance, the modern habit of declaring that no one is to blame for the breakup of a marriage. No doubt this is sometimes true, but one suspects that more commonly the explanation constitutes an unwillingness on the part of both partners to face the truth, to acknowledge the flaws in themselves. And is not the presence of these defects highlighted by the fact that second marriages are even more likely to end in divorce than first? Or take another common, but equally problematic declaration: 'I don't want just your acceptance, I want your approval.' Loving acceptance is declared not to be enough. What the person wants is a declaration they are just as good as the next person. In one sense this is of course true: we all stand in need of the mercy of God. But what it ignores is the obvious ways in which it is not true: not all of us are liars, adulterers or whatever. One illustration of this attitude is the way in which prisoners commonly place their own crimes on the right side of some imaginary divide: 'Everyone engages in a financial fiddle somewhere, even if it is just their income tax form'; 'She was asking for it anyway'; and so on, with only child molesters in the end left beyond the pale. Clearly such attitudes make reform of the prisoner difficult, but much the same could be said of those of us who may never see the inside of a prison cell but are equally indulgent of our own particular failings. It is almost as though what is desired is an easy society of mutual endorsement, whereas what the Bible calls us to is realistic repentance and a gradual appropriation under God of the full implications of what is meant by the indwelling of the Holy Spirit: 'God's temple is holy, and that temple you are' (1 Cor. 3.16–17).

It is interesting in this connection to contrast such attitudes with an allegedly more corrupt world, that of the Middle Ages. Corruptions there no doubt were, but at least there was full recognition of the arduous path before us. This can be seen even at the heart of its corruptions, in its penitential system, which had its origin in the severity of the Celtic penitential rules, but even if we look only to preaching, a similar seriousness is to be observed. For drawing on authorities such as Augustine and Gregory the Great, the raising of Lazarus (John 11.38–44) became the favoured text for explaining our need for continued repentance and re-formation throughout our

Christian lives. Sin, it was argued, was as bad as the death of Lazarus, with the stone against the tomb a symbol of our hard-heartedness, and burial 'the load of sinful habit pressing down upon us', our only possible release being Christ's summons out of the grave and the Church's help in loosening our bandages (v. 44). Those who took their faith seriously were thus left in no doubt (nor should we be) of the fact that, despite being forgiven, throughout a Christian's life there will continue to be the need to die afresh to sin, so that through God's grace we may live once more. To quote the exhortation to godparents with which the Prayer Book Service of Baptism ends: we are 'to follow the example of our Saviour Christ, and be made like unto him; that as he died and rose again for us, so should we who are baptized, die from sin and rise again unto righteousness, *continually* mortifying all our evil and corrupt affections, and *daily* proceeding in all virtue and godliness of living'.

Then in due course will come that other aspect of salvation as deliverance which we said we would discuss, escape from the divine wrath in the judgement that is to come. It would be unfortunate if, bewitched by the metaphor, we failed to take the notion of divine wrath seriously. We should not of course think of God seething with temper and resentment, ready to 'zap' us with his thunderbolt in due course, should we not obey him. The intention of the image is to tell us that God is utterly opposed to selfishness, social injustice and ruthless exploitation of resources. It tells us of the seriousness with which God regards human sin, that, though psychology and sociology may help explain the conditions which lead to the act, they do not exonerate: human wickedness remains a reality which precludes enjoyment of the vision of perfect goodness which is God.

What allows us to escape that judgement is not that we have necessarily passed beyond the point of wickedness. It is a commonplace to observe that it is usually the greatest saints who are most acutely aware of their own sin, but – more insidious and more problematic – it is not unknown for an otherwise saintly individual to have (unacknowledged by him or her) a character which is fundamentally flawed, for instance through pride or lack of self-perception. So it is certainly not passing beyond sin which makes the difference; rather, it is a matter of remembering that inseparable from the divine judgement is the Father running to embrace the prodigal son (Luke 15.20) and the outstretched arms on the cross which welcomed the penitent thief (Luke 23.34).

Suffering

If our discussion thus far has been along essentially the right lines, one interesting correction needs to be made to one of the most common contrasts drawn between Christianity's understanding of salvation and related concepts in other religions. For it is often said that western and eastern Christendom differ precisely in this, in what they see as the source of the problem: that whereas western Christians identify factors such as sin and death, eastern Christians locate this in ignorance. However, if the analysis given above is correct, then the twentieth-century decline in consciousness of sin has in fact brought us closer to the eastern understanding. For, as we argued above, forgiveness is always accompanied by, and perhaps only properly comes through, a simultaneous discovery of the depths of one's own depravity.

But, if that is now a point of analogy, a major contrast remains in attitudes to suffering. For, whereas Hinduism and Buddhism both see salvation as requiring detachment from suffering, central to the Christian claim is its potentially, redemptive quality. The aim is not so much escape from it, as a willingness to give it a new significance, a fresh dimension. However, this is not to say that the Christian should invite suffering; only that, should it befall, then it has the capacity to bear a redemptive quality, just as Christ's suffering also worked for the good. Moreover, Christians committed not only to praying for God's kingdom to come, but to working for it, may well find that commitment leads beyond hungering and thirsting for right into suffering for it, as in the long tradition of Christian martyrdom that began with Stephen and has continued in our own day with the many who risk torture or death for their faith. We need to remember that 'martyrdom' literally means 'witness', and thus that someone like Sheila Cassidy, tortured in Chile for treating wounded revolutionaries, was no less a martyr than Oscar Romero, assassinated for attempting to relieve the conditions of the poor in El Salvador.

But before considering further this question of suffering's potential role, the issue must first be set in its wider context. In ordering the world, God chose to give human beings freedom in such a way that it became possible for them to choose to rebel against him; in short, God valued that choice more than the production of mere automata who always obeyed the divine will. A tragic dimension therefore entered into the divine decision to create a world of the kind in which we live. God might have created one without suffering in which automata who looked like us always did what was right, but instead, because he wanted us freely to choose to love him, he risked a world from which the Lover must stand at a distance from the beloved, waiting and longing to be invited, yet at the same time knowing all the suffering which we as human beings are capable of imposing upon one another. The atheist declares the result not worth the candle, but before the Christian engages in oversimplistic debate, what needs to be recognised is that what is at stake has nothing to do with differing estimates of how much suffering there is in the world. Rather, it is all a matter of two entirely different, clashing value systems, with opposing estimates of the worth of that freedom and the resultant life which it makes possible. The Christian insists that God has personally encountered and disarmed human rebellion by taking the full force of it upon himself; not only did God by entering into our suffering on the cross endorse human protest against unjust suffering by identifying with that protest in his own cry of agony, he exhibited human freedom in accepting the cross, he honoured that same freedom in allowing himself to be nailed to it, and granted real freedom to us by opening up to us possibilities for new life. Moreover, no human suffering need be unmitigated; compassion is called forth by people needing help; courage flourishes in situations of fear, and so forth. This is not to say that the good result justifies the occurrence of some particular suffering or evil, but it can go some way to ameliorate it, and even to redeem it.

One further tragic dimension needs to be mentioned. Much, though not all, suffering that occurs is essentially arbitrary, and part of the reason that it is felt to be evil is precisely because it is inexplicable and undeserved. (We do not think to blame God for things which we have brought upon ourselves, though we may protest at such suffering.) It is for this reason that there is a thread of Old Testament witness which simply will not allow the easy connection found in other parts between rightness before God and prosperity. Such questioning as to why the wicked flourish is to be seen in some of the psalms, while the obverse side of the coin, the righteous suffering, is explored at length in the Book of Job. The New Testament is equally emphatic against any simple equation of suffering with deserts, or even attempts to lay blame (cf. Luke 13.4; John 9.2–3), even though it is also clear that none is guiltless before God.

In creating the world, God's plan involved the regular operation of laws for the natural order. Generally they are beneficial and proportionate; for instance, pain has at its root a fundamentally beneficial purpose, in warning us to take action, but sadly sometimes such action may well be beyond our present powers. On other occasions, generally beneficial laws can turn evil for all sorts of reasons, some beyond our present knowledge. Of course, God knew that suffering was a consequence of his creation, but it does not follow from this that he wills individual suffering. To suggest that all suffering arises for a person as a result of the divine plan, as if earthquake, cancer and so forth were deliberately intended to strike one individual rather than another, would make God sound like a moral monster. But we must also admit that occasionally Christians believe themselves to be called to suffer for their faith, and in freedom are able to respond. Equally, in suffering, they, and others are free to accept it, fight it, or overcome it, depending on what is the most appropriate response to the kind of suffering that it is. Later, finding God's grace in the midst of it, they can sometimes talk about it almost *as if* God caused it for this good effect, seeing parallels between their own suffering and the cross of Christ.

It is against such a background that the Christian's more positive understanding of suffering should be set. It is not that tragedy is absent from the world. The inevitability of it is at the very heart of God's decision to create, as Revelation reminds us, with its talk of 'the book of life of the Lamb slain from the foundation of the world' (Rev. 13.8 AV). Nor is it that God willed the pain of any particular individual: its essentially arbitrary quality should not be denied. Rather, the point is that through divine grace the possibility is there for its creative transformation, certainly in the response of others to the person experiencing the pain as their love and compassion are deepened, but also often in the people who are themselves experiencing the pain.

Of course one should not underestimate the debilitating power of much suffering, whether physical or otherwise. Yet it is true that, at least for the northern hemisphere, there never has been a period in history in which it has been so easily subject to human control. Think for instance of life before the invention of modern anaesthetics! But it is not for us to judge how others face pain. Human beings have very different psychological capacities. In response to the same physiological intensity of pain it may take little effort for one individual to continue working normally, while for another not only is early retirement and constant care necessary but it takes a supreme effort for that individual not to slip back into self-pity and resentment against all those better off. The point rather is that God offers each of us the necessary help or grace to respond positively in our situation, to the degree to which our psychology and antecedent experience permit. In other words, what is possible will vary enormously from individual to individual, and it certainly does not mean that the Christian must be able to accept his suffering without any inner conflict: some of the psalms and lives of the saints give ample endorsement to the need to work through towards acceptance, in the meantime giving full vent to one's natural resentment against God.

But more than psalter and saint one can appeal pre-eminently to the crucified one himself. Certainly the crucifixion's redemptive quality is seen most obviously in the fact that it was through such dreadful suffering that the supreme benefit for humanity came, the guarantee of divine forgiveness. But it is not just the possibility of external benefit to others to which it bears witness. Because our Lord fully entered into our humanity, it also demonstrates how such a transformation can be effected internally. For whether we compare the last words from the cross in Mark and Matthew with Luke and John or simply take Mark in isolation, the evidence suggests that Jesus' initial reaction to his suffering was that of all of us – fear, depression and uncertainty. But through prayer he moved beyond that to confident assurance in the ultimate loving purposes of his heavenly Father – a confidence which we can find detected in either the conclusion of the psalm from which he quotes the initial verse in Mark and Matthew or in the last words attributed to him in Luke and John. He is there then alongside us in our suffering as one who understands in the deepest sense of that term.

Salvation as our transformation: transforming grace and human freedom

Our discussion of suffering has already taken us beyond the more negative aspects of salvation as release to its more positive side, of how it can also effect our transformation. Though more prominent in later strands, this notion also finds its appropriate echo in Scripture. Particularly fine is the image used in 1 Peter: 'Like newborn infants, long for the pure, spiritual milk, so that by it you may grow into salvation' (1 Pet. 2.2). But occasionally Paul also talks of us 'being saved' (e.g. 1 Cor. 1.18), and indeed on one occasion even stresses its provisional character, as depending upon our response: 'Now I would remind you, brothers and sisters, of the good news that I proclaimed to you, . . . through which also you are being saved, if you hold firmly to the message that I proclaimed to you' (1 Cor. 15.1–2).

At this point it would be all too easy to allow traditional Reformation disputes to raise once more their divisive head, and to set grace and freedom, faith and works firmly in opposition to one another. But now through the welcome efforts of ecumenists in the churches it is possible for us frankly to acknowledge faults on both sides. So afraid has the Protestant tradition been of admitting anything whatsoever which might appear to detract from the absolute priority of grace that it has tended to ignore the key role assigned by Paul to works – passages which, if pulled out of context, might easily be mistaken for extracts from the Epistle of James! Romans 3.28 ('We hold that a person is justified by faith apart from works prescribed by the law') and James 2.24 ('You see that a person is justified by works and not by faith alone') may seem irreconcilably opposed, but in fact for Paul as much as for James good conduct is an indispensable element in our relation with God – 'faith working through love', as Galatians (5.6) puts it. One further difficulty with traditional Protestant approaches has been the way in which in their overspecification of the content of faith they themselves had been in constant danger of introducing a new system of merit, one based this time on intellectual belief rather than practical works. None of this is of course to deny the equally serious faults on the Catholic side, particularly in the degenerate scholasticism which treated 'created grace' as though once granted it then operated as a power at the individual's disposal, able to act quite independently of God, instead of as the medium of a continuing and personal relationship between creator and creature.

Against that we must emphatically assert the absolute priority of grace, that the initiative at every stage is always God's, not ours. But this is entirely compatible with acknowledging a key human contribution, that God carries us no further than our wills assent; hence the appropriateness of T. S. Eliot's repeated prayer in the *Four Quartets*, 'make perfect our will', or the Prayer Book request to 'make us to love that which thou dost command' (Collect for Trinity 14). How else are we to explain that sadly all too common phenomenon of otherwise outstanding Christian souls who have none the less totally blocked God from some aspect of their lives? The pride or self-deceit are all too obvious to the rest of us, but God chooses not to act, because he values something more, our free human response. At the same time we need to acknowledge that the free response need not always be fully conscious. For instance, as a way of making the terrible reality tolerable a woman who has been sexually abused as a child may throw all the blame upon herself. Yet there is also a deeper level at which she knows the truth, and, through response to which, God can eventually draw her into a starker, yet fuller and healthier reality.

One suspects that a major factor in generating Reformation and Counter-Reformation positions was their cultural background in Renaissance individualism, a stress which has of course continued to accelerate until our own day. For, so long as one thinks in purely personal terms of one individual (me) confronting another (Christ), it is all too easy to suppose that some sort of conscious transaction must take place, with our decision of faith or good action in turn generating a divine decision (justification) or action (gift of created grace). But that of which both Bible and early Church speak is of something much more intimate, of our personal identities transcended in such a way that all that we do, including faith, is not really ours at all but God's work in us – 'yet not I but Christ in me', as Paul puts it at one point (Gal. 2.20). Certainly the major Reformers as also the Counter-Reformation Council of Trent sought to avoid the worst of these faults, but the way in which the modern inheritors of the Reformation can so easily slip into talk of 'our decision of faith', a phrase Luther or Calvin would never have used, illustrates how easily the individualism which has been growing since at least the Renaissance can trap us into an inadequate grasp of the process of salvation. For the primary stress should be neither on our own faith nor on our own works, but on the gracious initiative of God, working at all levels and not just that of our conscious selves, and indeed working not just directly upon us but also indirectly through those with whom we live and work, as well as in the prayers of others, whether known to us or otherwise.

Our new identity in Christ

In the Old Testament the social assumptions implicit in this way of viewing things were given expression in a corporate understanding of the nation or its remnant. Such an idea continues into the New, with our interdependence upon one another within the Church continually stressed. But there is also something new, and wonderfully profound. For the divine presence is no longer externalised but seen as constitutive of the very identity of the Church, particularly in Paul's image of her as the Body of Christ and John's of the vine and its branches. It was a position which was then reinforced when the Church extended its mission into the Greek world. For a basic assumption of Platonism is that something only has reality in so far as it imitates or participates in the perfect exemplar of its kind (the theory of forms), and so through much of the Fathers' writings runs this subtext, that we are only really truly human in so far as we participate in the perfect human being, Jesus our Lord. It is also this same subtext which explains the recurring patristic theme of salvation as deliverance from death. It is not that Christ's resurrection offers hope for our own. Something much deeper is at stake: because Christ's humanity is infused with the power of divinity, we too can hope to share in divinity's characteristic attribute, eternal life, in so far as we become part of that humanity through participation.

The modern reader may find such mystical language obfuscating, but it is worth wrestling with, as it is as much biblical as patristic. How else are we to interpret verses such as 'as all die in Adam, so will all be made alive in Christ' (1 Cor. 15.22)? Paul is comparing the two human natures by which our identity may be given: one which rebelled and the other which embodied a life of perfect obedience. As 'Adam' is the Hebrew for man, it was possible to think more easily in inclusive terms, so that 'Adam' could come to stand for all human beings, both male and female, under the old order, just as Christ would include all under the new. Such an understanding is also a recurrent theme in the writings of the Church Fathers as they seek to explicate what they understand by the Nicene Creed's phrase, 'he became man': the Greek verb cognate with *anthropos* is taken to mean not that he became a male person (though of course he was that), but that he was inclusive in the widest sense. He was not only a human being, not only definitive of what it is to be a human being (though again he was of course all of that), he was also the human

134

being whose presence within us can save and transform all humankind. This does not mean the destruction of our individual personalities, but it does imply that we do not only exist as individuals; as part of Christ's Body, the Church, we are part of something much larger than ourselves, as Christ's humanity suffuses our own in ways not always accessible to our conscious selves. Unfortunately, English, unlike Greek or Latin, has hitherto used only one term, 'man', for both 'male' and 'male and/or female', whereas other modern languages are able to translate less ambiguously as in German's *ist Mensch geworden* (not *Mann*). But the English 'man' did at least have one merit in terms of this tradition of understanding: it could be used generically of humanity as a whole as well as referring to a specific individual. Such language of incorporation into the perfect humanity that is Christ's finds its natural application in the sacraments.

In Romans 5–6 Paul develops his baptismal theology through a contrast between Adam and Christ which seems to assume the historicity of Adam ('sin came into the world through one man and death through sin'). Even if we now read Genesis 3 rather differently, as the story of each and every one of us, Paul's basic point surely stands. In baptism we are symbolically moved out of the sphere of influence of 'fallen humanity', all those social influences around us that incline towards sin and which are prior to any conscious choices of our own. Then instead of being subject to such 'original' sin, all the sin that is prior to any reflection on our part, we are granted the presence of the Holy Spirit in our lives, there to conform us to the image of Christ, the definitive human being, will we but let him. Yet what is offered is more than mere conformity. We become one with him, a true part of his Body as the humanity God intended us to be. To extend the Pauline image, we have become his hands and his feet. For, as St Teresa of Avila once put it, 'Christ has now no body on earth but yours, no hands but yours; yours are the eyes through which to look with Christ's compassion at the world, yours are the feet, with which he is to go about doing good.' Through baptism Christ can thus become the primary social force working in and through us, gradually replacing the wider society in which we are set and to whose less healthy influences we can so easily fall prey without even being aware that this has happened.

Baptism, like Eucharist, is an essentially social activity. One cannot baptise oneself, and that very fact points us to the reality that being a member of Christ can never be only about the individual and Jesus, but about joining the company of all the faithful, in this life and the next. Being baptised, and continuing to enjoy in the Eucharist all the benefits of Christ's passion, commits us to one another and the whole creation for which Christ died. Baptism projects us into the ecumenical enterprise, for we all belong together in Christ; and, more widely, it projects us into the ministry of reconciliation, for God was in Christ reconciling the *world* to himself.

Such a life of increasing identification with Christ is also conveyed sacramentally in the Eucharist. By eating his Body and drinking his Blood and by feeding on him by faith we strengthen our identification with him, and thus continue one with him, part of his Body as the humanity God intended us to be. Therein lies the justification for those who insist that the Nicene Creed should continue to speak of Christ becoming 'man' (in some wider or more inclusive sense of the kind already outlined) and not only 'a man'. For the Fathers were right that what we identify with is a humanity valid for all ages, not the various idiosyncrasies of first-century Palestine which scholarship may happen to discover. That is why he comes to us in the Eucharist not as a stranger from a remote age but as the Lord of every age.

At this point it would be very easy to get side-tracked into a discussion of the sense in which he 'comes'. Paul speaks of some dying as a result of profaning the Body and Blood of the Lord (1 Cor. 11.27), and ever since most Christians have sensed that the Eucharist is an awesome mystery in which they are participating, one in which they are privileged to share in Christ's presence in a distinctive way. At times this has led to a crude and distorting literalism. However, more precise definitions of that presence have more often than not hindered rather than helped the building up of the Christian community. Elizabeth I wisely foreshortened controversy by declaring:

136

Christ was the word who spake it,
Christ took the bread and brake it,
And what his word doth make it
That I believe and take it.

Much more important than reviving old disputes is to identify that to which the symbolism points. As Cranmer put it, God the Father 'does assure us thereby . . . that we are very members incorporate in the mystical body of his Son'. What that means is the transformation of our lives both personally and socially through divine grace.

Our sacrifice in his

In the past, our personal transformation has often been understood in excessively passive terms, with the traditional theology of the Eucharist, whether Protestant or Catholic, unfortunately merely reinforcing such passivity. Thus the characteristic Protestant stress on thankfulness, ascribing all to God, has not always escaped degeneration into quietism and dismissal of the necessity of action on our part. Similarly, the traditional Catholic stress on a providentially ordered, hierarchical world has at times produced its own tragic consequences in the unnecessary acceptance of suffering, as the poor find their only relief in their identification with the suffering Christ of whom the liturgy speaks. One place that this has been most evident is in Latin America, and against such a backdrop present-day liberation theology surely represents a very understandable and natural revolt.

Christian endorsement of such passivity, whether Protestant or Catholic, has often found expression in the notion of 'sacrifice'. But the word 'sacrifice' literally means being made dedicated or consecrated to God, and so should more properly suggest not a giving up of something but some positive offering. Certainly, quiet acceptance, even resignation, can be on occasion the appropriate response, but in general we should see ourselves as summoned to action. This is not to suggest as an alternative endless activity. There remains a vital role for receptivity and response both in relation to God and to our fellow human beings. But such a capacity to listen and to react still remains essentially different from pure passivity, with us then like wet sponges merely absorbing whatever befalls us. Instead, we should see ourselves as called to let Christ's Spirit invade us, so that all we do, whether by action or response, is made sacred, made holy.

In this sense, we offer our whole lives as a positive sacrifice of joy and thanksgiving, as well as being willing to suffer birthpangs to bring new life to birth. Certainly not all that Paul lists under 'the fruit of the Spirit' could be described as passive – 'love, joy, peace, patience, kindness, generosity, faithfulness, gentleness, and self-control' (Gal. 5.22–3). Inner assurance is combined with a warm outreach towards others, and it is this pattern which we find confirmed in the life of our Lord himself. It is difficult not to read even some of his hard sayings as tinged with humour (for example, 'a camel through the eye of a needle'!), and of course it is of Jesus that it is remarked: 'Behold a glutton, and a drunkard' (Matt. 11.19). Leading graced lives, having thankful hearts will of course mean willingness to face sacrifice in the narrow sense, should that be required, but it must surely also be taken to include sheer enjoyment of the beauty and wonder of God's creation and all the blessings of human fellowship which it can bring.

Elsewhere in the book we have suggested that, despite some potential pitfalls, the idea of sacrifice can perform a valuable and important role in furthering our understanding of salvation. In the history of the Church the idea of sacrifice has often been at its most contentious in its application to the Eucharist. But, if difficulties can be overcome elsewhere, it is surely worth making the effort here also.

Though Protestant objections are much more common and familiar, it is a notion which has raised worries across the spectrum of Christian belief. To some of Catholic persuasion the doctrine has at times appeared to be presented with such stress on the efficacy of the divine action that any sense of personal responsibility on the part of the individual believer is either undermined or lost altogether. On the other hand, among Protestant objectors a major critique has been that any use of the concept leaves the principal role to the priest, who in consequence is almost taken to control what happens when he 'offers Christ in the mass'. Both protests have their legitimacy. The 'Catholic' realises that not all can be the result of divine action; the 'Protestant' that not all can be a matter of what we do. However difficult it may prove, we need an account of both Christ's sacrifice and Christian sacrifice in general that places an appropriate emphasis on both the divine and human contribution. The divine and the human were alike involved in the sacrifice of Christ on the cross, and in an analogous way it is the divine Spirit that makes possible a cruciform pattern to any life of Christian sacrifice today.

Some medieval writers wrote as though not only was the mass all that counted, its gifts were entirely at the disposal of the priest who celebrated the rite. But, however consistent such an account may seem with some liturgical practices as well as a popular tradition of piety, it is grossly unfair to most of what passed as official teaching or as theology. Chapter 5 has already alluded to 'the timelessness of liturgy', the belief that the eucharistic liturgy participates in the timeless worship of heaven, and this is certainly an important factor which needs to be taken into account. For often, when theologians or church formularies spoke of Christ being re-offered or re-presented what they had in mind is not that blood flows once more as on the cross, but rather that what Christ once did can be appropriated at any time or in any place. What is thus at stake is the eternal availability of the cross, rather than its repetition.

It is a point about the permanent relevance of what Christ has done on the cross; and, lest we become too narrowly confined within our twentieth-century perspective, it is worth adding that there is here an obvious parallel with the modern, Protestant stress on the continuing suffering love of the crucified God for his creation (an emphasis present, of course, also elsewhere in this book). For, not only are both concepts ways of mediating the permanent concern of Christ for our world, they also raise similar problems. Thus, just as the permanent availability of Christ our sacrifice needs expansion to be intelligible and defensible, so too does the parallel notion of a suffering God. For to make sense of the notion in both cases we must surely speak of a suffering that is of a differing order and significance from that experienced upon the cross; otherwise precisely the same objections that were once made to the agony of Christ being renewed in Catholic theology, must also now be raised against much Protestant theology. In respect of the issue which concerns us here, the difference in kind between cross and Eucharist may be expressed in terms of the double role of Christ as victim and priest. On the cross, unrepeatably, Christ suffered and died on our behalf, as the sacrificial victim; in the Eucharist, again and again, as we recall and celebrate that unique sacrifice, we are joined with, and participate in, Christ's continuing action in heaven, where, as our great High Priest, he offers himself, and indeed the whole world which he has redeemed, to the Father.

But if the divine element in the idea of eucharistic sacrifice needs careful explication and qualification, so too does the notion that the human role is preeminent. The priest as a wielder of power over Christ is deeply troubling; but so too, it must be added, is the idea of any Christian, whether priest or worshipper, as purely passive. It matters what we do; to say that we need to respond and accept that initial sacrifice of Christ implies a summons to action, not passivity. It has been a repeated theme of this book that the notion of sacrifice has been wrongly applied – as demanding passivity of those whose lives are already wrongly made too passive – the obvious, but by no means exclusive, instance among Christians (as chapter 1 emphasised) being that of women. Instead, we must think of us all as called to identify with Christ's sacrifice – whether we be priest or people – in active outreach to the world. This means that 'taking up our cross' (Mark 8.34) is a matter not only of 'completing what is lacking in Christ's afflictions' (Col. 1.24) but also of 'rejoicing in the Lord always' (Phil. 4.4), as we learn in obedience to our Lord 'both to be full and to be hungry, both to abound and to suffer need' (Phil. 4.12 AV).

It is this sense of active participation in Christ's original sacrifice that modern ecumenical documents (such as BEM, Lima, 1982 and ARCIC, Final Report, 1982) stress, and which we would also wish to endorse. Nothing that we can do can add to the perfection of Christ's sacrifice of complete obedience upon the cross, but what we can do is identify with that sacrifice in both word and deed, as its effects are made available to us once more in the drama of the liturgy. In seeing ourselves as drawn thus into the movement of Christ's self-offering, we approach more nearly the biblical notion of sacrifice which was never intended as a matter of something we do, but as something in which we are privileged to participate, most obviously perhaps in the notion of the shelem or communion sacrifice (Lev. 3); significantly, its celebration carried with it a summons to 'rejoice in the presence of the Lord' (Deut. 12.18).

The complexities of Christian history mean that inevitably not only great care ought to be taken in determining the appropriate expression of such a notion in the Church's liturgy, but that great care will in fact be taken! Nonetheless, such care will have been worthwhile; for without its expression something very valuable is lost. Cranmer in so sharply separating off as a post-communion response the offering of 'ourselves, our souls and our bodies' as 'a reasonable, holy, and lively sacrifice unto thee' intended something rather more than mere Reformation polemic. Not only were the corruptions of medieval notions of eucharistic sacrifice thus firmly circumvented, a very laudable stress on the manner and necessity of our response was appropriately highlighted. But, moving though the words undoubtedly are in their context, for many something significant and important was lost, which the restoration of the eucharistic prayer to a single unity in modern liturgies more effectively conveys. This is the fact that cross, Eucharist and response are all part of a single act: the gracious initiative of the Son who not only made – 'once offered' – a 'perfect and sufficient sacrifice . . . for the sins of the whole world', but also enables thereby whatever sacrificial response we are now able to make on our part. It is only in and through him that we can offer ourselves to the one Father whom by our adoption we and he both share. It is the desire to stress the single character of this act which explains why some also find it helpful to think at this point of the Passover prayers over the bread and wine – 'work of human hands' – which in all probability Christ used at the Last Supper.

Their use at the Eucharist may be interpreted as a sign of all creation being offered in and through Christ back to the Father.

What such sacrifice in detail will mean we have already sought to elucidate in earlier paragraphs: that it must firmly be seen as having a positive, joyful aspect, as well as involving a summons to self-denial. It is within that wider context that the traditional play on holiness as wholeness can find its natural setting. In this life the process of bringing our natures and their potentialities to their proper and integrated completion has already begun. We are being healed of our wounds. In understanding how such wholeness may be brought about, modern psychology has many useful insights to offer, and these should be gladly welcomed. At the same time two cautions need to be issued, even in respect of psychologists whom many Christians have found sympathetic such as C. G. Jung and Carl Rogers. Wholeness remains essentially only an ideal, for seldom will human brokenness and fragility ever be fully resolved this side of the grave. Secondly, and more importantly, such wholeness must never be pursued simply for its own sake; we are freed in order to serve others. There is much reason to suppose that such holiness and wholeness cannot be found outside of community. Even Christian hermits, if they are to flourish, need not only the prayers of the community but also to be in some form of continuing relationship. If we take seriously our baptism as making us fellow members of the Body of Christ, then it is not something to be pursued alone, but something to be received through mutual ministry, encouragement, fellowship and love.

That social dimension is a repeated biblical theme, which is well encapsulated by the Hebrew word *shalom*. We are most familiar with the translation 'peace', but it means so much more than the mere absence of conflict. Its field of meaning includes wholeness or well-being, but it means wholeness realised in the context of a society as a whole, with no aspect of human need neglected, which is why we find it sometimes translated as 'prosperity'. A famous verse of Jeremiah urges the Jewish exiles in Babylon to the realisation that in the 'welfare' of their enemy is their own 'peace' to be found (29.7).

Modern New Testament scholarship has helped us to recover the sense in which the Eucharist as messianic banquet was intended to symbolise a new social order, but full recovery of that social sense will be delayed for so long as the Church continues to be corrupted by secular individualism. We are all one in Christ and just as you did it to one of the least of these who are members of my family, you did it to me' (Matt. 25.40).

In other words, the Church is intended as the model of community, as the Body of him who will draw all people unto himself (John 12.32). Of course, individuality transcended can be narrow and jingoistic, as with Nazism or, at a more mundane level, with some football crowds. But it can also be what makes a community flourish. Christ is so much more than substitute or representative, more than just one individual relating to another (ourselves). For it is he who gives us the grace to see things from others' perspective, he it is who builds us up into a common whole, he who creates that peace of complete integration of ourselves and one another that will be finally ours beyond the shadow of death.

Augustine defines 'the sacrifice of Christians' as 'the many being one Body in Christ' (*City of God,* 10.6). Whether it be at the Eucharist or elsewhere, he argues, it is as individuals and as a society being made whole through him that the 'head' offers up its 'members'. But can such language be applied to those who seek after God in ways other than our own, in the pluralistic world of which we are all increasingly conscious? It is to that issue that we turn next.

7

Christ and world faiths

This report of the Doctrine Commission is the first to include a full chapter where Christian understanding of a key theological concept is considered in relationship to other faiths. This is appropriate because the inter-faith issue has in recent times become a kind of touchstone in some quarters in connection with the doctrine of salvation. It is also a subject on which theologians within the Church of England hold a variety of approaches. In view of the fact that some readers may not be familiar with the nature of the subject-matter, this chapter makes a number of references to recent literature. Details are given in notes at the end of the book for those who wish to follow them up.

In our introductory chapter, we considered some ways in which people of other faiths view the nearest equivalent concept in their faith to that of salvation in the Christian faith, and we do not intend to go over the same ground again. If a group of Buddhists were to write a doctrine report, they would be asking in a chapter like this how Buddhists see faithful Christians or Muslims in relationship to the Buddhist doctrine of *nirvana*. Here we are considering some Christian understandings of salvation and asking where they leave the faithful Hindu or Buddhist, not in Buddhist or Hindu terms, but in Christian terms. We are not pretending Christian salvation is '*moksha*' or '*nirvana*'.

We note that the status of adherents of other religions is only one aspect, if a very important one, of a general problem, the particularity of the Christian claims about salvation on which we have touched in chapter 3. There seems to be a paradox between, on the one hand, a 'universal' vision of Christian faith and the open generosity of God, and, on the other hand, the social situation of the early Christian churches; these communities included small groups of Jewish Christians who were living increasingly uneasily with other Jewish people, and of Gentile Christians who were trying to assert their identity within the powerful culture of the Greeks and the Roman Empire; in both types of community emerged a seemingly 'exclusive' position. The paradox received expression in the report of the Lambeth Conference of 1988: 'Anything that is "exclusively" true of the incarnate Lord, is true of one who is precisely the most "inclusive" reality, the divine life rejoicing in itself and seeking to share itself. All of creation is caught up in this moment, for all of creation has been called into existence by this moment of divine love.'[1]

This chapter is in three sections. In the first section, we outline some theological responses to experiences of living in multi-faith contexts, both in Britain and in other parts of the world. Then we consider the interpretation of some biblical passages and themes which may relate to other faiths. Finally we identify key elements in a theology of religions that can provide an appropriate framework for Christian understanding of salvation and other faiths. These sections will, incidentally, also enable us to reflect on the subject within the well-known Anglican appeal to Scripture, tradition and reason.

The context of experience

Experience should not be isolated from the Bible or from reason, for experience can be misleadingly subjective, particularly if not checked out with the experience of contemporaries and with that of the past expressed in Scripture and in the teaching of the Church. It can be ambiguous in itself, and be read differently by different people. People's experience, for example, of a religion like Islam varies enormously, depending on whom they have met, and in which contexts. At a recent weekend course for Christians on Islam and Muslims in Britain, participants found their views moving in many directions as they met the great variety amongst Muslims, and heard Muslim exponents of the theology and practice of their faith make their presentations. Equally, theology without experience is also in danger of great inadequacy, particularly in respect of other faiths, on which too many people have pronounced without having met people of other faiths at all.

The context of contemporary Britain

Only since the considerable immigration from the Indian sub-continent in the 1960s have members of the Church of England met people of other faiths on any large scale. Until perhaps the mid-1970s, apart from the long-established but comparatively small Jewish community, their presence was low key. They were seen largely as 'immigrants' whom we were concerned about 'integrating' into society, rather than as people of various faiths whom we had somehow to integrate into our theological thinking, whether negatively, neutrally or positively. Since then, the profile of Muslims, Hindus and Sikhs in particular has been much raised, at a time when Christian churches have been in decline, both absolutely and relatively to these other communities. It is reckoned there are about 400,000 Sikhs in Britain, 300,000 Jews, 300,000 Hindus, 25,000 Buddhists, and between 1,000,000 and 1,400,000 Muslims. It is hard to estimate the number who attend synagogues, temples and mosques regularly, but those involved with these communities are all clear that the number attending is a much higher proportion than that of those who are nominally Christian.

This higher profile is not merely numerical; it is the result of what Muslims, Hindus and others have done for themselves, as they have ceased to meet behind closed doors, and have converted or built places of worship and community centres throughout our major cities. In Birmingham, for example, there are now more than seventy mosques of various kinds, including several large purpose-built ones. The City Council has recently produced a religious map of the city on which Christian buildings are portrayed alongside mosques, syna-gogues, temples and gurdwaras, as the diversity of religious life is displayed and, indeed, celebrated. In the centre of Leicester, there is a Jain temple converted from a URC building, with not only richly artistic pillars and statues inside, but also a public facade of ornate carvings of high quality, carved by sculptors from India. Even Buddhism has been raising its profile, with much publicised four year retreats in rural Scotland, undertaken largely by European converts.

In addition, they have been fighting for various rights which are religious in origin. The Sikhs have demanded the right to wear their turbans on construction sites, the Muslims to have single-sex girls' schools, and now their own State-funded schools, the Hindus to build temples in suburban areas.

It is partly because of issues prominent in the media that Muslims have a higher profile: for example, the Salman Rushdie affair, the Gulf War and the various hostage crises. And some within the media seem to wish to build up Islam as 'the enemy', to replace 'communism'. So, also, to a lesser degree with Hindus and Sikhs and Buddhists, with the conflicts in India and Sri Lanka, and the repercussions amongst their British relatives here.

As a consequence of the widening spread of people of other faiths more Christians are meeting them on a day-to-day basis, and are forming attitudes, not just to them as people, but also to their religions. How are we to view them, how does God see them, can they be saved? Three 'positions' about salvation were set out ten years ago for British readers by Alan Race,[2] and then became established surprisingly quickly as broad categories; there are exclusivist, inclusivist and pluralist approaches to people of other faiths, or to those faiths themselves. We return to these later, but in brief, and generalising, the exclusivist sees salvation exclusively through explicit faith in Christ, or through the Church; the inclusivist sees salvation as being ultimately through Christ, but inclusive of all, or of particular people who follow other faiths, and indeed of those faiths themselves; and the pluralist sees there being as many paths to salvation as there are religions. This theological use of 'pluralism' needs to be distinguished from the descriptive use of 'plurality' as one popular way of describing British society, and the educational sector in particular. 'Pluralism' is also used in connection with the school curriculum in general and to assemblies and religious education in particular.

The General Synod document *Towards a Theology of Inter-faith Dialogue*, and the consequent debate leading to the commendation of the report in 1984, and the report on Multi-Faith Worship, with the debate in July 1992, mark points where the Church of England has begun to grapple seriously both with the practical realities and with the theological issues involved. In between came the Lambeth Conference Report of 1988, where a commitment was made by the Anglican bishops, to 'affirm all they can affirm in the faith of Muslims and Jews, especially when it resonates with the Gospel', and the report writes of the common hope for the kingdom, felt by both Jews and Christians, and 'the deep Islamic reliance on the grace and mercy of God'. 'Although often misunderstood and misrepresented by Christian theologians as teaching salvation by works, all schools of Islamic thought are marked by a deep sense of the gratuitous mercy of God.'[3] Such appreciation leads to the way of dialogue, understanding and sharing, which is commended to the Communion.

The world-wide context of mission

Mission is clearly an imperative everywhere, including Britain, but much can be learnt from the practice of mission in multi-faith contexts elsewhere, both at the present time and in the twenty centuries of Christian history. All we can give are a few glimpses from that history.

As the Christian gospel encountered the Gentile world questions inevitably arose about the relationship between the Christian faith and other religious traditions. In the writings of the Greek apologists, most notably Justin Martyr, there is a willingness to recognise the religious philosophy of Platonism in particular, as providing a preparation for the gospel. Just as the Jewish prophets pointed forward to Christ, so a preparation for the gospel can be traced in Greek philosophy. Just as the revelation of God to Moses at the burning bush was interpreted as the appearance of the divine Logos, so that same

Logos was seen as present in the 'seeds' of the word in the truth witnessed to by pagan philosophers. Christ is therefore the fulfiller of other religious yearnings as he is of the Jewish prophets.

Not all early Christian theologians were willing to follow this line. Others, most notably perhaps Tertullian, drew a sharp line between Greek philosophy and the Jewish/Christian revelation, asking 'What has Athens to do with Jerusalem?' There were many who characterised pagan religion as 'demonic'. And even those like Justin who had a positive attitude towards pagan philosophy, tended to combine this with a clear condemnation of pagan worship.

After the rise of Islam, large numbers of Christians (and Jews) continued to live in what came to be the 'Islamic world'. They were certainly restricted in many ways in their life and witness and often there were tensions between the communities. They made, nevertheless, a considerable contribution to the emergence of 'Islamic' civilisation, especially in the areas of philosophy, medicine and government. Already in the seventh and eighth centuries, St John of Damascus represented the Christian community in the court of the *Ummayad* caliph. He had a number of discussions with Muslims on religious matters and two of his 'dialogues' with Muslims survive to this day. His theological method, which became so influential in the Christian world, also greatly influenced the emergence of formal theology, or *Kalam*, in the Muslim world. The 'Nestorian' Patriarch Timothy also maintained a presence in the court of the great *Abbaside* caliphs and accounts have survived of his discussions with them and prayers for them.

These two examples of the oriental Christian encounter with Islam differ markedly in tone from the polemics of both Byzantium and the West. There Christian–Muslim relations were often polarised, from both sides, as is graphically illustrated in the sad story of the Crusades and of the struggle to dominate Spain. But even in the West a more respectful note can, on occasions, be heard. For instance, we read in a letter from Pope Gregory VII to the Muslim ruler of Bijaya (modern Algeria) in 1076: 'Almighty God approves nothing in us so much as that, after loving God, one should love his fellow man. You and we owe this charity to ourselves, because we believe in, and confess, one God, admittedly in a different way.' There was the celebrated meeting between St Francis and the Sultan, Melek-El-Kamil, around 1220, which is portrayed as a deep dialogue about truth, in which each was led to respect the other, even if they could not convince each other; St Francis' heart was moved to prayer out of deep compassion for the brother for whom also Christ died, and the Sultan out of great respect for the simplicity and humour of Francis and his companion, Illuminato.

Two further medieval pioneers of dialogue with Islam were Ramon Lull and Cardinal Nicholas of Cusa. Lull endeavoured to search out common principles of Christianity, Judaism and Islam, while Nicholas was provoked by the fall of Constantinople to the Muslim Ottomans in 1453 to write *De Pace Fidei,* in which he argued as one deeply engaged in the dialogue with Islam that there was only one religion but in a diversity of rites.

We note that many of the oriental Christian traditions have long missionary histories: the Copts in North East Africa, the Church of the East (or 'Nestorians') in India and China, and the West Syrians in India. The Sigan-Fu stone (set up in the eighth century) bears witness to the seriousness of the 'Nestorian' missionaries in expressing the Christian faith in Chinese terms. Similarly, the ancient churches in India had reached an accommodation with Hinduism well before the arrival of European missionaries. In the late seventeenth century, the Italian, Matteo Ricci, who spent over a quarter of a century in China, endeavoured to express Christianity in terms acceptable to the Chinese, and to make use of indigenous Chinese ceremonies in Christian worship, in much the same way as, so many centuries before, Augustine of Canterbury had been urged by Pope Gregory the Great to baptise as many customs as possible of the Anglo-Saxons.

Such experiences have long been those of both British missionaries and British people serving overseas, and also with local Christians, with whom they worked, and all have learned by interaction with adherents of other faiths among whom they lived. This has been particularly so in the Indian subcontinent which we give as our main example. Christians in Kerala have been posed with practical and theological questions related to their Hindu or Muslim neighbours for at least seventeen hundred years. If we consider missionaries from the Church of England, they came out in increasing numbers from the early nineteenth century. They came largely following what they saw was Christ's call to rescue the lost, typically expressed in the words of Sankey's hymn:

> Go forth, and rescue those that perish,
> Where sin and darkness reign;
> Go, lend a helping hand to save them,
> And break the tempter's chain.

This was the time when Mohammed was frequently condemned as 'that imposter', and where Hindu practices such as *suttee* (widow burning) or the self-immolation of worshippers before the Hindu deity on the juggernaut were highlighted vividly. The missionaries were bringing the possibility of salvation to the Hindu, Sikh or Muslim, and their view of those religions was completely or largely negative.

But experience gradually changed the attitudes of many of these missionaries. They began to experience the kindness of character of many people of other faiths, people who did not convert to Christianity, but responded to them personally; far from opposing Christian mission, they gave space for it and trusted its schools and hospitals. The missionaries began to read the Scriptures of other faiths and to see there a depth that had to be considered seriously. Also, for all the efforts of the missionaries, these religions did not collapse.

Such pioneers were faced with the critical question, what was the ongoing status in God's eyes, both of people who followed these faiths sincerely, appearing to gain a framework for their lives in doing so, and also of the faiths themselves? Did God have a purpose in these religions, even a saving purpose? And what of someone like Mahatma Gandhi, who responded to the person of Jesus Christ, and read the Sermon on the Mount regularly as well as the Gita, and appeared to put the teaching of Jesus into practice much more faithfully than most Christians? Could he be saved, who wrote, 'Today, supposing I was to be deprived of the Gita and forget all its contents but had a copy of the Sermon on the Mount, I should derive the same joy from it as I do from the Gita', and, 'The Cross is an eternal event in this stormy life . . . Living Christ means a living Cross, without it life is a living death.'? (We should note at the same time that such admiration was not related to the necessity of the historical Jesus, for Gandhi. He also wrote, 'I should not care if it was proved by someone that the man called Jesus never lived, and that what was narrated in the Gospels was a figment of the writer's imagination. For the Sermon on the Mount would still be true for me.') And what of the many ordinary Hindus, who admired and responded to Christ in various ways but did not wish to become part of a western colonial church, or would have faced ostracism if they had? Could they be saved?

Experiences such as these can be seen in relationship to various theological positions. Theologians such as Schleiermacher, in the nineteenth century, or Otto, in the early twentieth century, saw a common essence within religious experience. Karl Barth said that anyone who has not felt the compelling power of Schleiermacher has no right to criticise him. But, having said this, Barth regarded all religion, including the Christian religion, as man-made, and needing to be reformed by being centred on the singular revelation of God as seen in Jesus Christ.

But, in the 'mission field', and in India in particular, theologies of salvation were based on much deeper meeting. In 1913, J. Farquhar wrote his famous book *The Crown of Hinduism*. Here, he recognised and evaluated positively the achievements of Hinduism, the sincere aspirations of Hindus, and the good that many of them showed in their lives. But, in the end, 'Jesus, the Son of God, who died for our sins on Calvary, produces a religion which satisfies the modern mind, and which also proves to be the fulfilment and goal of all the religions of the world, the crudest as well as the loftiest.'

The first World Missionary Conference at Edinburgh in 1910 had shown great wisdom in its balance. It is a striking example of how creativity in theological reflection comes directly out of a concern for mission, rather than, as so often, doctrine and mission being held in separate compartments. It was unashamedly evangelical in that it called for the evangelisation of the whole world in one generation. But also, in its Commission 4 on inter-action with other faiths (thought essential more than eighty years before this Doctrine Commission is considering the issues), it began by drawing on evidence submitted from all parts of the world. There were no less than sixty-one extensive reports related to experience with Hinduism, with a range of opinion. Wesley Ariarajah analysed these replies and concludes: 'Almost all the replies received emphasised that Christians should possess and not merely assume a sympathetic attitude towards Hinduism. Such sympathy should be based on knowledge and not be the child of emotion or imagination.'[4] The Commission concluded: 'More harm has been done in India than in any other country by missionaries who have lacked the wisdom to appreciate the nobler side of the religion which they have laboured so indefatigably to supplant.' They studied also Hindu concepts of incarnation (*avatar*), devotion (*bhakti*), and salvation (*moksha*). Of the latter, the comment was made 'Though the idea of salvation (i.e. *moksha*) is always associated with the conception of rebirth, yet there is also connected with it an earnest longing and passionate desire for union with God.'

In contrast to both Farquhar and the searchings of Edinburgh, the conference at Tambaram, Madras, in 1938, affirmed a revitalised exclusivism. Hendrik Kraemer represented an approach to mission characterised by Dialectical Theology. He dominated the conference, as did his book *The Christian Message in a Non-Christian World*. Here he wrote: 'If we are ever to know what true and divinely willed religion is, we can only do this through God's revelation in Jesus Christ, and through nothing else', and, 'In this light and in regard to their deepest and most essential purport, other religions are all in error.' He therefore urged on converts a radical discontinuity from their former faith as they entered the Church of Christ.

This is still a powerful view, not least in India, and leads to a powerful missionary imperative. Salvation, in whatever form, is available only through Jesus Christ and explicit confession of him. It is the predominant voice that has led most Asian converts in Britain to deny any continuity with their past, and, indeed, this has been almost required of them by the zeal of those responsible for their conversion. It is experience-based, since Kraemer was a long-term missionary and represented a widely held view. Often such a radical discontinuity is demanded by the convert; otherwise why suffer what he/she often does? It is because in the new faith salvation is assured.

Since the Second World War, two other broad theological approaches have come alongside those of Farquhar and Kraemer. Both arise from the experience of mission as Christian presence with people of other faiths: (i) being alongside in presence, service and witness, and seeing where the Spirit leads (associated with the name of Max Warren); (ii) the dialogue movement, in its various forms – dialogue in daily life, dialogue in common social action and nation-building, theological dialogue, dialogue in depth (in spirituality).

C. Murray Rogers wrote of the last: 'I long for the only dialogue which will help me to realise more deeply the mystery of the Spirit in me.' It requires an acknowledgment that one does not know everything. Dr Gangadaran, one of the two Hindu observers at the WCC Assembly in Canberra, speaks of the basis of such dialogue: 'Only a person with the highest knowledge can understand their own ignorance. When they have understood their scriptures, such a person will leave a space. Only so can God find place to come in.' This reveals an essential willingness to learn. The same Hindu comments: 'If I do not understand now, this does not mean I may not understand later. I can never know that something is not going to be of significance for me in my search for truth.' Remarkably, he then quotes the story of the thief who hung beside Jesus on the cross, how he was given the promise of salvation, because at the end of his life he realised the significance of the one hanging next to him. The Roman Catholics, Abishiktananda and Bede Griffiths, are amongst those who have gone furthest in this identification with another faith while remaining committed to Christ.

Some theological responses to experience of other faiths

Amongst those mentioned above, some would call themselves, or be called by others, pluralists. Some may be described as inclusivists and others as exclusivists. Most pluralists in no way deny the centrality of Christ for the Christian tradition of which they are a part (though some who disagree with them have a suspicion that they have a tendency to diminish Christ in the interest of inter-faith harmony). But they see different world-views in other faiths which also seem to work for people of those faiths, enabling them to lead integrated and holy lives. Pluralists like John Hick have been deeply influenced by experience with certain people of other faiths. Like Schleiermacher and Otto mentioned above (p. 152), he has an experiential concept of religion. Instead of a christological centre, for Hick, there is now God at the centre (or more recently, 'the real'). In his now famous 'Copernican revolution' in religion, he writes: 'And we have to realize that the universe of faiths centres upon God, and not upon Christianity or any other religion. He is the sun, the originative source of light and life, whom all the religions reflect in their own different ways.'[5] There are different ways to salvation, however that is understood, different paths to the top of the mountain. Some would claim there was still one mountain top, one ultimate reality, which is seen in different ways. Others, that the idea of one mountain is beyond reach, we are on different mountains, and this does not matter, provided that we reach the clear air at the top of our mountain. This allows each faith to keep its own integrity, but little motivation for mission, in the sense of a call for conversion, which is merely a distraction. Mission is about working for the kingdom, with our neighbours of all faiths and none. This has been described by a Hindu scholar as 'mutual dynamic mission in which God wants us to be partners'.

Stanley Samartha, in a recent book, puts it like this:

> When alternative ways of salvation have provided meaning and purpose for millions of persons in other cultures for more than two or three thousand years, to claim that the Judaeo-Christian-Western tradition has the only answer to

all problems in all places and for all persons in the world is presumptuous, if not incredible. This is not to deny the validity of the Christian experience of salvation in Jesus Christ, but it is to question the exclusive claims made for it by Christians, claims that are unsupported by any evidence in history, or in the institutional life of the church, or in the lives of many Christians who make such claims. If salvation comes from God – and for Christians it cannot be otherwise – then possibilities should be left open to recognise the validity of other experiences of salvation.[6]

To this challenge this entire report seeks to respond.

Others are often grouped together as 'inclusivists', and they are a very broad category. But, basically, again from experience, their contact with people of various faiths has led them in two directions, which may seem contradictory, but which they wish to hold together. On the one hand, they have come to respect not only the persons of the other faith, but also that faith itself, very deeply, not just for the good works that may flow from its adherents, but also for the spirituality that evidently lies behind it. On the other hand, through encounter, they have become more, not less, committed to the place of Jesus Christ in questions of salvation, and of what he reveals uniquely, as they see it, of the nature of God. Holding these two together, they wish to see Christ at the centre, and that means his cross and resurrection, as well as his teaching and incarnation, and, at the same time, to include within God's saving grace the possibility of salvation in every respect for people of other faiths. Some would say they are saved as people, outside their religion; others would include elements given to them in their faith. We would prefer to use the term 'inclusivist' for the second group. As a criterion for what can be included, they would tend to use what conforms to the ethos and teaching of the New Testament, or what they estimate Christ would accept. And they would use such criteria for what is acceptable in the Church.

Anglicans from the Church of England historically have made a significant contribution to the development of these various theologies. F. D. Maurice and Bishop Westcott can be seen to be amongst those who before their time struggled to some extent with these questions. In his book *The Religions of the World, and Their Relations to Christianity* (1847), Maurice sets out a positive view of the religious aspirations of humanity combined with a need for the Christian to prevent such religious aspirations becoming idolatrous and superstitious. Maurice saw Christianity not as the destroyer, but the preserver of what is strongest and most permanent in Hindu life and character, a kind of fulfilment theology sixty years before J. Farquhar. Recognising how Hinduism reveals a desire and longing for converse with the unseen world, Maurice writes: 'I contend that he who is able to give the answers to the Hindoo's deepest questions is not a destroyer, but a preserver: that he will have a right to boast of having upholden all that was strongest and most permanent in the Hindoo life and character.'[7] C. F. Andrews, Verrier Elwin and Jack Winslow were three Anglicans who allowed experience with the people of India to transform their theology; Henry Martyn and Temple Gairdner became pioneers in mission and dialogue with Islam. In the modern period, we can think of bishops such as Kenneth Cragg, Stephen Neill, George Appleton, John Robinson, John V. Taylor, David Brown, Lakshman Wickremasinghe (of Sri Lanka) and Michael Nazir-Ali, all of whom contributed diverse and significant writings, as have Max Warren, Roger Hooker, Christopher Lamb and others. Common to all these is a link between mission, experience and theology.

In what has sometimes been recognised as a growing trend of Anglican theology of inter-faith encounter,[8] Max Warren speaks of 'the unknown Christ' who saves even when 'unrecognised as the Saviour'. Through his method of Christian presence, Kenneth Cragg seeks to 'unveil the hidden Christ, that is the elements that are already "in Christ" within the other religions'. John Taylor points out that every religion has its 'jealousies', its tenets that carry a 'universal significance and finality' for all humankind. For Christians this jealousy is the assertion 'that Jesus is central to God's purpose for mankind . . . that from the beginning the world was held in existence by the Redeemer who was to die'. This Christ is 'the invisible magnetic pole that draws all peoples in their quest for the Ultimate.'

All three views, exclusivism, inclusivism (of both a wide, and the more specific sense which we are using) and pluralism, are present today within the Church of England, and also increasingly related to experience within Britain. But the difference may be that those in the 'exclusivist' area are less willing to be influenced by experience, positive or negative. They may be just as friendly and accepting of people of other faiths at a human level, 'loving your neighbour as yourself'. But theological presuppositions will determine attitudes finally. This is illustrated by the much quoted story of the conversation between D. T. Niles, the Sri Lankan ecumenical theologian, and Karl Barth. D. T. Niles asked Barth how he could know that Hinduism was unbelief if, as he had admitted, he had never met a Hindu. Barth's reply was 'I know that *a priori'*. (On the other hand, Barth can be said to be extremely inclusive in the sense that he sees all people, though not of course their religions, already included in the crucified and risen Christ. This would make him inclusivist in the wide sense, but not in the specific sense we are using the term.)

Wesley Ariarajah's book mentioned above suggests that the non-Roman Catholic churches are still dominated by the Tambaram spirit, even if it is subtly expressed. Dialogue is enshrined in the WCC structures, but has not brought a decisive move away from exclusivism at any of the major resolution-making conferences. Edinburgh 1910 is shown as all the more radical in the light of the decades since.

As we have seen in chapter 1, during these same years, the Roman Catholic Church has moved from the position that there is no salvation outside the Roman Catholic Church. Vatican II represented a sharp shift. In *Nostra Aetate* it is affirmed that 'the Catholic Church rejects nothing that is true and holy in these religions', and that they 'often reflect a ray of that truth which enlightens all men'. But Christ remains the way, the truth and the life. 'It is in him, in whom God reconciled all things to himself (2 Cor. 5.18–19), men find the fullness of their religious life.' Writing of Christ's redeeming sacrifice, Vatican II teaches:

All this holds true not only for Christians but for all men of
good will in whose hearts grace works in an unseen way. For
since Christ died for all men, and since the ultimate vocation of man is in fact one and divine, we ought to believe
that the Holy Spirit in a manner known only to God offers
to every man the possibility of being associated with this
paschal mystery.[9]

In similar vein, Karl Rahner made two clear points in relationship to
salvation. He said that people of other faiths are saved *through*, and
not *despite* their religion and faith. And there followed the phrase for
ever associated with him, 'anonymous Christians' – they are saved
because they are inspired by Christ, though they do not know it; this
phrase has been much criticised, but it is a consequence of Rahner's
desire to honour the positive experiences of many, while being true
to his conviction about the centrality of Christ. Hans Küng added
the distinction between other religions as 'ordinary' ways to salvation, and Christianity as the 'extraordinary' or special way. The
present Pope, John Paul II, in his encyclical *Redemptor Hominis*,
embraces what has gone before: 'The human person – every person
without exception – has been redeemed by Christ; because Christ is
in a way united to the human person – every person without exception – even if the individual may not realise this fact.'[10]

Pluralism can mean there are no absolutes, and each finds their own
way, and even creates their own reality. It fits also with a
Christianity which has lost its confidence. We can leave others to
follow their own way, while we do our best to be faithful Christians.
It avoids the necessity for the rather uncomfortable task of evange-
lism and witness. More positively, it takes seriously the cultural
diversity experienced in modern Britain, and shows genuine respect
for the various faiths around, without either threatening them or
suggesting their adherents need to be converted. It also fits well with
the obvious fact that good and devout people are to be found in all
our religious communities. But, even with this open approach, there
still remain the key questions of criteria and limits. In the face of
cults and sects, or the loosely defined New Age movement, most

pluralists would draw the line at some point. If we return to the image of the paths up a mountain, is anything a path? Are there not paths that fade out like sheep tracks, or even end at the top of precipices half way up the mountain? Is it possible to find salvation through something that is not true, even if it seems to satisfy its adherents? There is a question to be addressed by pluralists as to whether they take seriously the necessary exclusivity of truth.

The witness of converts

Finally, in terms of experience, it is vital to hear the witness of converts, who of all people have actually lived on the margin between different faiths, and have often suffered in consequence. While pluralism admits of the possibility of conversion, there is little point in it, as salvation is already available within each faith, in terms which satisfy within that faith. Yet there is hardly a convert who is a pluralist, unless perhaps converted for convenience or marriage. The genuine religious converts, whether to Christianity or to any other faith, certainly believe that their conversion makes a difference, and that is why they face whatever befalls them. Such converts usually either deny any continuity with what came before, and see salvation coming only through the new, or they accept the past with thanks, seeing their relatives in the old faith as preparing the way.

For example, a Christian convert from Sikhism writes of his Sikh family:

> They know how important they, and my Sikh upbringing, are to me. Over the years they have developed respect for me, as a Christian, just as I respect them. I wear the Sikh bracelet as a sign of my pride for my roots, and as a sign of my commitment to stand for God's truth and justice that it demands.

Such a person has suffered for his conversion, for his commitment to the calling to be a disciple of Jesus Christ, experienced as read in John 15.16: 'You did not choose me but, I chose you.' But he is convinced that the same Jesus Christ reveals a God who will include his relatives as well as himself. He echoes the approach of his great fellow Sikh, Sadhu Sundar Singh. The well-known story is told of him that when someone said that his mother, a saintly Sikh woman, would go to hell if she did not become a Christian, he replied: 'Then I will ask God to send me down to hell so that I may be with her there.'

A Hindu convert in Britain became a Christian as he observed the way a particular fellow Christian student lived his life, and moved with people. He hardly knew him, but observing was enough. As he had been brought up, he had been deeply influenced by the holiness of a particular older Hindu, who died after the conversion of the student. He comments:

> I cannot believe my old Hindu will not be accepted by the love of God. 'The fruits' were so evident in him. From my limited understanding of missionaries throughout the ages, the attitude has often been one of the missionary offering their knowledge of God to others. Often it appears to me that people are not led to understand Christ as the fulfilment of the quest, but that their quest itself is demolished.

A convert from Islam in Britain put it like this:

> I was already seeking for God as a Muslim. Muslims have the same hopes and fears. I know that it is the same God who has created us all, Christians and Muslims. Both as a Muslim and as a Christian, I worshipped that same God. But I have come into a new and personal relationship with God through Christ. Before I was in awe of God, and felt every small evil I did would be weighed against my good works. Now I feel the love of God.

From a very different context, Bishop Clement of the Diocese of Central Zambia, tells how when the missionaries first came to Zambia, as it became, the people recognised the God the missionaries spoke of as the God they already knew who was creator of the great plains and mountains and forests of Africa.

But other converts do not see this type of continuity of experience of God, or acknowledge common experience of worship, or possibility of salvation in their previous faith. Another convert from Islam spoke of how she felt the continuous need of prayer for protection since she had experienced so much suffering and real persecution leading to the break up of her family life, due to her conversion. She saw things in terms of spiritual warfare. The assurance of salvation is felt by her to be radically discontinuous with anything understood before.

Such individual responses often depend on the overall context. How Muslims and Christians see each other and relate to each other is a very different question in Britain as compared with certain Middle Eastern countries, and how they relate in one part of Africa is very different from another. Hence the need to look at these questions both in general, and within the specific context for which this report is written.

The Bible

Faced with this wide-ranging and complex set of questions, we naturally turn to the Bible. Both Old and New Testaments are confessional documents, written out of faith, to encourage faith. They are written out of particular cultures, to encourage loyalty, commitment and conversion within particular traditions. The major faiths of the world today were either unknown to the writers because they did not exist, or were beyond their geographical experience. So we are not able to read off easy biblical answers, even if we wished to. We look for insights which may illuminate our doctrinal task from several sources: from the ways in which the Jewish people reflected on their relationship with Canaanite and other religions among which they lived, from the way the Church reflected on the parting of the ways between Judaism and Christianity, and from the way the Church expanded into the world of Greek culture and Roman imperial rule.

In doing this, we recognise a dynamic relationship between Scripture, tradition and reason. We need to interpret Scripture in the light of the experience of the centuries in between; thus this section should not be abstracted from the first part of this chapter. Nor must we neglect reason, as we reflect on what has been handed down to us. Nevertheless, we hold by the Anglican understanding, as in Article 20 of the Thirty-Nine Articles, that 'It is not lawful for the Church to ordain any thing that is contrary to God's Word written.. . .' We should be wary of a doctrine of salvation in relationship to people of other faiths that was not consonant with Scripture in its main thrust.

Old Testament

In the Old Testament there is no doubt that the God who revealed himself to Israel as Yahweh is the God of the whole world and of all the nations. The early chapters of Genesis set a universal context for the rest of the Old Testament story. From Adam and Eve to the Tower of Babel the story concerns the common origins of all the nations. It tells not only of rebellion against God, but also of people, such as Abel, Enosh, Enoch and Noah, who knew God in primeval times. It is only after this universal context has been set that the story narrows to Abraham and Sarah, the man and the woman through whose descendants, Israel, all the nations of the world are eventually to be blessed.

Once the Old Testament story becomes that of Abraham and Sarah and their descendants, the religions of the other nations Israel knew are usually represented in wholly negative terms, as idolatrous. But there are four ways in which the Old Testament portrays Gentiles (non-Israelites) in a positive relationship to the one true God. In the first place, God acts for and through other nations without their acknowledging him. He calls Cyrus to be his servant (Isa. 45.1) and leads Gentile nations in exodus events of their own (Amos 9.7).

Secondly, Israel's knowledge of the God revealed to them can be and is shared with non-Israelites who also come to worship Yahweh. The Old Testament never suggests that it is necessary to be a born Israelite in order to know and to serve Yahweh. In some cases, such as Rahab (Josh. 2.1–21; 6.25) and Ruth, members of other nations not only turn to Yahweh but also join his people. In other cases, such as Naaman (2 Kings 5) and Nebuchadnezzar (Dan. 2–4), they acknowledge the God of Israel as the true God without becoming Israelites. Jonah is a reluctant missionary to the people of Nineveh because he knows that they can be saved by repentance and faith in the true God. The message of the book of Jonah is that God desires the Gentiles, even Israel's bitterest enemies, to turn to him.

Thirdly, the prophets, especially of the exilic and post-exilic periods, predict the time when no longer will there be merely a few Gentile converts to the God of Israel, but the nations in general will turn to God. Egypt and Assyria will worship Yahweh and, like Israel, will be his peoples (Isa. 19.24–5, cf Zech. 2.11). God's word will go out from Zion, and the nations will be drawn to the light of the restored and glorified Jerusalem (Isa. 2.2–3; 61.1–3). All people will worship Yahweh in Jerusalem (Isa. 66.23; Zech. 14.16–19).

In the second and especially the third of these categories, we see the development of the kind of universalism which is the most characteristic of the biblical tradition. It is a movement from the particular to the universal. Yahweh chooses one people so that he may become known to all peoples. God reveals himself to Israel so that this revelation may be shared with others (cf Isa. 49.6). These are the roots in the Old Testament of the Church's mission in the New Testament to preach the gospel to all nations. This kind of universalism need not imply that there is any true knowledge of God in other religious traditions.

However, there is a fourth theme in the Old Testament's portrayal of Gentiles, which is not so often noticed, but which may have implications for a positive Christian evaluation of faiths other than those which derive from the Israelite-Jewish-Christian tradition. There are a few Gentiles in the Old Testament narratives who know and worship the true God quite independently of Israel. Their knowledge of God does not derive from his revelation of himself to Israel, but is nevertheless acknowledged as valid by the biblical authors. For example, Melchizedek is priest of God Most High (Gen. 14.18–20), who is identified with Abraham's God (14.22). Jethro, Moses' father-in-law, the priest of Midian, seems already to worship the same God as Moses, before recognising this God's activity in saving Israel from Egypt (Exod. 18.8–12). Balaam, the prophet, is commissioned and inspired to prophesy by the true God, even though he tries to disobey this commission out of a reluctance which is the Gentile counterpart of Jonah's (Num. 22–24). Job and his friends are also Gentiles (Job 1.1; 2.11; 32.2) whom the book of Job does not place in any relationship to the Old Testament salvation-history. We are told that God says about Job that 'there is no one like him on the earth, a blameless and upright man who fears God' (Job 1.8). Though no doubt they are fictional characters, they show that an Old Testament wisdom writer could easily imagine devout worshippers of the true God unrelated to the Israelite context.

More generally, the wisdom literature, in both the Hebrew Scriptures and the Apocrypha, sometimes displays a notable openness to the thought and language of Gentile cultures. In incorporating elements from other cultures and sages, these books provide some basis for a broad understanding of God's activity in the world and human society. In this literature an extensive role is played by the increasingly personified figure of Wisdom, emanating from God, preexisting creation and active throughout it. Her activities (according to Proverbs 8, Wisdom 7, Ecclesiasticus 24) seem to be without boundary: 'The first man never managed to grasp her entirely, nor has the most recent one fully comprehended her' (Ecclus 24.28).

In Jewish Wisdom literature, however, wisdom is also firmly linked to the tradition of Israel. Thus Wisdom is firmly identified with the Torah in Ecclesiasticus 24, and dwells in Israel: 'All this is no other than the book of the covenant of the Most High God, the law that Moses enjoined on us' (v. 23). (At the same time, a book like Ecclesiasticus also centres firmly on a Messianic hope for Israel (ch. 36), and on the story of the illustrious who stood by the covenants (chs 44–50). Wisdom (chs 10–19) concentrates on the Exodus and on salvation history, and it has extremely strong strictures against idol worship.) Some of the teaching in Proverbs emerges later as the background to some of the teaching of Jesus. And Paul often incorporates general wise teaching as current in popular Hellenistic philosophy in the lists found in some of the Epistles. Wisdom 7 and Proverbs 8 prefigure Colossians 1, where the language is now applied to Christ. Such borrowing is also seen in early Christian art, in the way helpful models from pagan mythology can be found in the painting of the catacombs.

In general, in the Old Testament, the focus of attention is not on the question of salvation or otherwise for non-Jewish people, either as communities or for the good amongst them. They had their own ways to salvation or otherwise (though it should be noted that righteous Gentiles mentioned in the Old Testament are normally monotheists).

New Testament

While the Old Testament is primarily concerned with the present and future destiny of the Jewish people and is only tentatively missionary, Christianity developed in its early stages a strong sense of commitment to a universal mission, since God 'desires everyone to be saved and to come to the knowledge of the truth' (1 Tim. 2.4). A confidently missionary religion is unlikely to be positive towards other faiths whose adherents it is seeking to convert; it is likely to look either for a complete break from those faiths, or for bridges from them, which will then be left behind after conversion.

With very limited exceptions, the books of the New Testament direct attention to the death and resurrection of Jesus Christ. Salvation is deeply related to those events, and the assumption through and through is that they are decisive; they are decisive both because of the Person who was on the cross and in the tomb, and because of the subsequent effect. A doctrine of salvation which is in any real sense biblical must focus significantly on this fact. Jesus in no way can be seen biblically as one among many examples. The God to whom he points is a very specific one, the God of Abraham, Isaac and Jacob, the God whom he calls Abba and with whom new possibilities of relationship are established through his ministry. Though it is true that much of the ethics of Jesus can be found elsewhere, his cross and resurrection, both as events and in the interpretation given to them, stand in a class apart. No book could be more cross-centred than the Epistle to the Hebrews, where the sacrifice of Christ is seen as abolishing the sacrifices of the Old Covenant, and being something once and for all.

As has been seen in the chapters on the meaning of salvation in the Old and New Testaments, there is a general sense of being enabled to escape from what destroys life on this earth, and produces health, peace, prosperity and blessing. As well as most of the Old Testament references, many of the New Testament references lie in this area. As we consider the world around us, and the effect of different faiths within their various contexts, corporately and individually, we may be led to recognise diversity in the understanding of salvation in practice. We do, in fact, find that the major faiths bring salvation in this sense to their followers in varying, but significant degrees. If we wish to use a term from the Jewish-Christian tradition, we seem to see signs of the kingdom of God. The pluralist would say that such are there in their own right. The inclusivist would say that they are there because of the Spirit of God, revealed in Christ, whether recognised as such or not. The exclusivist would say that these are signs, good in themselves, but ultimately not significant in terms of final salvation.

Another important strand in the meaning of salvation in the Bible is about forgiveness, escape from eternal punishment, and citizenship of the renewed heaven and earth. There is no question that, in the New Testament, this normally becomes inextricably linked to the death and resurrection of Christ. The assurance of such forgiveness is possible only because of the length to which God has gone, in Christ, in order to reconcile the world to himself. It is not mere wishful thinking that God is love and will forgive. Since that is so, there is no way that the cross can be by-passed, in order to include people of other faiths. They must in some way be included through the cross and resurrection, as Christians are, because there is no other way. In the Fourth Gospel, it is in the hours before he goes to

167

the cross that Jesus says 'I am the way, the truth and the life'. In John 14.6 he continues: 'No one comes to the Father except through me.' Such passages are accepted by many exclusivists as expressing Jesus' definitive self-understanding; inclusivists tend to point out that they need to be interpreted in terms of the logos Christology of the Prologue that pervades the Gospel as a whole, while pluralists tend to assume that the logos Christology was a mistaken development. But 'the way' can be seen as the way of the cross, and that is why this way of salvation is a scandal. And the initiative remains with God: 'No one can come to me unless drawn by the Father who sent me' (John 6.44).

Clearly there are parts of the New Testament which can be read as strongly exclusivist. A much quoted verse, for example, is Acts 4.12: 'There is salvation in no one else, for there is no other name under heaven given among mortals by which we must be saved.' But we must see this statement of Peter, speaking to the Jewish rulers and elders, in the context of the healing miracle that has just happened at the Beautiful Gate. He is answering the question in interrogation, 'By what power or by what name did you do this?' It is a question of power in healing primarily, not of ultimate salvation in an inter-faith context. Of course, physical healing and salvation are linked, not least in Luke's use of the same Greek word. But even then, Acts 4.12 clearly centres on Jesus and is compatible with an inclusive theology, of either of the kinds mentioned above (p. 156), as well as forms of exclusivism.

There are also elements which can be read in an inclusivist way in terms of the meaning of ultimate salvation. The parable like that of the sheep and the goats (Matt. 25.31ff) has been argued as indicating a way whereby those of other faiths can be included, who do works of mercy for their own sake, not seeking a reward, and find themselves, to their surprise, welcomed into heaven. The occasions when Jesus commends the faith of a Gentile, such as the centurion or the Canaanite woman, can be argued as being a commendation, not of their faith as such, but their faith in his authority and healing power. Yet on these occasions Jesus commends in striking terms deep stirrings in the hearts of these people who come from such diverse backgrounds. Some passages would seem to go further. For instance in the parable of the Pharisee and Publican (Luke 18.9ff) the despised tax-collector not only is commended, but goes away 'justified', and this because of his willingness to acknowledge his utter dependence on the forgiveness of God: 'God be merciful to me, a sinner.' Also it is the behaviour of a good Samaritan who, astonishingly, is chosen as the example of what we are to do to enter eternal life (Luke 10.25ff). Whatever our exegesis be of any particular verses, however, we should not hang our whole theology on isolated texts or on one or two verses, rather than on the overall picture we get from Scripture. In general terms, it is by fruits that we can recognise authenticity of faith. And if we consider the Beatitudes (Matt. 5.1–12), we find that appropriate reward is given to surprising groups of people – the poor in spirit, the gentle, those who mourn, those who hunger and thirst for right, the merciful, the pure in heart, peacemakers, and those who are persecuted in the cause of right. Romans 1.18ff would suggest that in principle not only knowledge of God but also appropriate response to God is possible outside the Jewish tradition. Romans 2.15 speaks of conscience as providing a guide for those who do not have the Law. Admittedly Paul mentions these things only to support his argument, that therefore everyone is without excuse since, in practice, no one can respond appropriately and so all are equally dependent on the action of God in Christ and the Spirit.

This openness to the affirmation of the righteousness of some outside the believing community does not normally extend to an affirmation of their religious quest. Paul is as uncompromisingly hostile to Gentile idolatry as any prophet in the Old Testament. Only in Acts 17 is there a suggestion that people of all nations may 'feel after and find' the unknown God, and only there poets quoted as giving them already an understanding of God as creator. The altar to the 'unknown God' may represent only a kind of insurance, but nevertheless this is something that Paul feels he can build on. Yet Paul faces the problem that the majority of Israel has rejected Christ, and he finds himself unable to judge them lost. In the end 'all Israel will be saved' (Rom. 9–11). This is a matter of eschatological hope, grounded in the unfathomable providence of God; one aspect, maybe, of the hope for the redemption of all humanity in the Last Adam (1 Cor. 15.45; cf. Rom. 5.12ff).

The New Testament concentration on Christ is often seen as a stumbling-block to more open inter-faith theology, because it encapsulates 'the scandal of particularity', that it is only through Christ and his cross that God's salvation is mediated, and that is through a Christ who lived at one time, in one province of the Roman Empire. This is what was such a scandal for Mahatma Gandhi, attracted as he was by the figure and teaching of Christ. But it could be argued that for Paul and the Pauline tradition Christ represents a universalisation of God's dealing with humanity, not a contracting of it. Christ's death and resurrection releases the love and salvation of God for the whole world, and indeed for the whole of creation. It challenges all human pretensions ('religion' in Barth's terms), and also affirms the possibilities of universal redemption. We see this in Romans 8.18ff, where it is the whole of creation that groans for release. We can see this also in the first chapter of the Epistle to the Ephesians, in particular in verse 9: 'He has made known to us the mystery of his will, according to his good pleasure that he set forth in Christ, as a plan for the fullness of time, to gather up all things in him, things in heaven and things on earth.'

Theological perspectives

Christian theology seeks to be loyal to biblical and church tradition, and also open to the experience that encounter and mission have brought, not only in the present, but from biblical times. It is also concerned with reason, and in particular it poses the question, 'What is God's purpose for those who came before Jesus and his cross and resurrection, and those who have come after but followed faithfully other traditions?'

We believe that the terms exclusivism, inclusivism and pluralism have performed a useful function in laying out a map of some possible ways of describing where people are in terms of our subject. But, at their best, they remain ambiguous, and are places on a spectrum rather than separate options. At worst they can label people, often in a judgemental way. Pluralists can see exclusivists as bigoted, and inclusivists as lacking the courage of their convictions, trying to have it both ways, and being 'the same old exclusivists' in disguise. Exclusivists can see pluralists as betraying the mission of Christ, and easily slipping into mere relativism. To some extent they may agree with pluralists in the way they see inclusivists. Exclusivists and pluralists may also agree in seeing real differences between faiths, for example, between Buddhism and Christianity. Where they will differ is in assessing the significance of these differences in terms of salvation. Inclusivists can see exclusivists as being dogmatic and hard-hearted, while pluralists have lost the centrality of Christ, and so they can feel superior to both, though their position can lack the clarity of the other two.

Both as individuals and as a Commission, we find ourselves moving beyond any one of these three positions; indeed, it may be that our statements can be found to give support to all three at various points.

It has been suggested that the big divide is between pluralism on the one hand, and the other two positions on the other, both of which centre in some implicit or explicit way on the work of Christ as being critical for all humanity.[11] With this understanding, readers might see in what follows a position that could be labelled 'an open and generous exclusivism' or 'a Christocentric inclusivism', or 'trinitarian pluralism', and all may be right. Another view would be that it is pluralism and exclusivism that have a clear commonality, in that they both take seriously the difference between religions, while inclusivism blurs that distinction, as in the name of Christ all religions are claimed for Christianity.

The common assertions we are able to make are based upon our understanding of God's Love, Spirit and Word, and their pivotal expression in the cross and resurrection of Jesus Christ.

God's Love is unconditional, beyond restriction, for all, not only for some. The guarantee that God is love is shown by the ministry of Jesus. As women and men experienced this ministry and linked it with the person of Jesus, this conclusion about the nature of God was confirmed. That love cannot be narrower than a love which includes tax-gatherers and sinners, penitent thieves and quarrelling disciples. These are the very people whom 'religion' excluded. Is it to include these, but not the good Hindu or Muslim? – or indeed the bad Hindu or Muslim, who throw themselves on the mercy of God, as they experience it? Such a love is not so restricted that it cannot reach out across religious barriers.

It is also love related to justice and holiness. God does not save despite his justice and his holiness (1 John 1.5: 'God is light, and in him there is no darkness at all'). Such love and justice are at the very heart of the concept of the kingdom of God which is also inextricably linked to salvation through the proclamation of Jesus. Those reflecting theologically on experience outside Europe have shown us how salvation, unrelated to liberation and participation in a just society, as God intended, means little to the struggling majority of the world who live in grinding poverty. Every religion needs to take this into account, whenever it drifts towards spiritualising the centres of its faith. Such spiritualising has left many Hindus as outcasts, untouchables, now Dalits (the oppressed and crushed ones) by their own naming, despite the subtle philosophy in the Hindu tradition. Another terrible example is the acceptance of slavery for so long within the Christian tradition.

Secondly, there is the concept of the Spirit. There is an essential continuity between the Spirit moving over the waters at creation, experienced by prophets and rulers in the Old Testament, and then publicly displayed in the person of Jesus Christ, through his baptism and then through his Church. Some may say the Spirit moved more widely before Christ's time and that afterwards the Spirit is confined to the Church. We do not say that. Certainly, the character of the Spirit is now revealed by Christ. St Paul writes of the Spirit of Christ, the Holy Spirit, the Spirit, the Spirit of God, but he appears to mean the same personal reality. The last Doctrine Commission report on the Spirit clearly argues for the view that the Spirit is not confined to the Church, however named or described:

> The Spirit, though particularly at work in the Christian Church by covenant and promise, is also at work outside it, in the lives and characters of people of other faiths and none . . . Naturally the touchstone of the quality of the Spirit's activity in the life of any person, whether Christian or not, is the evidence of a Christ-like spirit. Wherever that spirit is to be found, it must surely be attributed to the unseen, inward working of the Holy Spirit. (p. 12)

The Spirit's fruit is described in Galatians 5 as love, joy, peace, patience, kindness, goodness, trustfulness, gentleness and self-control. This fruit of the Spirit is to be seen in the life of Christ, who brings us to a realisation of the character of the Spirit. As such, he is the criterion for judging whether the Spirit is present in any context or situation or person. Thus our judging that the Spirit may be found outside the Church is not an arbitrary one, nor does it mean that the work of the Spirit can be identifird everywhere. Those of other faiths and indeed of none who display such fruit are we believe amongst those who have responded to the Spirit of God; there is evidence that God is savingly at work in them, and he will bring his work to fulfilment. 'The doctrine of the Holy Spirit allows us theologically to relate the particularity of the Christ event to the entire history of humankind.'[12]

It is timely to listen once more to the witness of those who have lived closely with those of other faiths over a long period:

> The simplicity of life of a South Indian Hindu woman who has the sense of detachment that enables her to give a clear message to those around her: 'Whether I live or die, I am the Lord's.' Within that ultimate security, she gives out so much love to others. The row upon row of Muslim men, prostrate in prayer, each morning and evening in so many mosques in the midst of a Westernised secular city. The witness of a young Western Buddhist about to go on a four-year retreat

as a novice monk, and who testifies to how he has been saved from a hopeless life of drug addiction through this new faith. The witness of peace of Buddhists as they walk in procession . . . The unshakable faith in God displayed by the Jewish community, even in the deepest darkness of the Warsaw Ghetto, as they recited the psalms daily, and sang a song they had learnt from the Vilna Ghetto:

> Never say that you have reached the very end,
> though leaden skies a bitter future may portend,
> and the hour for which we've yearned will yet arrive,
> and our marching step will thunder, 'We'll survive.'
> From green palm trees to the land of the bitter snow,
> we are here with our sorrow, our woe,
> and whenever our blood was shed in pain,
> our fighting spirits will now resurrect again.[13]

Other examples can be added like that of the Sikh lay person who leads evening worship every day, for more than two hours, in a local Sikh gurdwara, and where about two hundred are present each time, of all ages, as he expounds the Scriptures on which the Sikh faith is based, and truly ministers to the community in the spirit of love that flows from his faith. His openness is such that if a Christian minister is present whom he knows, he will often invite him up to share a word. The writer adds 'Such is the trust of this remarkable leader that I feel free to witness to Jesus Christ, reading and commenting directly from the New Testament, in the heart of this community.' Or the Hindu who, staying in a Christian college for three months attended the Eucharist daily, receiving a blessing, and, in the quiet, listening and absorbing all that was going on.

We would affirm that such people live as they do through the grace of God and through his Spirit. However, as we look around our world we can give many contrary examples from people of all faiths and none, who show that they do not live by that Spirit, whatever they profess with their lips. We need not rehearse such: for example, the list of places of religious conflict is endless at any one time. Mahatma Gandhi rightly said that it is those who want to save religion who so often destroy it. Again our judgement is not arbitrary, it is by the Spirit of Christ.

Thirdly, there is the concept of the Logos, the Word of God, the cosmic Christ, without whom was not anything made that was made. The possibility of life, meaning eternal life, is there within all human beings, through the Logos. This cosmic Christology is reflected in John 1, Colossians 1 and Hebrews 1, the opening chapters of three major works in the New Testament. To have a Christ-centred under-standing of salvation does not mean that we need to be confined to what happened to Jesus of Nazareth in the first century AD. This is the conviction of Raymond Pannikar, with his understanding of Christ transcending time, being incarnate in Jesus of Nazareth but not confined to him:

> The ultimate reason for this universal idea of Christianity, an idea which makes possible the catholic embrace of every people and religion, lies in the Christian concept of Christ: he is not *only* the historical redeemer, but *also* the unique Son of God, the Second Person of the Trinity, the only ontological – temporal and eternal – link between God and the world.
>
> Whatever God does *ad extra* happens through Christ.[14]

God is creator of all through his Word and Spirit. God wills all to be saved that he has created. This can only happen through that same Word and Spirit. The Word is made flesh in Christ, and so we are given a criterion for the presence of that same Word elsewhere. It is the poor, the lost, the little ones who are given as examples. The Spirit can be seen specifically in the Church, both corporately and through its members. But the Spirit also blows where the Spirit wills. The Church extraordinarily is to include, not just Jews and Greeks, but those beyond the pale, barbarians and Scythians. God is surely not confined after the birth of Christ and after Pentecost, any more than he was before. The Spirit is the one who points to the future, as he leads us to all truth, beyond what we can bear now. That will not be contrary to the teachings of Christ (John 16.12–15), but it will build on them. Maybe people of other faiths, and indeed of no religious faith, will teach us more than we yet know ourselves, as we interact with them and discover new things together.

Fourthly, there is the distinctive understanding of God as Trinity, which should be at the centre of any inter-faith reflection. As Gavin D'Costa puts it:

> Without Jesus, we cannot speak of God, but that speaking is never completely exhausted in history, for the Spirit constantly and in surprising ways calls us into a deeper understanding of God in Christ. In this way, the Trinity anchors God's self-revelation in the particularities of history, principally focused in Jesus Christ, without limiting God to this particularity through the universality of the Spirit.[15]

He writes of a 'Trinitarian Christology', which reconciles the exclusivist emphasis on the particularity of Christ and the pluralist emphasis on God's universal activity in history. The instruction to love our neighbour opens us to people of the world religions.

The recent book by Clark H. Pinnock, written to persuade his fellow-evangelicals to hold open attitudes towards questions of salvation, concentrates interestingly on the Logos, the Spirit and Trinity. He writes of the Logos as connecting Jesus of Nazareth to the whole world and guarding the incarnation from becoming a limiting principle, and of the Spirit as the overflow of God's love, 'active in human cultures and even within the religions of humanity'. Referring to the breadth of this activity of the Spirit, he returns to the Trinity: 'The doctrine of the Trinity means that God, far from being difficult to locate in the world, can be encountered everywhere in it. One needs to take pains and be very adept at hiding not to encounter God.'[16]

He ends by quoting the well-known hymn by Frederick Faber:

> There's a wideness in God's mercy
> Like the wideness of the sea;
> There's a kindness in his justice
> Which is more than liberty.

For the love of God is broader
Than the measures of man's mind;
And the heart of the Eternal
Is most wonderfully kind.

But we make his love too narrow
By false limits of our own;
And we magnify his strictness
With a zeal he will not own.

Where then does the cross and resurrection come into the picture? Here the challenge is different in connection with people of other faiths only in one particular way. Even with regard to Christians, we are required to say how this apparently obscure event in the past is connected with our salvation today. We refer the reader to our discussion in chapters 4 and 5. The particular difficulty with people of other faiths is that they do not express a particular faith in Christ or that they may explicitly deny the central and saving importance of the cross. We have to explain how our belief that 'Christ died for all' relates to them.

What saves is not the cross itself, but God. We have elaborated this in considerable detail in earlier chapters, and here we can give but the briefest outline. In essence, God alone saves, and that is his mission. God saves as Trinity, Father, Son and Spirit; all save, and none saves without the others. He wills to save all people, as he created them all. All fall short of his will for them, and so all need his forgiveness and acceptance. Salvation is not something that can ultimately be earned, but comes as sheer gift, as happened to those surprised people in Matthew 25. The cross and resurrection are God's gift to us. They both reveal and save. They reveal the love of God because of the nature of him who is on the cross. And they change human history because here we believe is uniquely revealed the depth of God's love for us. Here also, however it may be expressed, something occurs which makes a decisive difference to human destiny, indeed to the whole of creation. Salvation is opened up to the whole world by the cross. For some, this leads to a direct response to that love, as they become witnesses to it as members of

177

the Body of Christ, the Church. But the death and resurrection remain objectively the ultimate victory of good over evil; in sacrificial language, they show the seriousness of human sin and the degree to which God will go to show a way beyond it. He does something once and for all, on the cross. What is revealed is not the narrowness of God's action, but the sheer breadth of it. And that breadth, with all the suffering involved can be effective beyond the limits we try to put upon it. The Lamb of God who takes away the sins of the world gives his life as a ransom for many and is the passover sacrificed for us. We see 'the world', 'many' and 'us', as inclusive and not exclusive categories.

In the past, much of the discussion about salvation has rested on the cross alone. But as we focus our attention on eschatology, we focus our attention also on the resurrection of Christ and its relationship to our future destiny. Inter-faith dialogue brings out sharply the differences between the Christian understanding here and that of other faiths. The resurrection of Christ is not an optional addition to any discussion about salvation; it is at the core of Christian understanding, and that is why Paul says that if it did not happen, then we are of all people the most to be pitied. Is it to be an exclusive rising, though it was an inclusive creation and fall in Adam? And what are to be the criteria for judgement? They are about attitude, whether there has been an awareness of grace, and a sense of unworthiness and need for forgiveness; and along with this our lives can be judged by what has flowed from that response to grace.

The question of salvation is not only about whether we have responded to the Christian message, if we have been lucky enough to be born into it, or to have heard it clearly as we grew up or in later life. For there is forgiveness at the heart of God, which is the very centre of the Christian message, and that is most specifically proclaimed on the cross, in Christ's words in St Luke: 'Father, forgive them, for they know not what they do.' The prayer is that those who crucified Christ should be forgiven; are not the humble and good followers of another faith to be the recipients of the same prayer? Christian assurance about salvation can go along with a deep hope that others may be included in God's saving purpose both now and finally. We can never say that someone is not saved.

Two Hindus, both prisoners in an Indian jail, witness to this centre of Christian revelation in the God of forgiveness. The first was a life prisoner, who had also been operated on for a brain tumour and had continually to wear a bandage round the scar on his head. He remained a Hindu, but attended the weekly Christian worship service. In Holy Week, he asked to give a testimony. He said, pointing to his bandage, 'Only someone who is guilty of killing a man, and who has suffered a disease like mine, can understand how much Jesus and his cross can mean.' As a Hindu, he felt included in the saving power of the cross and indicated with sure conviction where that power lay.

The second had killed a relative in a family fight. He was also a Hindu. He attended the Eucharist month by month, at first out of curiosity. But then he began to receive unconsecrated host which was given to Hindus, as is done for catechumens in the Orthodox Church. One day he asked if he could join the Christians and share the cup. When asked why he wanted this so much, he said that since coming to the service, he had realised for the first time that he was guilty of sin, not just that he had made a mistake. He longed now for forgiveness and acceptance by God. He was told that he received this by the absolution pronounced each time. He said: 'That is not enough. Unless I can kneel shoulder to shoulder with the priest, and receive from the same cup, I may know with my head that I am forgiven by God, but I cannot feel it!' As a Hindu, again, he had seen where the centre of the Eucharist lies.

An example has even come to our attention of a Muslim who, contrary to all doctrinal orthodoxy, as a young student in Palestine and reflecting on the suffering following the Gulf War, wrote: 'Every day they crucify him, every day they hang him.' People under persecution so often seem to identify with the crucified Christ, of whatever faith they are. One of the Indian newspaper headlines, reporting the news that Gandhi had been assassinated, wrote 'Gandhi meets his Calvary'. A Jewish example in similar vein comes in the novel *My Name is Asher*

Lev, by Chaim Potok. The novel turns on the quest of an Orthodox Jew who is an artist to express the pain of being a Jew in the modern world. To the horror of his community, he chooses to paint crucifixion scenes.

All finally focuses on what flows from our doctrine of God. As we have seen, it is God alone who saves, and God saves only according to, and not against, his nature. At the centre of our Christian faith is the belief that God is love. This is revealed through Christ's birth, his teaching, his ministry, his death and his resurrection. That love is expressed memorably in a parable like the Prodigal Son, where the father goes out in love to receive back the child who has wilfully wasted the inheritance which he had demanded.

Conclusion

It is incompatible with the essential Christian affirmation that God is love to say that God brings millions into the world to damn them. The God of Love also longs for all to come into relationship with him, and this is his purpose in creation. When he chooses certain peoples, such as Israel, or certain persons such as the prophets or Apostles, he chooses them not for exclusive privilege or salvation, but for a purpose in the expression of God's self-revelation and showing of his saving love for all.

In practice, all religions are open to grave distortion, as Barth rightly asserts. The history of religions, including the Christian religion, reveals this graphically, as does the present map of conflict in our world. This is so corporately, between individuals and within persons. It is by the criterion of Christ, his life, teaching, cross and resurrection, that all faiths, including Christianity, are judged and/or affirmed. It is by the criterion of Christ that we in practice discriminate provisionally between different religions as we consider how to relate to them.

As a fact there are conflicting truth claims made by religions. As Christians, we cannot agree with Muslims, for example, in saying

Christ did not die on the cross, or with Hindus, in accepting reincarnation.

In terms of ultimate salvation the decision is entirely God's. As Christians we cast ourselves on the mercy of God as revealed in Christ, assured that God will receive those who respond to him in faith. Trusting in his just and merciful treatment of ourselves, so we are able to trust that God will act in the same just and loving way towards all his children, including those of other faiths. Ultimately, we believe, and this is why we are Christians, that it is through Jesus Christ that God will reconcile all things to himself. How that will come about, we can only be agnostic about, whether it is through some real but unconscious response to the Christ within them now, or whether it is in response to some eschatological revelation, or by some other means.

Meanwhile, we live in a world of many faiths, and it is our very Christian calling that leads us to feel humility and respect before the transparent goodness of many within other religious traditions (and indeed, many of no overt religious faith). We do assert that God can and does work in people of other religions, and indeed within other religions, and that this is by his Spirit. Such is an essential basis for genuine dialogue with them. We do assert that God has not only worked through the peoples of the Middle East, but that he did intend, for example, some significant experience of his presence in the Indian subcontinent in the centuries before Christ, and indeed amongst many of those who follow the so-called 'primal religions'. This is to be expected, since God created the potential for a religious sense in all human beings, and this is indicated in the diverse and widespread phenomena of the religions of humanity.

We can see empirically that people are enabled to live better lives through loyally following other faiths, and this must mean that God is at work in these faiths, even if it cannot determine the question whether those faiths have value for ultimate salvation or not. God can and does encounter people graciously outside the Christian religion, making it possible for them to come into relationship with himself and to receive his gifts. Several of us would also affirm from personal experience their authenticity as we would judge it by the above criteria already mentioned: the lives and also the spirituality of particular people coming from other faith traditions. We can be ready to affirm this without prejudging the issue of salvation: 'People sometimes fear that to affirm the presence of any encounter with God outside Christianity is to imply that any truth to be found there may in its own right be "saving truth". We wish to affirm that the only "truth" which has saving power is God.'[17]

We would also sensitively and firmly assert that fullness of relationship with God is possible only in Jesus Christ, who is the definitive revelation of God. For many this may happen only in an eschatological dimension (cf. 1 Cor. 15.22–8). But it is from this assertion that comes the imperative, expressed throughout the New Testament of the universal mission of the Church, to proclaim the gospel to all nations.

A Pakistani Christian woman working in London, reflecting on what she sees as the reticence of people in Britain about witnessing to people of other faiths, and comparing it with the difficult context in which she lives, reflects: 'If we love our neighbours, it is our duty, out of that love, to tell them about the sacrifice Christ has made for them. Otherwise we are keeping them in the dark, forgetting our mission of love and the sharing of good news. And that love will make us work at finding the language that will be understandable by them.' An Indian Christian woman, working in a British city amongst people of various faiths, echoes this: 'Our mission is to show people life in its fullness as experienced in Christ. Standing by our Muslim brothers and sisters, as they fight for a better deal in education, health and recreation, standing by them when they face racism, that is part of the Christian mission of love.'

Hence, we read in the report of the Lambeth Conference of 1988:

> We are called to proclaim God's love and forgiveness by word and deed. We must use every means available to spread the message of salvation. Our proclamation must be sensitive to the culture and beliefs of others. Nevertheless Christ calls all

people to turn from evil and all that hurts or enslaves, and to receive the fullness of life that he alone can give.[18]

Unfortunately, as we well know, the Church often gets in the way of such a proclamation: 'Christ is not the property of us Christians, and if we rejoice when the Holy Spirit opens men's eyes to His glory, we must at that moment remember how often the church has blinded them, and pray that we may be not once more a stumbling block.'[19] But, as John Taylor also points out, the Holy Spirit, who has been at work in all ages and cultures, often breaks through, not by evolution, but revolution, with the experiences of awakening and disclosure that the Spirit gives in encounters between Christians and people of other living faith.

Lakshman Wikremasinghe, the former Bishop of Kurunagula, Sri Lanka, died prematurely, as on his troubled island he struggled in his ministry to hold together people of different races and faiths. In the Lambeth Inter-Faith Lecture of 1979, in similar vein to the quotations above, he said:

> Now we see the goal of dialogue but darkly. In the realised realm of truth and righteousness, recorded in the last chapters of the Book of Revelation, we shall see face to face. The servants of God shall see him, who is the Source, Guide and Goal of all that is, and adore. The riches of other streams of salvation will be drawn into that realm by the Divine Light that illumines and attracts. What is now hidden will be revealed. Until then, we follow the path open to us in this era, and seek to have foretaste of what mankind in its fullness can be. Then togetherness will enrich uniqueness, and uniqueness will illuminate togetherness. To that final dawn may the Father of all lead us.

So there is a plurality of ways by which people are being made whole in the here and now; these are ways the Spirit of God is working. And there is an expectation in the future, that, while people may have the freedom to reject the salvation that is available to all, through God as Trinity, God will save ultimately those who are willing to be saved, by their penitence and acceptance of the love which stretches out to them, in the way that it meets them in their lives and within their traditions. There is only one way, but that way is one that is without barbed wire or boundary fences, so that all may join this way. If we think of salvation in the broadest sense as encompassing all that heals and enhances human life, then clearly aspects of salvation are available in many ways, not only explicitly through Jesus Christ. In the ultimate sense, salvation is defined by having Jesus Christ as its source and goal. To use the terms we deliberately put aside earlier, this pluralism and this exclusivism are reconciled, not in some form of inclusivism (in the usual sense) but eschatologically, in the final purposes of God. To recognise the life, death and resurrection of Jesus as 'constitutive' of salvation as well as revelatory, as Christians do, is to anticipate that he will prove to be the definitive focus of salvation in its fully comprehensive meaning. It may be, too, that our understanding of Christ will itself be enhanced when people of other faiths are gathered in.

Because this ultimate salvation is found in Christ, mission remains the central task of the Christian Church. The task is to proclaim by word and to display in action that God has created a world that is good, and that we are responsible for that creation; that the Kingdom of God, a kingdom of justice and peace, has already begun in Christ, and that we can be assured of its future consummation through him; that the gift and assurance of salvation and eternal life is available now, and the mark of this life is love. We deny the fullness of that love if we deny the truth and goodness which Christ, as Logos, and God by the Spirit, can also inspire in those of other faiths and of none. We believe that God has chosen to provide the fullest revelation of himself in Christ, and the fullest revelation of his love for all humanity in the cross and resurrection. Hence we naturally pray that God will bring all people, including those of other faiths, to explicit faith in Christ and membership of his Church. This is not because we believe that the God revealed in Christ is unable to save them without this, but because Christ is the truest and fullest expression of his love, and we long for them to share it. In the Lord's words in St John's Gospel, 'I came that they may have life, and have it abundantly' (John 10.10).

Notes

1 *The Truth shall make you free* (Church House 1988), p. 83.

2 Alan Race, *Christians and Religious Pluralism*, (SCM 1983).

3 *The Truth shall make you free* (Church House 1988) p. 304–5.

4 Wesley Ariarajah, *Hindus and Christians*, (Eerdmans 1991).

5 John Hick, *God Has Many Names*, (Macmillan 1980), p. 52.

6 Stanley Samartha, *One Christ, Many Religions* (Orbis 1991), p. 97.

7 F. D. Maurice, *The Religions of the World* (6th edn, 1886), p. 56.

8 For example, these quotations are taken from the Roman Catholic writer, Paul Knitter, in his section on Anglican views in *No Other Name?* (SCM 1985), p. 135.

9 *Pastoral Constitution on the Church*, para 22.

10 *Redemptor Hominis*, 14.

11 As suggested by Michael Barnes in *Religions in Conversation*, (SPCK 1989).

12 So writes Gavin D'Costa in his essay 'Christ, the Trinity and Religious Plurality', published in the volume he co-edited, *Christian Uniqueness Reconsidered* (Orbis 1990), p. 19.

13 Andrew Wingate, *Encounter in the Spirit* (WCC, 2nd edn, 1991), p. 82.

14 Raymond Pannikar, *The Unknown Christ of Hinduism* (DLT 1964), p. 82, 83 and 167.

15 Gavin D'Costa, *Christian Uniqueness Reconsidered* (Orbis 1990), p. 18–19.

16 Clark H. Pinnock, *A Wideness in God's Mercy* (Zondervan 1992), p. 104.

17 *The Truth shall make you free*, op. cit. p. 95.

18 *ibid*, p. 30.

19 J. V. Taylor, *The Go Between God* (SCM 1972), p. 196.

8

Ending the story

Towards the end of the preceding chapter we referred to the final purposes of God and to the eventual consummation of God's kingdom. Christian people live in this hope, a hope which springs from Easter faith and from the knowledge of the love of God in Christ from which 'neither death, nor life . . . nor things present, nor things to come . . . nor anything else in all creation' will be able to separate us (Rom. 8.39). We live by this hope in a world of injustice, flawed by sin, and marked by an ultimate futility, for, as we have already commented in chapter 1, the universe as we know it will sooner or later die. Our hope is therefore of a new creation, new heavens and a new earth. It is a resurrection hope of cosmic dimension. But because it is a hope grounded in the victory of the love of God who loves each one of us so uniquely that even the very hairs of our head are numbered, it is a personal hope for us in the face of the darkness of death. So in the Nicene Creed we confess that we 'look for' – that is to say we 'wait with longing expectation for' – 'the resurrection of the dead and the life of the world to come'. It is a hope that is corporate, cosmic and personal.

The character of Christian hope

Christian eschatology, or the endeavour to understand the 'last' or 'ultimate' things, covers a wide and complex area, and in Christian history has been expressed in different ways. But there is a consistent theme in the hope of believing people that their incomplete present experience of God will be resolved and their present thirst for God fulfilled. Christians have looked for a final vindication of the good and definitive revelation of the consistency and purpose of God in his provident action in history. It is a hope that has taken many forms in the history of the Church. In times of oppression and persecution a sense of crisis and imminent expectation of the end has prevailed. Apocalyptic images of final judgement and catastrophe, a cosmic violence that destroys the world and its sinful institutions to let God begin again, have been the predominant note. At other times there has been a more muted note – of the world 'growing old' and running out of resources, coming to an end, but an end which will be God's new beginning. Faced with the world's evil, Christians have prayed in longing, even anguished, hope for the coming of God's kingdom.

> When comes the promised time,
> When war shall be no more,
> Oppression, lust and crime,
> Shall flee thy face before?

Eschatological hope has also meant a different emphasis: an ordered doctrine of the last things, personal expectation of final justice and retribution and a personal longing for rest and satisfaction in a new life that will begin at death. In the Christian mystical tradition, union with God in knowledge and love, already known in part in this life, will be consummated in that final transfiguring union when the understanding of the thinker and the contemplation of the lover are made one. But Christian hope is not only personal, it is cosmic. The whole universe itself is condemned to eventual collapse or decay, so that if it is really a cosmos, making ultimate sense of its history, it too must have a destiny beyond its death. God must surely care for all of his creation. Matter matters to him and it will not be abandoned to futility. A credible eschatology must be one of cosmic scope.

The Christian waits with expectation for a 'new heaven and a new earth' (Rev. 21.1), and lives in and by the Easter faith that in Christ God has defeated death and overcome the power of the grave. In baptism the believer shares sacramentally in the death and resurrection of Christ. In the Eucharist Christians are fed with the bread of heaven, the bread of the Day of the Lord, the banquet of heaven. In the Lord's Prayer we not only pray that God's kingdom may come and his will be done; but we also pray that we may be sustained, both by our earthly food and by that true and living bread which is Christ's own life. In being so fed we have a foretaste of the life of the world to come.

The language in which Christian hope has been expressed is necessarily imaginative and pictorial. It has also been shaped by different philosophical outlooks and understandings of the world. An uncritical literalism has contributed to the sense that Christian eschatology is largely attenuated to a life beyond death, and even then, as the Rural Church Project found, for instance, among churchgoing people only 69 per cent believed in a destiny beyond death, whilst for the general public that proportion was reduced to 42 per cent. There can be no doubt that Christians need to articulate in a coherent way a doctrine of the 'Last Things'.

In the strictest sense, of course, it is God who is the one 'Last Thing' of creation. The creator, who is Alpha, the source and origin of all that is, is no less Omega, the final horizon of history and the ultimate reality existing at the end of time. In his self-giving, God brings the created order into being. It is sustained by and dependent upon his will and purpose, but that will and purpose sustain it in its own freedom. The present universe is a creation *ex nihilo*, 'out of nothing', and, in so bringing it into being, God has 'made way' for it as an entity other than himself. Its evolutionary history is understood as the divine gift of 'freedom' by which creation is allowed to make itself, exploring and realising the fruitful potentiality with which it is endowed.

Within the complex patterning of creation, life and personality have emerged, and that which we might characterise as the realm of spirit. That realm of spirit may well include orders of being beyond human personal being. In the creed God is confessed as the creator of 'all things visible and invisible', and the worship of heaven in the Scriptures and Christian liturgies is portrayed not only as the worship of redeemed humanity, but of angels and archangels.

188

In the Scriptures the description of human nature as made 'in the image and likeness of God' (Gen. 1.27) is at the heart of the Christian understanding of our human existence as persons. Human nature is only understood rightly when it is seen as having an openness towards, and a capacity for, communion with God. The potentiality of human personhood finds its consummation in that relationship, and that 'capacity for God' is the ground likewise of our being as persons in relationship with each other. It is no accident that the two great commandments are the love of God with all our heart, and soul, and mind, and strength, and the love of our neighbour as ourselves. From those made in his image God calls a people to be his own, and enters into a covenant relationship with them. God promises a future to his people and to each unique human person he has created, whose uniqueness is fulfilled in communion with Christ. Those made in God's image are called to grow into his likeness and receive the gift of God's eternal life. Already Christians receive the gift of the Spirit and so are united to Christ. Their ultimate salvation is *theosis*, participation in the life of God himself. We are to be 'participants of the divine nature' (2 Pet. 1.4) and, 'seeing the glory of the Lord as though reflected in a mirror, are being transformed into the same image from one degree of glory to another' (2 Cor. 3.18).

Death and resurrection

Human hopes, human aspirations, and human achievements, the thirst for eternity and immortality, are mocked by death. It cuts across all human hopes. It denies and breaks relationships, it sunders the love which is at the heart of our personhood. Although in earlier and in less developed societies the ravages of disease and natural disaster meant that death struck very often in the prime of life, in our generation and in western culture many live into frail old age with severe diminishment of their mental and physical faculties. That pre-death diminishment places the same question marks against life and hope. Humanity born to die makes life a 'tale told by an idiot, full of sound and fury, signifying nothing'.

As we have already seen in chapter 4, for the faith of Israel, death is the taking away of breath, perceived as the gift of God which makes human beings truly alive. As the Psalmist writes: 'when you take away their breath, they die and return to their dust' (Ps. 104.29). In the Old Testament the wraith-like existence of *Sheol,* the place of the departed under the earth, is a place of non-being, far removed from the gift and fulfilment of eternal life. Such non-being is the triumph of death, often envisaged as an engulfing power opposed to God. Such a destiny provokes sharp questions. Is this non-being the destiny of those made in God's image and likeness? Are the holy ones of God to see corruption? Is the end of the righteous to be one with that of the wicked? Is there to be no ultimate redressing of the moral balance? No, the answer came. God *will* vindicate his people. He will deliver them not only from sin but also from death, and death was seen as the consequence of disobedience (Rom. 5.12) and as 'the wages of sin'. Salvation, liberation, deliverance will come on the Day of the Lord, when his righteous judgement will triumph, his will at last will be done, and the dead will be raised to life. The hope of the righteous, of the people of God, is resurrection. The wicked also will be raised to judgement. The Day of the Lord, the day of messianic hope, is the day of resurrection.

The predominant theme of first Jewish and then Christian hope in the face of death is that of the resurrection of the body. Language about the immortality of the soul is also found in the inter-testamental period. The passage from Wisdom 3.1, 'The souls of the righteous are in the hands of God, and no torment will ever touch them', has been used in the later Christian centuries to support a dualist view of death as being the release of an immortal soul from a mortal body, a view which came to predominate, though still combined with a doctrine of the resurrection of the body. The modern inclination to understand human nature in terms of a psychosomatic unity (chapter 1) makes this form of expression of the Christian hope highly problematic. Even before this modern questioning, the relation between the destiny of the world and the destiny of the human person, between 'corporate' and 'individual' eschatology, was often strained. The fate of souls after death, and their judgement at that point, were uneasily integrated with the apocalyptic drama of the final judgement and the resurrection at the Last Day. If today we are to continue to use language about the soul we may perhaps best understand it as the 'information-bearing pattern' of the body, as we have suggested in chapter 1. Death dissolves the embodiment of that pattern, but the person whose that pattern is, is 'remembered' by God, who in love holds that unique being in his care. The strong sense of the worship of the Church being set within the communion of saints, witnesses to the life to come as a present reality as well as a future expectation. When Jesus rebukes the Sadducees, who denied there was a resurrection, he quotes the words of God to Moses at the burning bush. God is the God of Abraham, Isaac and Jacob, who are not simply figures of the past. 'God is not God of the dead, but of the living; in his sight all are alive' (Luke 20.38). Moses and Elijah appear on the mountain of the transfiguration. Even though there is still a final transformation to which we look forward at the resurrection at the Last Day, already there is a sharing in the life of heaven. For some this will be adequately characterised as the holding in the mind of God of the information-bearing pattern that is the meaning of the soul. Such a state is less than fully human (since it is disembodied), but it is certainly not unreal (since it is in the mind and heart of God). Nor need it be purely static, for it would be open to the possibility of some degree of pattern-changing activity. For others, if we are to take the sense of ourselves as a psychosomatic unity with full seriousness, this needs to be envisaged in terms of an appropriate bodiliness. But, however conceived, all will agree that there remains a fuller realisation of God's purpose for us all at the end.

If we speak of the resurrection of the body it is not to be supposed that the material of the resurrected body is the same as that of the old. Indeed, it is essential that it should not be, for otherwise the new creation would simply be a re-run of the old creation, and presumably it would recapitulate the latter's transience and death. St Paul warned that 'flesh and blood cannot inherit the kingdom of God, nor does the perishable inherit the imperishable' (1 Cor. 15.50). In that context, Paul speaks of a 'spiritual body' (*soma pneumatikon*), a phrase which does not mean 'a body consisting of spirit' but 'a body animated by the Holy Spirit'. The only clue we have to this bodily reality is the glorified body of the Risen Lord, for the resurrection of Jesus is the seminal event of the new creation. In his victory over death, the Last Day has arrived. The resurrection of Jesus is the beginning within history of a process whose fulfilment lies beyond history, in which the destiny of humanity and the destiny of the universe are together to find their fulfilment in a liberation from decay and futility (cf. Rom. 8.18–25).

'Christ has died, Christ is risen, Christ will come again'

In Jesus the kingdom of God comes, the Day of the Lord is here. He 'empties himself' in the self-giving of love to live and die in solidarity with humanity. He refers to himself as 'Son of Man', which, in one interpretation, is 'mortal man', 'man born to die'. Yet, so living, he embodies no less God's eternal life, so that in his presence the kingdom comes, and with it the judgement of God. In his being judged by Pilate, the representative of the political authorities of this world, the judgement of the world takes place. '*Now* is the judgement of this world; *now* the ruler of this world will be driven out' (John 12.31).

In Jesus the divine gracious freedom coincided with our human obedient freedom to the point of death itself. The Apostles' Creed confesses that he descended into the place of the departed. That is the meaning of the term 'hell' in that particular clause of the creed, though there is also Christian truth in the understanding that God in Christ freely chose to go to the point of utter estrangement from the Father, so that, we might say paradoxically, for the sake of the love which is his nature, God chose to know the darkness of the utter absence of love. In this understanding, the cry of dereliction from the cross, 'My God, my God, why hast thou forsaken me?' signals the 'descent into hell' in which the love of God plumbs the farthest depths of alienation and apartness from God. Not only the cry of dereliction, but also the silence of Holy Saturday express the cost of

Christ's saving work. Love's redemption encompasses the dead and contends victoriously with the powers of evil.

The Easter hope in the victory of Christ, 'who has overcome death and opened the gate of everlasting life' is known not only in the mythical drama of the harrowing of hell, but in contemporary theologies of liberation, which find in that victory salvation from political and social oppression, from the principalities and powers of the secular world. An essential part of Christian hope is the anticipatory realisation of God's new creation, in the bringing into being of a foretaste of that new order, 'when God will wipe away all tears from their eyes, and there will be no more death, and no more mourning or sadness' (Rev. 21.4).

In the creed, we confess our hope that Christ 'will come again in glory to judge the living and the dead'. Our human destiny, and that of the world, is centred on Christ himself. When God remakes the whole world, as he has promised, Jesus Christ will be personally present as the living heart and focus of all.

The New Testament uses a variety of quite different images to express this vital belief. 'He is coming with the clouds; every eye will see him' (Rev. 1.7). 'This Jesus, who has been taken up from you into heaven, will come in the same way as you saw him go into heaven' (Acts 1.11). 'The manifestation [the Greek word is literally 'epiphany'] of the glory of our great God and Saviour, Jesus Christ' (Tit. 2.13). 'Your life is hidden with Christ in God; when Christ, who is your life, is revealed, then you also will be revealed with him in glory' (Col. 3.3f). All these ways of saying essentially the same thing draw on the rich symbolic language of the Old Testament, not least the book of Daniel. They are not intended to provide literal depictions of the event, as though Jesus were (for instance) a space traveller returning to earth. They refer, in the far more profound language of biblical imagery, to the manifestation in this world of that which is already true of Jesus Christ in heaven, that is, that dimension of reality which is immediate to God. In that dimension, Jesus is already victorious over all evil, ruling over all things, mediating the Father's love for the world and embodying the true response of humankind to that love. When God creates the 'new heavens and new earth', this same Jesus will be manifest as the victor, the Lord, the mediator and the high priest of all creation.

These are among the things which in the present we know 'only in part'. But, as John insists, we know that 'when he is revealed, we will be like him, for we will see him as he is' (1 John 3.2). In this faith and hope we live as Christians, not towards the horizon of death and futility, but towards the horizon where 'the Sun of righteousness shall rise, with healing in his wings' (Mal. 4.2 AV).

A new creation

Our Christian hope is also that at the End and in the End God's new creation will mean the vindication of the oppressed, and the establishment of that kingdom, for which we pray every time we say the Lord's Prayer – the kingdom in which the righteous will of God will be done, 'when justice will be throned in might, and every hurt be healed'. Then 'the kingdoms of this world will indeed become the Kingdom of our God and of his Christ', and of that Kingdom there shall be no end.

The present creation is characterised by disease and disaster, with mortal transience as the necessary cost of new life. An evolutionary universe, allowed by its creator to explore and realise its God-given potentiality, cannot be otherwise. The same processes of cellular variation which produce new forms of life will also produce the possibility of malignancy. If the new creation is to be free from physical evil and mortality (Rev. 21.4) then the laws which govern its 'matter' will have to be radically different from those with which we are familiar. If this is the case, the question immediately arises, why the first creation was not made by its creator so that it would not be subjected to suffering. A clue to answering the problem of physical suffering may lie in the direction of the old creation being a world allowed to exist as something 'other', given by God the freedom to be itself. The new creation will be a world freely reconciled to God in Christ (Col. 1.20), a transfigured universe completely suffused with the divine presence. The 'matter' of such a world can coherently be supposed to possess new properties not seen in our present experience, so that the new creation is not a second attempt at creation out of nothing, but it is the eschatological transformation of the old creation. It will be a *cosmos pneumatikos* – a universe animated by God's Spirit, in the most intimate connection with its creator.

It is an old accusation that Christians have so stressed a future salvation beyond death that they have neglected to realise that '*now* is the acceptable time, *now* is the day of salvation' (2 Cor. 6.2), and have failed to live as those who are already in Christ part of the new creation. But there is, in reality, no essential opposition between a concern to live as citizens of the kingdom of God in this world, and a longing for that final consummation which must include victory over death. In fact they belong together, and the hope of the coming of God's kingdom is a living hope, which already breaks into a realisation in the present in Christian worship participating in the life of heaven, and Christian service, participating in the life of the world. The value of the old creation is implied by its redemptive transformation being the raw material of the new creation.

Christian dying and the Communion of Saints

The present gift of life in which Christians share does not mean they do not die, but that their death, as their life, is now *en Christo*, 'in Christ'. They die as sharers in the common life of the Body of Christ. Their life is 'hidden with Christ in God' (Col. 3.3). So Christians die in hope – a hope that is depicted both as resurrection at the Last Day and life already with Christ.

Living by the Spirit and in Christ we are brought home to the Father, and to that eternal life which is Christ's gift and promise. Heaven is the name we give to that reality. The Book of Revelation portrays it in vivid symbols as the life of the new Jerusalem, the heavenly city, which has as its centre, the Lamb both slain and victorious, the triumphant sign of sacrificial love. As Austin Farrer said, heaven is 'the pattern of perfect relations . . . an endless beginning, a ceaseless wonder, perpetual resurrection in the unexhausted power of him who makes all things new'. In heaven God will be manifest in his works 'but his works will there be like music in the hands of the master, the mere utterances of his mind.'[1]

Participating by grace in the communion of God's love, here and now we have a foretaste of that union, and the Christian life of prayer opens us up to that reality. The great Christian teachers of prayer remind us that Christian mysticism speaks of union, not absorption, for God is love, and love unites and does not overwhelm. In heaven we shall know as we are known, perfectly ourselves and perfectly related one to another. It is because heaven is such a participation in the communion of God's love that it is right to believe that we shall see and know those whom we have loved, but we shall see and know them in God. In heaven, 'Christ is himself through taking us all into his heart, and we shall be ourselves by taking him to ours'.[2] All whom we love will be loved in Christ the source of love.

Human destiny in heaven will not be the attainment of an eternal and static perfection, but rather an everlasting participation in the exploration of the inexhaustible riches of the divine nature. Because the 'time' of the new creation is a new time, it need bear no simple or sequential relationship to the time we presently experience. Though we die at different times, we may all enter into our destiny together.

Since heaven is participation in the life of God, only those fitted to share that life may fully enter into it. Heaven is a communion of saints, a communion of those made holy by the work of the Spirit in the response of faith. Sanctification, growth in holiness, is the condition of heaven. And there is no holiness without God's grace because only God can make holy. Yet such holiness requires our human response; it is not the product of a mechanistic determinism, but a fruit of our love freely given, won from us by God's transforming love for us. Those Christians who have wanted to speak of 'purgatory' have by this language wanted to stress that God's love and mercy reaches out to fit for heaven those who still at their dying need to grow in that holiness which is the very condition of communion with God. Those who have resisted the language of purgatory have done so because they believe that God uses death itself as the instrument to complete the necessary task of dealing with that sin which, up to that point, still distorts the life of all Christians. This view claims support from such texts as Romans 6.7: 'Whoever has died is freed from sin.'

We confess our belief in the Communion of Saints, and Christian prayer is one expression of that communion. It is therefore appropriate to mention the Christian dead in Christian prayer, in thanksgiving for their lives and as an affirmation that they are in the hands of God who works in them the good purpose of his perfect will. This kind of prayerful remembrance of the faithful departed is prayer in Christ, and an expression of love for them. In the Spirit, through Christ, we are made free to remember and love the faithful departed, in a trusting love which overcomes the barrier of death.

Furthermore, because Scripture makes it clear that God created, loves and sustains all humanity, and that Christ died for the sins of the whole world, to pray in the name of Christ for God's will to be done may appropriately include a prayer of commendation 'for those whose faith is known to God alone', as is included in the ASB litany. It is for this reason that the Doctrine Commission of 1971 commented: 'We do not know the ways of God with those who have died outside the faith of Christ, but we do know his saving will for all, and we recognize the pastoral urgency from which the need for this prayer arises.'[3]

When death occurs and we bid farewell, we rightly seek to commend the soul of the departed into the hands of God, and in this context language about the soul indicates that living centre of human personality, which is no longer present in the dead body before us. A commendation into the hands of God is a commendation into a deeper participation in the communion of love which is God's being, and so into the communion of saints. The earliest funeral prayers were rich in images of refreshment after a journey (green pastures and springs of water), fellowship with the saints (the Old Testament patriarchs and the martyrs), and rest after struggles and conflicts. Liturgical prayers for resurrection at the Last Day, the final consummation when God will be all in all, co-exist with prayers which emphasise that the heavenly places are a present reality, for each Eucharist is offered 'with angels and archangels and with all the company of heaven'. Here and now in our worship we anticipate the life of the new creation, and share in the life of the world to come. We wait in expectation for that Last Day, when God will complete his purposes in creation by making all things new.

In the Communion of Saints, heaven and earth are united in a common worship, and it is in this context that the prayers of the Christian dead should be seen. Christians pray for one another on earth; this of course does not take away from the centrality of Christ as the one High Priest who intercedes for us. We join our praises with those of the saints, and that praise is always the praise of God's holy, loving and righteous will; praise and prayer are united in the longing that God's will may be done. In the end it is Christ, the true once and future King, who is the Lord of both the old and the new creation, and it is in him that the mystery of the prayerful relations between the living and the departed must find its true expression.

Final judgement

No one can be compulsorily installed in heaven, whose characteristic is the communion of love. God whose being is love preserves our human freedom, for freedom is the condition of love. Although God's love goes, and has gone, to the uttermost, plumbing the depths of hell, the possibility remains for each human being of a final rejection of God, and so of eternal life. As John Burnaby has written:

> Dogmatic universalism contradicts the very nature of love, by claiming for it the kind of omnipotence which it refuses. Love cannot, because it will not, compel the surrender of a single heart that holds out against it . . . Love never forces, and therefore there can be no certainty that it will overcome. But there may, and there must, be an unconquerable hope.[4]

Final judgement therefore remains a reality. Moral and spiritual choices are ultimate and serious choices. In the past the imagery of hell-fire and eternal torment and punishment, often sadistically expressed, has been used to frighten men and women into believing. Christians have professed appalling theologies which made God into a sadistic monster and left searing psychological scars on many. Over the last two centuries the decline in the churches of the western world of a belief in everlasting punishment has been one of the most notable transformations of Christian belief. There are many reasons for this change, but amongst them has been the moral protest from both within and without the Christian faith against a religion of fear, and a growing sense that the picture of a God who consigned millions to eternal torment was far removed from the revelation of God's love in Christ. Nevertheless it is our conviction that the reality of hell (and indeed of heaven) is the ultimate affirmation of the reality of human freedom. Hell is not eternal torment, but it is the final and irrevocable choosing of that which is opposed to God so completely and so absolutely that the only end is total non-being. Dante placed at the bottom of hell three figures frozen in ice – Judas, Brutus and Cassius. They were the betrayers of their friends, and through that they had ceased to have the capacity for love and so for heaven. Annihilation might be a truer picture of damnation than any of the traditional images of the hell of eternal torment. If God has created us with the freedom to choose, then those who make such a final choice choose against the only source of life, and they have their reward. Whether there be any who do so choose, only God knows.

The God of hope

The images of Christian eschatology are rich and complex. They developed historically in ways that do not enable them to be fitted into a single coherent and systematic picture. In particular the integration of talk about the end of the world, time and history, is uneasily related to what we want to say about the death of those we love, or about our own future dying. Nevertheless, as we have seen, there are important Christian affirmations to be made.

St Paul reminded the Christians of Corinth that, if the hope of Christians was for this life only, then we were of all people the most to be pitied (1 Cor. 15.19). Death remains a deep challenge to belief in a God of love. And yet it is only a God of love who can overcome death and make of it 'the gate of life immortal'. It is such a God who in Christ entered our human living and dying, and gave us at Easter the sure hope of eternal life. St John of the Cross said that 'at the end he will examine thee in love', for love is both judgement and salvation. The One God in Trinity, whose being is communion in love, is the true Last Thing of every creature: 'gained He is heaven; lost He is hell; purifying He is purgatory; encountered He is judgement'.[5] In Christ his gift to us is the Easter life of the new creation, which sweeps us into that heaven where we shall praise, and we shall love, and we shall adore, because we shall be made like Christ and know him as he is, 'changed into his likeness from one degree of glory to another'. And that praise will flow out of the life of the new creation, when the kingdom of justice, and love and peace, will be established, and all will be gathered into the city, whose light and glory is sacrificial love, 'for behold, I make all things new'.

Notes

1 Austin Farrer, *Saving Belief*, p. 143; *The Brink of Mystery*, p. 51.

2 Austin Farrer, *A Celebration of Faith*, p. 90.

3 Doctrine Commission, *Prayer and the Departed* (1971), p. 55.

4 John Burnaby, *Amor Dei*, p. 318.

5 Hans Urs von Balthasar, *Word and Redemption* (1965), p. 147.

Conclusion: That nothing be lost

In these words Jesus asks his followers to gather up the surplus pieces of bread after the feeding of the multitude: 'that nothing be lost'. They are words that leap off the page of the Gospels as a statement of God's limitless ambition to save. They tell of the depth of God's longing, the expansiveness of God's design and the unwavering care with which God continues to pursue the completion and perfection of the whole of creation. The words tell, in short, of the breadth and length and depth and height of a love that passes knowledge. That is the gospel of salvation.

To speak in this way, however, might seem to confine the scope of that gospel within the limits of our perception. It might suggest a God of limitless ambition waiting to be fulfilled and undying love waiting to be requited; that is just a part of the story. For the bread was gathered up, and what might have been lost has again and again been saved. In the God who saves we have to do not with mere dreams and hopes, with what might be and one day, we hope, will be; we testify to a gift already received and signs already enacted of that gathering up which is God's will for all things. Already God's realm is inhabited by those who have known God's grace and lived lives empowered by it; already many who were plagued by oppression or sickness of body and mind have experienced release. If it is the case that we are part of a world where pain and alienation still abound and where therefore anything that might reasonably be called salvation is still far off – and such is the world we inhabit – it is nevertheless also and equally true that God's salvation has already drawn near.

It is the vast scope of God's design for salvation that requires the breadth and complexity of the topics over which this report has ranged. At the outset we sought to point to some critical aspects of the particular context in which we find ourselves. We observed the plurality of our society, our sense of individuals and communities going their own way. We reflected on the absence of any generally accepted diagnosis of the needs of humanity, let alone a commonly agreed religious framework for meeting them. Our world presents what can appear as an entirely hostile environment, one which the gospel of salvation has therefore simply to confront. But even when features of our contemporary world seem hostile to Christian faith and the values it seeks to promote, is it open to the community of faith to write them off as wholly negative? What would that say about a God who is determined that nothing be lost? So we have found ourselves required in this report to consider how God's gift of salvation can be discerned and received within human history; we seek in our generation, as all the generations of faith have done, for the wisdom to discern God's saving action even within experiences of suffering and at times when there seems to be no sign of the fulfilment of God's promise.

Similarly, we felt compelled to face at the outset the enormous scale of the universe in space, its duration in time and above all its inevitable mortality, even if its final decay is billions of years away. We noted the huge question mark which all that places against the weight Christians have traditionally given to the history of the human species, let alone that apparently minute piece of human history that is covered by the Christian Scriptures. It can sound immensely bland to continue using the language of the 'scandal of particularity'; how much more scandalous has that particularity become in the light of what we now know. Yet the infinite range of God's concern to save all that has been created has still to be declared, though in the face of that vastness of scale and inescapable dissolution which cosmologists now take for granted. At the same time our message must not lose the particularity of God's love, imaged by Christ as a love that numbers the hairs on our heads and lets no sparrow fall to the ground unnoticed.

The salvation God offers to the world has always engaged particularly with the needs of the poor in each generation, those who have been victims of deprivation, discrimination and oppression. Theirs is the history that is often unread and even untold. Yet the God who is concerned that nothing be lost has a particular care for those whom the world counts lost, or who find themselves to be so. We could not write this book unaware that this century has generated overpowering examples of the human capacity for cruelty and injustice: it has seen the Holocaust as well as other less chronicled instances of national and racial persecution and wars of enormous scale and violence; it closes with unprecedented numbers of starving and displaced persons. The conviction we share with Christians world-wide is that the gospel of salvation has to be declared in the face of those realities and in a way that both responds to them and inspires and enables us to engage with them.

Among the forms of injustice of which the awareness is so much stronger in our generation than has previously been the case, and which we constantly kept in mind, are the disparities of power and resources available to women and to men: to those disparities the God who saves invites us to respond. Yet in doing so we have needed to face the fact that this particular issue of justice, that between women and men, has come to involve as one of its aspects a sensitivity to the way in which language reflects, and in turn affects, our apprehension of the Christian tradition. For the language of faith, not least in the way it has spoken of salvation, has presented, for centuries unconsciously, what now appears as an unmistakably 'male' perspective. We have sought to address this very current issue, aware that our observations and suggestions are made in a situation where forms of speech are in a state of constant and rapid change.

If the relations between the sexes have been topical in the life of the Church, and therefore have needed to be addressed in a statement of our belief about salvation, so has that other issue of our time to which we referred in our opening chapter: that is, the Christian understanding of whether, and how, God saves the adherents of the world's other faith traditions. It might seem easy enough to say that the God who desires that nothing be lost continues to offer the gift of salvation to all, from whatever culture they come. But we have had to reflect further on this matter: for is there not a question how the God who desires that nothing be lost regards the history, culture and achievement of the world's various faith communities? The God who sent his Son as saviour of all ensures also, we believe, that the richness of other faith-traditions, the fruits of prayerfulness and compassion they have borne, are also not to be lost. In what we have said about this vitally important issue, therefore, we have maintained three essential points: the centrality for Christian faith of the person and work of Jesus Christ, the universal range of the salvation God bestows through him and the real gifts bestowed upon humanity through the world's great communities of faith.

These issues are raised for us not simply because we are people of this time; they are raised also because we are part of the Church, ourselves beneficiaries of the gift of salvation as Scripture and the life and witness of God's people down the ages testify. This double imperative, deriving from our being people of this time and from our being people of this faith, has driven us afresh to the resources of faith and tradition in the search, if not for conclusive answers to the needs of our time, at least for means of living creatively and faithfully in it. In that encounter we have been aware both of the need for new ways of expressing the faith, and at the same time of some central themes which, however problematic, are constant features of the Christian message of salvation at any time.

Principal among these is the conviction that there has been no salvation without sacrifice. No other word suffices to describe the character of what Christ offered; if nothing is to be lost – and that is Christians' undying hope – then it required, and requires, paradoxically, the expenditure of everything. That desire and gift of God are presented to the world on the cross, claimed by the Church in the experience of worship and prayer, baptism and Eucharist, and called for in the life of disciples at all times. Such sacrifice is not to be understood as a requirement that human beings degrade themselves, or allow themselves to be degraded, a demand which not least those who experience the oppressive yoke of injustice would reject for good reason; rather it consists in God's willingness to risk all to save all, and to reveal the glory of humanity supremely in losing all. We are called to follow in that way, and the Christian testimony is that those whom the world considers of no account can claim their true dignity in this way as in no other.

Throughout our reflections we have seen the need to hold on to the sheer scope of God's design, recognising that God's promise is for this life and not only for this life; it is for persons one by one, and no less for the communities and nations of the world. It is for humanity, and no less for the enormous variety of creatures with which we share our planet; it is for our world, and no less for the vastness of the universe. All things are 'returning to their perfection through him from whom they took their origin'; our calling is to act faithfully in all the situations which cry out for that salvation to be revealed in this life, sustained by the hope that ultimately God will be all in all.

Appendix: Salvation
and the Anglican heritage

As Anglicans, we shall want to ask whether the historic formularies of the Church of England, especially the Book of Common Prayer and the Thirty-Nine Articles, contain any particular version of atonement doctrine. We may also find it instructive to compare these historic formularies, which still have canonical authority, with the *Alternative Service Book 1980* and more recent supplementary liturgical material in respect of the doctrine of the atonement.

But before turning to the liturgies and Articles, we are bound to take note of the fact that these are by no means fully representative of Anglican piety in practice. For example, the theology of Richard Hooker, the sermons of Lancelot Andrewes, the poems of George Herbert, the hymns of Charles Wesley and the spiritual writings of Edward Pusey all serve to remind us that the tradition of Anglican spirituality draws on deep resources of catholicity that transcend those particular notions of salvation and the atonement that dominate our historic formularies. In particular, the doctrine of union with God, participation in God, and transformation by the power of God into the likeness of Christ is strongly present in these authors and stems from the Greek Fathers of the Church with their concept of theosis. This motif is not absent from the Book of Common Prayer – the Prayer of Humble Access includes the words 'that we may evermore dwell in him and he in us' and in the post-communion prayer communicants thank God that 'we are very members incorporate in the mystical body of thy Son' – but it is hardly conspicuous. These themes have recently come to enrich our ecumenical theology of communion (*koinonia*).

Classical doctrines

The Thirty-Nine Articles were promulgated in 1563, though they drew heavily on earlier formularies, and received their final form in 1571. It is probable that they did not intend to define positively a particular doctrine of the atonement. The Articles were not intended to serve as a summary of Christian belief, a potted systematic theology. They deal with points of contention in the sixteenth century, over against the Church of Rome, the Anabaptists and rigorous Calvinists. The atonement as such was not in dispute and the Articles allude to it merely incidentally. Their aim was to be inclusive not exclusive. They gave theological liberty within the bounds of legal conformity. The laity in general have never been required to subscribe to the Articles. The clergy are now required to make only a general assent that the historic formularies 'bear witness to Christian truth' as set forth in the Scriptures and creeds, and to affirm their belief in 'the doctrine of the Christian faith as the Church of England has received it' (ASB Ordinal). (See further on the nature of the Articles: the Doctrine Commission report *Believing in the Church* (1981), pp. 109–41). Nevertheless, a particular tradition of the interpretation of the atonement can be clearly discerned in the Articles. Let us now look at some of the evidence.

Article 2, in stressing the true deity and true humanity of Jesus Christ against alternative Christologies advanced by some strands of the radical Reformation, affirms that he 'truly suffered, was crucified, dead and buried, to reconcile his Father to us, and to be a sacrifice, not only for original guilt, but also for all actual sins of men'. Read in the light of Article 9 ('Of Original or Birth-sin'), this statement makes it clear that the framers of the Article believed, in accordance with the traditional doctrine that stemmed from St Augustine, that Christ's death removed our guilt before God in three respects: the guilt believed to have been imputed by God's decree to all humanity on account of the first disobedience of their putative progenitor Adam; the guilt incurred by the present depraved condition of our human nature; and the guilt incurred by individual sinful acts.

Article 31, which was directed against the propitiatory conception of the Roman mass, stresses that the death of Christ on the cross constituted a 'perfect redemption, propitiation, and satisfaction, for the sins of the whole world, both original and actual'. These words echo the wording of the Prayer of Consecration in the service of Holy Communion as found in both Prayer Books of Edward VI (1549 and 1552) and the Book of Common Prayer (1662): 'Almighty God, our heavenly Father, who of thy tender mercy didst give thine only Son Jesus Christ to suffer death upon the cross for our redemption; who made there (by his one oblation of himself once offered) a full, perfect and sufficient sacrifice, oblation, and satisfaction, for the sins of the whole world . . .'.

The Litany (which predates the Edwardine Prayer Books, having been composed by Cranmer in 1544, drawing on Roman, Eastern and Lutheran sources) invokes the active as well as the passive obedience of Christ (to use a traditional theological distinction) and rehearses the history of salvation from the incarnation to the sending of the Holy Spirit upon the Church in words that had been used in England since the Anglo-Saxon church: 'By the mystery of thy holy Incarnation; by thy holy Nativity and Circumcision; by thy Baptism, Fasting and Temptation, *Good Lord, deliver us.* By thine Agony and bloody Sweat; by thy Cross and Passion; by thy precious Death and Burial; by thy glorious Resurrection and Ascension; and by the coming of the Holy Ghost, *Good Lord, deliver us.'* It thus sets the cross at the centre of an unfolding drama of redemption, emphasises Christ's sufferings as truly human, and balances the victory of Easter with the solidarity of Christ with our needy human condition.

The collects of the Book of Common Prayer contain a wealth of profound theological reflection. Do they also teach, explicitly or implicitly, a particular doctrine of the atonement? Sometimes they merely echo the phrase of the creeds 'for us': ' . . . circumcised and obedient to the law for man' (The Circumcision); 'who for our sake didst fast forty days' (Lent 1). The Easter collects state that Christ 'overcame death and opened unto us the gate of everlasting life' (Easter Day); that he died for our sins and rose for our justification

(Easter 1); and that he is given to us 'both as a sacrifice for sin and also an ensample of godly life' (Easter 2). But they do not appear to bind us to any particular theory of how Christ overcame death, died for our sins or became a sacrifice for sins. The collect for Palm Sunday contains an exemplarist doctrine of the atonement (in the weak sense of exemplarist – setting us an example – rather than showing forth or exemplifying the reconciling love of God) when it affirms that God, of his tender love towards mankind, sent his Son 'to take upon him our flesh, and to suffer death upon the cross, that all mankind should follow the example of his great humility'.

The Proper Preface for Easter in the BCP is rich in atonement imagery. The crucified and risen Christ is seen as 'the very Paschal Lamb, which was offered for us, and hath taken away the sin of the world; who by his death hath destroyed death and by his rising to life again hath restored to us everlasting life'. The Paschal or Passover Lamb is a sacrificial image; to take away the sin of the world is an expiatory motif; and the Christus Victor theme is sounded in the destruction of death and the bringing of life. Here certainly we have the raw material of atonement theology, but no actual explanatory theory of why sacrifice, expiation and victory were achieved by the death and resurrection of Jesus Christ.

This summary of the teaching of the historic authoritative documents of Anglicanism suggests several reflections.

These sources clearly depict Christ's atoning work in terms of sacrifice – both explicitly and in the implicitly sacrificial language of oblation and offering. But within the broad sacrificial framework of the doctrine of the atonement that is present in the BCP there are a number of important distinctions to be discerned.

Personal and impersonal

The tradition in which the Anglican formularies stand is often labelled 'objective' in discussions of the atonement because it looks for a transaction 'out there' between God the Father and God the Son, independent of the response made by the beneficiaries of that transaction ('something accomplished, something done'). The alternative tradition, associated with Peter Abelard (1079–1142), is often dubbed 'subjective' because it focuses on the human response to the sacrificial love of God, and 'exemplarist', not, as is sometimes assumed, merely because it proposes Christ as the perfect model or example of the human response to God in obedience and love, but because his faithfulness unto death on the cross for our sake shows forth or exemplifies the love God has for us in a way that nothing else could. Clearly this Abelardian concept of the atonement is just as 'objective' in that it postulates an objective act of divine revelation intended to awaken human response. Moreover, the juridical models of the atonement obviously have their subjective aspect in the human appropriation of Christ's atoning work through repentance, faith and the sacraments of the Church. Evidently the terms 'objective' and 'subjective' are of limited value and ought to be employed with caution, if at all.

The model of atonement presupposed by the Thirty-Nine Articles belongs to the so-called 'juridical' tradition: the model employed is provided by legal concepts and has primary reference to the law court. The juridical tradition is associated particularly with Anselm of Canterbury (1033–1109) and John Calvin (1509–64). Anselm interpreted the atonement in terms of the principle of feudal obligation that gave cohesion to early medieval European society. Sinful humanity owed a debt of honour to its creator – a debt that could only be repaid by someone who belonged to Adam's erring race yet was able to offer a virtually infinite compensation to God: the sinless God-man Jesus Christ. This is presumably one source of the term 'satisfaction' that appears in the Articles and the Prayer of Thanksgiving. Calvin, influenced not by feudal law but by the recently revived Roman criminal law, thought of Christ's death as dealing with the punishment required by God's justice rather than as making reparation to his honour. This is the significance of the term 'propitiation' in the Articles (in the liturgy 'propitiation' is used only in the recitation of the Comfortable Words, from 1 John 2.1–2; it is not used in the Prayer of Consecration).

Since the dominant model of atonement in the Articles and Prayer Book is juridical, it is constructed in terms of the impersonal considerations of law and justice rather than the personal categories of relationship and response. To say that is not by any means to disparage the notions of law and justice, for without them what hope would there be for the oppressed, the victims of cruelty and exploitation? But while justice must have the first word, it cannot be allowed to have the last (cf. Jam. 2.13). Justice must give place to mercy, even while mercy presupposes justice. The claims of retributive justice equate to the seriousness of wrongdoing or sin and therefore must be heard, but retributive justice alone can never effect reconciliation. Only mercy inspired by love that reaches out to the wrongdoer and absorbs the barrier of hostility, hatred and fear can reconcile. This is precisely the emphasis of exemplarist theories of the atonement – they are framed in personalist concepts. Juridical theories of the atonement have often pictured God's law, God's wrath, and human sin and guilt not as aspects of the relation between God and humanity, but as though they were actual objects or things that had somehow to be dealt with. That is to say, these concepts were 'reified' – as though they were objectively existing entities which curtailed the freedom of divine action so that God could not forgive sins if God wanted to without some equally reified compensation or satisfaction being offered to the supposedly implacable attributes of God. The alternative Abelardian or exemplarist tradition in its most radical form sees no barrier to God forgiving sins except the barrier of our own hardness of heart, while in a more moderate form it regards the death of Christ as an acknowledgement of the dire consequences of sin and therefore of the price paid by God to reconcile humanity to God.

Moral issues

Strong moral objections have often been made to juridical theories of the atonement. Juridical concepts include moral factors and so enable the atonement to be interpreted in moral terms. But juridical theories of the atonement tend to make legal considerations primary and moral ones secondary. Ultimately, they seem to confuse moral and legal categories. In the realm of law a debt must always be paid and a penalty must always be enforced. But in the moral sphere there is no such necessity. Loving parents will often waive a debt owed to them by their own child and they will do all they can to spare the child the self-destructive effects of its own wrongdoing. Again, in the legal sphere one person can sometimes pay the debt owed by another (though they cannot undergo their punishment), but in the moral sphere each person must be responsible for their own obligations. Moral responsibility is ultimately incommunicable. The great weakness of juridical theories or models of the atonement is that they appear to eclipse moral considerations by legal ones. This runs counter to our best theological instincts which suggest that personal analogies are the most appropriate ones for the character of God as revealed in Christ.

The view of the atonement reflected in the Thirty-Nine Articles is *substitutionary* in that Christ acts in our place and stead. In Anselm, Christ as substitute pays our debt; in Calvin, Christ as substitute bears our punishment. Thus Calvin's is a *penal* substitutionary theory while Anselm's is not.

In addition to the moral difficulties of the notion of substitution, there is also the question how we are involved in Christ's atonement and how we benefit from it. There is certainly a vital truth enshrined in the notion of substitution: Christ does indeed act 'in our place' and does for us what we cannot do for ourselves. But the danger of using substitutionary language in isolation is that it can appear to make the work of Christ external (or extrinsic) to us; in itself it cannot show how we have a saving interest in our redeemer. The term 'vicarious', however, which has the dominant sense of an action performed by one person on behalf of another, while preserving the intention of the Reformers, is not open to this objection. Our unity with our redeemer may be effected retrospectively, so to speak, by faith, the sacraments and the indwelling of the Holy Spirit.

Propitiation?

Finally, the Articles employ the term 'propitiation' (Article 31) and state that Christ 'reconciled his Father to us' (Article 2). When combined with the penal substitutionary interpretation of the atonement, this terminology seems bound to suggest that Christ's death was a divinely inflicted punishment which appeased the wrath of God against sinful humanity and enabled God to change God's attitude towards us, from one of rejection to one of acceptance. This interpretation is consistent with the translation in the Authorised Version of *hilasterion* (mercy-seat) and its cognates by 'propitiation', etc. (Rom. 3.25; 1 John 2.2; 4.10), where the AV is guided by the literal meaning of the Greek (to propitiate) rather than by the Hebrew meanings lying behind the text (*kipper*: to cover, wipe away).

The 1938 report of the Doctrine Commission was clear that 'The notion of propitiation as the placating by man of an angry God is definitely unchristian' (p. 146). It is significant that modern biblical translations render *hilasterion*, etc., not as 'propitiation', but as 'sacrifice of atonement', 'atoning sacrifice', 'expiation' or 'means of expiating sin'.

In this they are influenced, as were the Reformers themselves, by the fundamental biblical principle that God is primarily the subject of the atoning action. Thus in the key text, Romans 3.25, we read that God *put forth Christ* as a *hilasterion* to bring redemption through his sacrificial death. Whereas the object of the propitiation is God, the object of expiation is sin. To propitiate means to assuage wrath or displeasure. To expiate means to remove the sin that is the cause of separation, and to offer an atoning sacrifice means to reconcile two parties who have become estranged. It is nevertheless true that in Paul's thought the effect of expiation is the same as that of propitiation – to neutralise the sin that is the cause of God's displeasure and so to avert God's wrath (however that should be understood).

The nineteenth-century Anglican theologian Frederick Denison Maurice insisted that the mercy-seat of the Old Testament does not represent the propitiation of divine wrath against the sinner, but rather reveals that 'he who had established the mercy-seat was the Lord God of that earth from which the foulest steam of human sacrifices was ascending to the Baals and Molochs. He was testifying there that from him came freely down the blessings which they were hoping to buy of their gods; that he blotted out the transgressions of which the worshippers were seeking, by the cruellest oblations, to escape the penalty' (*Doctrine of Sacrifice*, p. 150). Christ's work is rightly understood as God's way of reconciling the world to God (2 Cor. 5.19) through a perfect sacrifice which we make our own in penitence and faith. It is in this sense that the Church sings (in the words of William Bright):

> Look, Father, look on his anointed face,
> And only look on us as found in him;
> Look not on our misusings of thy grace,
> Our prayer so languid and our faith so dim:
> For lo! between our sins and their reward
> We set the passion of thy Son our Lord.

God is the sole author of atonement. The expression 'propitiation' may obscure the truth that Christ's saving work originates with God, that it is the expression of God's infinite love for God's human creatures that no sin can ever destroy ('God so loved the world that he gave his only Son . . .' – John 3.16), and that Christ's will was entirely one with that of his Father, not pitted against it in order to wrest forgiveness from a reluctant and hostile God, as the cruder, popular expressions of penal substitution tend to suggest.

Some interpreters have attempted to avoid the unacceptable consequences of a doctrine of propitiation (i.e. that God's attitude to sinners is capable of being changed or that God's love and God's justice are at loggerheads) by entertaining the paradox that God propitiates himself. Athanasius spoke of God's act of self-reconciliation. Augustine confessed: 'In a manner wondrous and divine he loved even when he hated us.' Calvin employed the strongest language of propitiation (Christ 'procured the favour of God for us', 'appeased the wrath of God' and 'rendered the Father favourable and propitious towards us') and penal substitution (our sins were 'transferred to him by imputation' and by his death 'the justice of God was satisfied'). But Calvin acknowledged that this doctrine presents us with an irreconcilable paradox: 'How could he have given us in his only begotten Son a singular pledge of his love, if he had not previously embraced us with free favour?' Calvin appealed to the words of Augustine already quoted.

It can never be right to speak of God hating God's human creatures. The Prayer Book collect for Ash Wednesday (here echoing Wisdom 11.24) supplicates God 'who hatest nothing that thou hast made'. We should surely say, God always loved us even though God condemned us as sinners. It is precisely because God is already and eternally gracious to us and lovingly disposed towards us that God has, in Christ, demolished the barrier of alienation and bridged the gulf of separation so that his children might be restored to full and free communion with God.

The Alternative Service Book

The *Alternative Service Book 1980* contains a rather different emphasis in its implied doctrine of the atonement and draws on other aspects of the varied range of images to be found in the New Testament.

In Rite A, the First and Second Eucharistic Prayers are content simply to state that God gave his Son 'to be born as man and to die upon the cross' in order to free us from the slavery of sin and make us a Spirit-endowed people for God's possession.

The Third Eucharistic Prayer is more eloquent. It recalls that Jesus Christ was sent by God in his great goodness to be our saviour. He 'took flesh', 'was seen on earth' and 'went about among us' (perhaps an attempt to express the thought in John 1.14 of the Logos dwelling or 'tabernacling' among us – this passage reads like a poetic paraphrase of that key verse). The reference to the cross is evocative: 'He opened wide his arms for us on the cross; he put an end to death by dying for us' (note the repeated biblical and credal 'for us'). He 'revealed the resurrection' (which sounds like 'showed that it was there hidden all along', rather than constituting it and making it a reality).

The Fourth Eucharistic Prayer broadly follows the lines of the alternative order of the Communion in the 1928 Prayer Book (as does Rite B), except that where 1928 retains the 1662 Prayer Book's '. . . to suffer death upon the cross for our redemption; who made there (by his one oblation of himself once offered) a full, perfect, and sufficient sacrifice, oblation and satisfaction for the sins of the whole world', the ASB omits the language of oblation and satisfaction. It has instead: ' . . . to suffer death upon the cross for our redemption; he made there a full atonement for the sins of the whole world, offering once for all his one sacrifice of himself'.

The language of penal substitution and propitiation is avoided in the ASB. The theme of *sacrifice* that runs through the BCP is usually retained in the ASB and the vicarious nature of that sacrifice is affirmed ('his offering of himself made once for all upon the cross': First Eucharistic Prayer). However, the theme of Christ's sacrifice is strangely absent from the Second Eucharistic Prayer, though this prayer refers to the transformation of the communicants into the likeness of Christ, a theme on which we touched at the beginning of this note.

Some of the most evocative language of the ASB is found in the Proper Prefaces. The Rite A Proper Preface for Easter retains the substance of the BCP Preface which refers to the Paschal Lamb who has taken away sins, destroyed death and restored everlasting (now 'eternal') life. An alternative Preface invokes victory and healing: 'in his victory over the grave a new age has dawned, the long reign of sin is ended, a broken world is being renewed, and man is once again made whole.'

A richer, more evocative liturgical language is also found in the recent supplementary material published with the authority of the House of Bishops: *The Promise of His Glory* and *Lent, Holy Week and Easter*. It is naturally the latter which provides, especially in the 'Prayers on the Passion', references to the atonement. Through the cross, we are reminded, Christ blotted out our sins, bore our sins, unlocked the gates of paradise, perfectly revealed the loving nature of the Father, won a complete victory over evil, and made a perfect and eternal sacrifice to God.

Index of biblical references

General index

Abel 163

Abelard, Peter 110, 112, 210f

Abishiktananda 154

Abraham 13, 78f, 106, 163, 166, 191

Ackroyd, Peter 4

Adam 17, 53, 118, 134, 163, 178, 207

After-life 87f, 190ff

Alienation from God 43, 102f

Alternative Service Book 1980 215f

Andrewes, Lancelot 206

Andrews, C. F. 157

Angels 117, 188

Anselm, St, of Canterbury 67, 108, 210, 212

Appleton, George 157

Aquinas, St Thomas 12, 115f

Ariarajah, W. 153, 158

Aristotle 12

Arius 41

Articles of Religion, Thirty-Nine 162, 207ff

Assyria 164

Athanasius, St, of Alexandria 120, 214

Atonement 87, 96ff

Augustine, St, of Canterbury 150

Augustine, St, of Hippo 35, 116, 125, 143, 214

Augustinianism 54, 207

Babel, Tower of 163

Balthasar, Hans Urs von 200

Baptism 126, 136, 142, 187

Barnes, M. 171, n.11

Barth, Karl 65, 123, 152, 158, 170, 180

Beckett, Samuel 3f

Betjeman, John 68

Betrayal 104f

Big Bang 10

Biochemical manipulation 14

Bonhoeffer, Dietrich 112f

Book of Common Prayer 108, 111, 126, 132, 206ff, 215

Bright, William 214

Buddhism 20ff, 69, 127, 144ff, 171, 173

Bultmann, Rudolf 68, 72

Burnaby, John 198

Calvin, John 210, 212, 215

Canberra, WCC Assembly 154

Cassidy, Sheila 128

Chadwick, Henry 61, 73

China, Church in 150

Christ, in our place 102ff; the friend betrayed 104ff; two natures of 106, 207; who justifies 106ff; who makes amends 108; four representative 110ff; and suffering 112ff; our sacrifice 114ff; the victor 117ff; as High Priest 140; reconciliation of all things to God in 180

see also: Cross, Incarnation, Logos, Kingdom, Resurrection, Trinity

Christmas, Service of Nine Lessons and Carols 64f

Church, and history 64ff, 78ff

as the Body of Christ 88, 134ff, 142f, 177

Commandments, Ten 18; two great 189

Communion of Saints 191, 195ff

Consciousness, emergence of 10

Converts, witness of 160f

Coptic Church 150

Cosmology 13

Covenant 75, 79, 106f, 116, 166, 189

Cragg, Kenneth 157

Cranmer, Thomas 137, 141, 208

Creation 49ff, 66, 72f, 80f, 188f

221

Index